THE
LEGENDS OF THE SAINTS

AN INTRODUCTIO

FROM THE FRENCH OF
PÈRE H. DELEHAYE, S.J.
BOLLANDIST

WITH AN INTRODUCTION BY
RICHARD J. SCHOECK

TRANSLATED BY
V. M. CRAWFORD

UNIVERSITY OF NOTRE DAME PRESS • 1961

Nihil Obstat.

HERBERTUS THURSTON, S.J.
Censor deputatus.

Imprimi potest.

✠ GULIELMUS
EPISCOPUS ARINDELENSIS,
Vicarius Generalis.

WESTMONASTERII,
die 7 Junii, 1907.

PREFACE

This is a book that is indeed "penetrating in judgment and perfect in form," as Dom David Knowles has characterized it. And there can be no better entry into the magisterial scholarship of Hippolyte Delehaye, or an introduction to hagiography, than this little book.

"What is a saint? Who were saints? What are the tests for sifting out bogus, ghost and bilocating saints?" These are some of the questions that hagiography raises, and, Dom Knowles continues: "The hagiographer is plunged at once into the nightmare of early medieval diplomatic and forgery, into all the tangled chronological difficulties of the *fasti* of half the sees of Europe, into the labyrinthine ways of martyrologies, necrologies and calendars, into the linguistic, social and psychological varieties of Christian sentiment—Greek, Persian, Egyptian, Syrian, Slav and Oriental, into the magical mists and colours of the Celtic wonderland, and into the changes and translations that lapse of centuries and popular devotion can bring about in a matter that is of its nature peculiarly dependent upon personal knowledge and popular acclaim." To these factors must be added "the theological background and the judgment of credibility, possibility and moral and spiritual sanity inseparable from the subject-matter": that extraordinary group of gifted Jesuit scholars known as the Bollandists have not had to worry for problems and material to keep them occupied. To all the technical and critical problems with which the Bollandists, who have devoted themselves to hagiography, have been concerned during their three centuries of activity will doubtless someday be added an examination of "the frontiers of natural and supernatural activity." That society (never more than six strong) is indeed an immortal group blessed by "the uncovenanted gift of genius," and one may well echo Knowles' Vergilian wish that the fortunes of such a house stand firm and that their successors' names be numbered on the roll.

There are few fields of scholarship that touch so many others, and that reach out into those other fields to bring tools and results to bear upon their own, as does hagiography: folklore and anthropology, mythology and iconography, liturgy and ecclesiastical history, literary history and even literary criticism, place-names—these are but the major fields touched by hagiography.

Yet, "there is no form of literature into which people rush so frequently without any sort of preparation," as Delehaye writes (p.214), and the primary concern of his introduction is to classify methods and texts:

> To indicate briefly the spirt in which hagiographic texts should be studied, to lay down the rules for discriminating between the materials . . . to place people on their guard . . .

In his Preface to the third edition twenty years later, Delehaye indicated that there had been an insistent demand for a new edition and it has been nearly impossible to obtain a copy of the English translation for a long time. "Naturally the text has had to have some touching-up: in twenty years, scientific hagiography has made progress and we would not want to fail to take account of it. But we also wanted to keep the first appearance of this little book; and to handle over again, to introduce there all the developments one would wish, would have forced us to repeat what we have had occasion to say in special works, to which we shall send the reader."

There were misunderstandings: some had thought that saints were *hors de cause* of scientific investigation; that hagiographical texts are the only documents studied for the history of the saints; òr that Delehaye himself manifested a destructive criticism. The aim first, this later preface emphasizes, has been not to crowd this book with details that would here be digressive—there have been two books devoted to these special questions: *Les origines du culte des martyrs* (1912) and *Les passions des martyrs et les genres littéraires* (1921). And in this preface he concludes: "Let them be persuaded that we do not make war on the legends; that would be a foolish enterprise. All the Academies have joined to declare that the torment of Saint Lawrence could only have been as narrated—until the end of the world the *gril* [grill] will be the one emblem in which one will recognize the famous Roman deacon. The work of the legend can count among the great unconscious forces of nature. It is impossible that the popular soul be forcefully impressed by a great event or by some powerful personality without its feelings finding expression in its stories where fantasy throws off all restraints. To declare that legend has flourished abundantly around the sanctuaries is simply to state the importance of the cultus of saints in the life of the people. The legend is the homage of the Christian people to its protectors. One cannot slight this title. Only, one should not take it for history. That is a confusion which the zeal for the glory of the saints does not require and which offers serious troubles."

In Hippolyte Delehaye (1859-1941) are to be found the great attributes of the early Bollandists. For about a quarter of a century, until his death, he was the leader of the group; and he was hailed by the whole world of learning as a great scholar and the Bollandist par excellence. ("One of those supreme masters that arise from time to time among the Bollandists," writes Nigel Abercrombie in his biography of the great English liturgist, Edmund Bishop.) He was honored by l'Académie Royale de Belgique, l'Académie des Inscriptions et Belles-Lettres, l'Académie pontificale romaine d'archéologie, the British Academy, the Mediaeval Academy of America, and many others. A selected bibliography of his writings follows.

To borrow from the biographical sketch by P. Peeters: perhaps the best epitaph for Delehaye would be a repetition of his own words inscribed in the dedication of his *Origines du culte des martyrs* to his predecessors De Smedt and Poncelet: *In pace cum sanctis.*

v

A SELECTED BIBLIOGRAPHY

The Bollandists:

There is no full treatment of this group, and the best accounts are those of De Smedt in the *Catholic Encyclopedia* (1907) and of A. de Bil in the *Dictionnaire d'Histoire et de Géographie Ecclésiastiques* (1937). The section in Aigrain's *L'Hagiographie* (cited below) is largely based upon Delehaye's essay—*A travers trois siècles*: *L'Oeuvre des Bollandistes, 1615-1915* (1920), and to this should be added P. Peeters, 'Après un siècle (1837-1937),' in *Analecta Bollandiana*, vol. lv. Biographical sketches by Peeters of De Smedt, Poncelet, Van den Gheyn, Van Ortroy, Delehaye and Bosmans, which originally appeared in *Analecta Bollandiana*, have been reprinted as *Figures Bollandiennes* (Brussels, 1948). Father Peeters, who died in 1950, has been memorialized by Devos in *Analecta Bollandiana*, vol. lxix. There is a brilliant essay by Prof. David Knowles—an address to the Royal Historical Society, 'The Bollandists,' first published in the *Transactions R.H.S.*, 5th ser., vol. viii (1958)—which is to be reprinted in a volume on Great Historical Enterprises; I have quoted from it above and have found it to be altogether admirable as a survey.

Delehaye:

During a half-century of productivity Delehaye published more than a hundred dissertations, editions of texts, lists of manuscripts, etc., in *Analecta Bollandiana*. The following are his more important general works:

Bibliotheca Hagiographica Graeca, Brussels, 1895.
Les légendes grecques des saints militaires, Paris, 1909.
Les origines du culte des martyrs, Paris, 1912—2nd ed., 1933.
Les passions des martyrs et les genres littéraires, Paris, 1921.
Les saints stylites, Paris, 1923.
Sanctus, essai sur le culte des saints dans l'antiquité, Paris, 1927.

Of his "four classics of critical scholarship"—an edition of the Byzantine synaxary, 1902, a commentary on the martyrology of St. Jerome, 1931, a study of the Roman legendary, 1936, and a commentary on the Roman martyrology, 1940—one may adapt Knowles' praise of Peeters' work on Oriental hagiography: "it is for the specialist to appreciate and for the profane to admire such work."

Recent Scholarship:

There has been a flood of scholarship during the past two decades in matters hagiographical, but it would be a rash and profaning student who would presume to annotate Delehaye's work. Fortunately, there is the recent work of René Aigrain, *L'Hagiographie—Ses Sources, Ses Méthodes, Son Histoire* (Paris, 1953), to bring together the bulk of this recent work; and the student will soon turn to the richnesses of the *Analecta Bollandiana*.

There is much on saints' lives in the work of Urban T. Holmes: see his *History of Old French Literature* . . . (New York, 1948), Chapters 4 and 24, and his Bibliography of medieval French literature, vol. I in *A Critical Bibliography of French Literature* (Syracuse University Press, 1947), ed. D. C. Cabeen. There will soon be available a revision of J. E. Wells, *A Manual of Writings in Middle English* under the general editorship of J. Burke Severs, to guide the student through the mediaeval English sources and treatments; still useful are G. H. Gerould, *Saints' Legends* (Boston, 1916), and especially C. W. Jones, *Saints' Lives and Chronicles in Early England* (Cornell University Press, 1947).

In the field of folklore stories one may single out the work of Stith Thompson; his *Motif-Index of Folk Literature* (Bloomington, Ind., 1932-1936), is now appearing in a revised and enlarged edition (Indiana University Press, 1955—.).

THE TEXT

The text for the present edition is the English translation by Mrs. V. M. Crawford (London, 1907), which was made from the second French edition; that translation has been compared with the third French edition of 1927, and later bibliographical changes and additions have been incorporated, or noted, in brackets.

R.J.S.

Feast of St. Basil the Great 1961
Notre Dame, Indiana

AUTHOR'S INTRODUCTION

RECENT progress in scientific hagiography has given rise to move than one misunderstanding. Historical criticism when applied to the lives of the saints has had certain results which are in no way surprising to those who are accustomed to handle documents and to interpret inscriptions, but which have had a somewhat disturbing effect on the mind of the general public.

Religious-minded people who regard with equal veneration not only the saints themselves but everything associated with them, have been greatly agitated by certain conclusions assumed by them to have been inspired by the revolutionary spirit that has penetrated even into the Church, and to be highly derogatory to the honour of the heroes of our faith. This conviction frequently finds utterance in somewhat violent terms.

If you suggest that the biographer of a saint has been unequal to his task, or that he has not professed to write as a historian, you are accused of attacking the saint himself, who, it appears, is too powerful to allow himself to be compromised by an indiscreet panegyrist.

If, again, you venture to express doubt concerning certain miraculous incidents repeated by the author on insufficient evidence, although well-calculated to enhance the glory of the saint, you are at once suspected of lack of faith.

You are told you are introducing the spirit of rationalism into history, as though in questions of fact it were not above all things essential to weigh the evidence. How often has not an accusation of destructive criticism been flung, and men treated as iconoclasts, whose sole object has been to appraise at their true value the documents which justify our attitude of veneration, and who are only too happy when able to declare that one of God's friends has been fortunate enough to find a historian worthy of his task.

One might have thought that this simple analysis of the attitude of suspicion which so many devout souls assume in regard to historical criticism would suffice to demonstrate the injustice of their prejudices. Unhappily, it is less easy than might be supposed to efface an impression which, as they think, can only have been inspired by piety.

The conditions under which so many accounts of martyrs and lives of saints have been put together are, as a rule, too little known for any common ground of criticism to be available. Many readers are not sufficiently on their guard against the vague sentiment which endows hagiographers with some mysterious privilege of immunity from the errors of human frailty to which all other categories of writers are liable.

We therefore believe that we shall be doing a useful work if we try to classify, more definitely than has been done hitherto, the various methods pursued by pious writers, to sketch in broad outline the genesis of their compositions, and to show how far they are from being protected against errors which exact history is bound to denounce.

It may, perhaps, be as well to warn the reader from the first against an impression that might be gathered from a study which is mainly devoted to the weak points of hagiographic literature.

To give assistance in detecting materials of inferior workmanship is not to deny the excellence of what remains, and it is to the ultimate advantage of the harvest to point out the tares that have sometimes become mingled with the wheat to a most disconcerting extent.

The simple narrative of heroic days, written, as it were, with pens dipped in the blood of martyrs, the naive histories, sweet with the perfume of true piety, in which eye-witnesses relate the trials of virgins and of ascetics, deserve our fullest admiration and respect.

For that very reason they must be clearly differentiated from the extensive class of painfully-elaborated biographies in which the features of the saint are hidden by a heavy veil of rhetoric, and his voice overborne by that of his chronicler. There is an infinite distance between these two classes of literature. The one is well known, and its own merits recommend it. The other too often passes undetected and prejudices the first.

It must surely be admitted that from this simple task of classification, the need for which we are anxious to demonstrate, it is a far cry to that work of destruction which we may be suspected of having embarked upon.

Moreover, if we recommend any one who feels drawn to hagiographic studies to plunge boldly into the realm of criticism, we should advise no one to advance blindfold, neither have we dreamed of disguising the fact that by misapplying methods of research, however efficacious they may be in themselves, there is danger of being led to quite inadmissible conclusions.

It is easy to satisfy oneself on this point by glancing through the chapter in which we have discussed the questions touching upon mythological exegesis, so much in vogue at the present day. Certain brilliant displays which have taken place in that arena have dazzled a public more preoccupied with the novelty of the conclusions than with their trustworthiness. It has been our duty to lay down the necessary limitations, and to show how they may best be observed.

We do not profess to have written a complete treatise on hagiography. Many points which may suggest themselves to the reader have not even been touched upon, and we make no pretension of having exhausted any one of the subjects of which we have treated.

The quotations and examples might have been multiplied almost indefinitely. We believe ourselves justified, however, in resisting the temptation to impress the reader by a cheap display of erudition, and in avoiding everything that might have encumbered our exposition without adding anything to the force of the argument.

To indicate briefly the spirit in which hagiographic texts should be studied, to lay down the rules for discriminating between the materials that the historian can use and those that he should hand over as their natural property to artists and poets, to place people on their guard against the fascination of formulas and preconceived systems, such has been the aim of this volume.

Controversy—an evil counsellor—has been banished as far as may be from this little book. Nevertheless we shall occasionally be compelled to call attention to other people's mistakes. Defective methods, alas, frequently take shelter behind names of the highest credit, and sometimes, when attacking erroneous views, one may give the impression of attacking persons. For the critic it is a real cause for regret that in the thick of the fight blows sometimes fall on those at whom they were not aimed. Let it be understood, once and for all, that we have aimed at nobody.

Some chapters of this study first appeared in the *Revue des Questions historiques* (July, 1903). We have slightly revised and completed them in a few places. Except for two or three unimportant additions, this new edition of the book is simply a reprint of the first, which appeared in March, 1905.

CONTENTS

CHAPTER I.

PRELIMINARY DEFINITIONS.

CHAPTER II.

THE DEVELOPMENT OF THE LEGEND.

CHAPTER III.

The Work of the Hagiographer.

CHAPTER IV.

The Classification of Hagiographic Texts.

CHAPTER V.

The "Dossier" of a Saint.

CHAPTER VI.

PAGAN SURVIVALS AND REMINISCENCES.

CHAPTER VII.

CONCERNING CERTAIN HAGIOGRAPHIC HERESIES.

CHAPTER I.

PRELIMINARY DEFINITIONS.

Hagiographic documents—Imaginative tales. Artificial compositions
—Romances—Popular   inventions—Myths—Tales—Legends—
The hagiographic legend : its two principal factors.

LET us, in the first instance, attempt to define what
precisely is to be understood by a *hagiographic document*.

The term should not be applied indiscriminately to
every document bearing upon the saints. The chapter
in which Tacitus in vivid hues paints the sufferings of
the first Roman martyrs is not a hagiographic document, nor can the expression be rightly applied to
those pages of Eusebius's Ecclesiastical History across
which the victims of the great persecutions defile in
serried ranks. It was Eusebius, too, who composed, in
four volumes, a panegyric of the first Christian emperor
who, in the Greek Church, participates in the honours
reserved to the canonised saints. Nevertheless the Life
of Constantine is not a saint's life, whereas the book of
the Martyrs of Palestine, written with the object of
edifying the faithful by an account of the sufferings of
these heroes is at once a hagiographic document and
an historic record of the first order. So too the Acts
of St. Theodore, which in their present form possess

I

nothing in common with history, should, from the standpoint of hagiography, enjoy similar consideration. In the same class again, though under a special category, we may range the calendars or martyrologies in which the anniversaries of martyrs are recorded, together with official inscriptions, such as those of Pope Damasus, placed upon their tombs.

It thus appears that, in order to be strictly hagiographic, the document should be of a religious character and should aim at edification. The term may only be applied therefore to writings inspired by devotion to the saints and intended to promote it.

The point to be emphasised from the first is the distinction between hagiography and history. The work of the hagiographer may be historical, but it is not necessarily so. It may assume any literary form suitable to the glorification of the saints, from an official record adapted to the use of the faithful, to a poetical composition of the most exuberant character wholly detached from reality.

It is obvious that no one would venture to assert that everywhere and at all times hagiographers have submitted themselves to strict historical canons. But by what standard must we measure their digressions? That is a point to be determined in each individual case. Before attempting to suggest any rules on this subject, let us begin by laying down a few definitions less familiar than might at first sight be supposed.

In order to describe any narrative which is not in accordance with fact, a free use is made of the terms myth, fable, tale, romance, legend. Taken in a general sense these words are frequently used as though they were synonymous. The result has been a constant

confusion of thought which we shall hope to avoid by
a more rigorous definition of terms.[1]

We need, however, scarcely discuss the *fable*, which,
in its widest sense, may be held to include any imaginary narrative, and in its more restricted acceptation is
synonymous with the apologue, more especially when
the persons brought upon the scene are represented by
animals. This does not mean that hagiographers have
wholly neglected this form of imaginative composition.
The author of the *Life of SS. Barlaam and Joasaph*
has incorporated into his compilation various apologues
which have been the subject of individual studies.[2]
Nevertheless these are exceptions, and the critic of
hagiography need not, as a rule, trouble himself about
the emulators of Æsop and La Fontaine.

Myths, tales, legends and romances all belong to the
sphere of imaginative writing, but may be divided into
two categories, according as they are the spontaneous
and impersonal expression of the spirit of the people,
or artificial and deliberate compositions.

Romances, in the more usual acceptation of the term,
belong to this second category. The author selects
and studies his subject, and applies the resources of

---

1 The following are the titles of works dealing with this question,
which we give without questioning the conclusions of the authors,
who do not always agree among themselves. J. F. L. George,
Mythus und Sage, Berlin, 1837. J. Fiske, *Myths and Myth-makers*,
London, 1873. H. Steinthal, *Mythos, Sage, Märchen, Legende, Erzäh-
lung, Fabel*, in the *Zeitschrift fur Volkerspsychologie und Sprachwissenschaft*, vol. xvii., 1865, pp. 113-39. E. Bernheim, *Lehrbuch der
historischen Methode*, 3rd edition, Leipzig, 1903, pp. 317, 349, 457-
68. E. Siecke, *Mythologische Briefe*, Berlin, 1901. E. Bethe, *Mythus,
Sage, Märchen*, in *Hessische Blätter für Volkskunde*, 1905, pp.
97-142. [Fr. Lanzoni, *Genesi, svolgimento e tramonto delle leggende
storiche*, Rome, 1925 (Studi e Testi, 43).]

2 S. J. Warren, *De Grieksch christelijke roman Barlaam en Joasa
en zijne parabels*, Rotterdam, 1899, in 4to, 56 pp.

his talent and his imagination to the work of art he
has conceived. If he has chosen for his theme the
character and adventures of an historical person or of
a period of history, he will produce an historical
romance. If everything, both characters and incidents,
is pure invention it will be a novel of imagination; and
if, by means of a series of incidents, partly true, partly
fictitious, the author has attempted to depict the
soul of a saint honoured by the Church, we ought to
speak of his work as a hagiographic romance, although
the expression is one that has scarcely passed into
common use.

Romances of this type are exceedingly numerous,
and a few of them date back to very early times.[1]
One might instance the Acts of Paul and of Thecla, and
that collection of the apocryphal Acts of the Apostles
which enjoyed such long and extraordinary popularity.
The romance of the Clementine Homilies and Recog-
nitions is widely known, its main portions figuring for
a prolonged period in all the most celebrated hagiographic collections.[2]

Tales and legends, to which reference must now be
made, should not, strictly speaking, be placed in the
category of artificial compositions. It is true that the
name of tale is frequently bestowed upon short works
of fiction, and the novelist sometimes devotes himself
in his study to the composition of a narrative of which
the form recalls the legend or tale properly so called.
These learned imitations need only be mentioned here;

[1] An interesting account is to be found in E. von Dobschütz, *Der
Roman in der altchristlichen Literatur* in the *Deutsche Rundschau*,
April, 1902, pp. 87-106.

[2] H. U. Meyboom, *De Clemens-Roman*, Groningen, 1904, 2 vols.
Concerning this work and the most recent studies on the Clemen-
tines, see *Analecta Bollandiana*, vol. xxiv., pp. 138-41.

it is unnecessary to dwell on them further. We must reserve our attention for those works of fiction which have come down to us without any individual parentage, being the anonymous product of that abstraction known as the spirit of the people.

Let us first consider the *myth*. The term is frequently applied to anything that has no real existence, while the title of mythical personage is bestowed upon any hero who has lived solely in the imagination of the poet. Such, however, is not the technical meaning of the word, and it would be wrong to class as mythical personages figures such as Abner in *Athalie*, although the confidant of Joad was wholly invented by Racine.

The essence of the myth consists in the personification of a force or of an abstract idea; or, if you prefer it, the myth is simply an explanation of natural phenomena adapted to the capacity of a primitive people.[1] Whether we insist on treating it as a poetic symbol or whether, as has been ingeniously suggested, we should prefer to regard mythology as a treatise on physics for primitive times, it is none the less certain that natural phenomena supply the proper matter for the myth. The sun, the moon, the stars, lightning, the succession of night and day and the vicissitudes of the

---

[1] M. S. Reinach in *La Revue Critique* (3rd June, 1905, p. 425) questions this definition of a myth. "A myth," he says, "is essentially a story which humanity has believed to be true at a particular stage of its intellectual development." This formula appears to us too vague to serve as a definition. M. Reinach may have more reason on his side when he adds: "To attempt to draw a rigorous distinction, as the author has done, between the myth on the one side and the legend and tale on the other, is to demand from words a precision which they are unable to supply". The definition that we have adopted, being on the whole, the one most commonly accepted by specialists, we may perhaps be permitted the use of it in order to avoid confusion.

seasons are represented by gods and heroes, and by the adventures attributed to them. Aurora, with rosy fingers, opens the portals of the Orient, Phæton drives the chariot of the sun: such are the graceful fables with which the study of antiquity has familiarised us.

I do not wish to multiply examples, for before classifying a narrative it is essential to ascertain definitely its real significance, and were we to follow the methods of a certain school there would be very few works of fiction that could not be included under the category of mythology. There are men, so an ill-tempered critic has declared, who cannot even watch a cat and dog fight without some reference to the struggle between darkness and light. The exaggerations denounced in this sally are only too real, and we shall be careful not to make use of the term myth without solid reason.

Is there such a thing as a hagiographic myth? Or have the hagiographers made use of mythical elements? I see no difficulty in admitting it, and shall show later on that they have transferred to the saints more than one narrative which belongs to ancient mythology.

The *tale* proper is an invented story referring neither to a real personage nor yet to any definite place. "Once upon a time there were a king and queen who had a very beautiful daughter. . . ." This classical beginning of the story-teller [1] is exactly characteristic of its style, in which everything is made accessory to the plot of the narrative, intended solely for the entertainment of the listener, or calculated to set in relief some practical truth as in the case of moral tales.

---

[1] This is almost literally the opening phrase of Apuleius in *Cupid and Psyche*: "Erant in quadam civitate rex et regina. Hi tres numero filias forma conspicuas habuere," *Met.*, iv., 28.

Contrary to what one would imagine, there exists no great variety of popular tales. All may be traced back to a certain number of types, none of which appears to belong exclusively to a particular nation or even race ; they are the common patrimony of humanity.

Much has been written concerning their origin.[1] Without entering into a detailed study of the various theories propounded by specialists, mention must be made of two principal ones which have won more favour than the rest, and which may be considered as extreme solutions. Some explain the repetition of the same themes and the similarity in their forms by the uniformity of the human mind. Others take refuge in a less simple and less metaphysical explanation, which coincides more nearly with ascertained facts. According to them India is the one and only cradle of all popular tales disseminated throughout the whole world,[2] and whatever one may like to assume concerning their original author, they had their birth there and thence set out on their travels to become in the widest sense the common possession of all nations. It is in

[1] Emmanuel Cosquin, *Contes Populaires de Lorraine*, vol. i., Paris, 1886, i.-lxvii.; *id., L'Origine des contes populaires européens et les théories de M. Lang,* Paris, 1891; *id., Quelques observations sur les "Incidents communs aux contes orientaux,"* London, 1892. M. Cosquin is a definite partisan of the Orientalist theory, which has been combated more especially by M. J. Bédier, *Les fabliaux— Bibliotheque de l'École des Hautes Études,* vol. 98, Paris, 1893, pp. 45-250. Concerning other systems and their variations, the following may be consulted: Ch. Martens, *L'origine des Contes populaires* in the *Revue Néo-Scolastique,* vol. i., 1894, pp. 234-62, 352-84. L. Sainéan, *L'état actuel des études de Folk-lore* in the *Revue de Synthèse historique,* vol. iv., 1902, pp. 147-74. [In the 3d ed. Delehaye deletes the citation of Sainéan and in its place cites: G. Huet, *Les contes populaires,* Paris, 1923, 189 pp.]

[2] Among the advocates of the Orientalist theory, there are some who regard Egypt as the birthplace of popular tales. See, for instance, S. Reinach in the *Revue d'histoire et de littérature religieuses,* vol. ix., 1904, pp. 319-20. We cannot discuss the subject here.

no way necessary to commit ourselves here to any theory
of the first origin of popular tales. We need only remember that, like those light seeds that the wind carries
beyond the seas, they are for ever floating in the atmo-
sphere, and may be found in every country and every
clime without their being connected in any definite
way with either name or place.

The *legend*, on the other hand, has, of necessity, some
historical or topographical connection. It refers imaginary events to some real personage, or it localises
romantic stories in some definite spot. Thus one mày
speak of the legend of Alexander or of Cæsar, of the
legend of the Castle of the Drachenfels on the Rhine,
or of that of the Red Lake, Lough Derg, in Ireland.
Such, in accordance with common usage, is the precise
meaning of the terms we have to employ.

It must, however, be observed that in practice classification is less easy, and the various categories are less
clearly differentiated. One of these winged tales which
fly from nation to nation may for a moment settle on
some famous monument, or the anonymous king who
was the principal personage may take to himself some
historic name. At once the tale is transformed into a
legend, and one might easily be misled if some other
version of the same story did not reveal the purely accidental introduction of the historical element.[1] In the

1 In certain cases the various disguises are easy to recognize, as
in the stories in which Jesus Christ and St. Peter are brought on the
scene. Here, for example, is a legend of the Basque country, chron-
icled by Cerquand: "Our Lord and St. Peter one day, when out
walking, came across a man kneeling in the middle of the road and
praying to God to extricate his cart from the ditch into which it
had fallen. As Jesus was passing on without paying any attention to
the carter's prayer, St. Peter said to Him, 'Lord, wilt thou not come
to the help of this poor man?' 'He does not deserve our help,' Jesus
replied, 'for he makes no effort to help himself.' A little farther on

same way the myth itself may also readily assume the appearance of a legend.

On the other hand, if you despoil the legend of all that connects it with reality, you give it the external features of a mere tale. Hence the difficulty of disentangling legend and tale in the celebrated collection of the *Arabian Nights*, for in spite of the highly fantastic character of the stories that compose it, portions have been identified with some sort of historical basis.[1] Contrariwise it may occur that what is apparently a highly distinctive legend will suddenly re-appear in the guise of a folk tale. It was a long time before men recognised an adaptation of the celebrated tale of the ass's skin in the legend of Saint Dymphna, or before the touching history of Geneviève de Brabant[2] proved to be a theme which had previously been turned to account by the epic poets of India.[3]

As we have just seen, legends, considered as connected narrations, in contradistinction to myths and tales, presuppose an historical fact as basis or pretext : such is the first essential element of the species.   This

---

they came upon another man in similar plight, but shouting and swearing and doing his utmost. Jesus hastened to his assistance, saying: 'This one deserves our help for he is doing what he can'." Every one is familiar with this incident as told by the fabulist concerning Hercules. See R. Köhler, *Kleine Schriften*, Berlin, 1900, vol. ii., pp. 102-4. Consult also the admirable apologue: "Why men no longer know when they are going to die," *ibid.*, pp. 100-2.

[1] M. J. de Goeje, *De Arabische Nachtvertellingen* in *De Gids*, 1886, vol. iii., pp. 383-413.

[2] *Acta* SS., May, vol. iii, pp. 479-86.

[3] On the variations and derivatives of this story see H. Suchier, *Oeuvres poétiques de Beaumanoir*, Société des anciens textes Français, vol. i., 1884, pp. xxv.-lxxxi., clx. Marie de Brabant, whose story is identical has been the object of ecclesiastical veneration. *Acta SS.*, Jan., vol. ii., p. 180; April, vol. i., p. 57.

historical fact may either be developed or disfigured by popular imagination : and here we have the second element.   Both elements may be combined in very unequal proportions, and according as the preponderance is to be found on the side of fact or on that of fiction, the narrative may be classed as history or as legend.

As it is the fictitious element which determines the classification of legendary narratives, people have naturally formed the habit of applying to it the name of the species itself, and thus the term legend has been extended to every unconscious distortion of historic truth, whether there be question of a series of incidents or of a solitary episode.

However we interpret the term, it seems scarcely worth while to insist on the considerable part played by legend in hagiographic literature, which is emphatically popular both in its origins and in its aim. Indeed it is from hagiography that the name itself has been borrowed.   In its primitive meaning the legend is the history that has to be read, *legenda*, on the feast of a saint.   It is the passion of the martyr or the eulogy of the confessor, without reference to its historical value.   " Legendarius vocatur liber ille ubi agitur de vita et obitu confessorum, qui legitur in eorum festis, martyrum autem in Passionariis," wrote John Beleth,[1] in the twelfth century, thus differentiating the passion from the legend, contrary to the custom that was subsequently to prevail.   For, as early as the thirteenth century, the *Legenda Aurea* sanctioned the wider meaning which includes at once the acts of the martyrs and the biographies of other saints.   We

---

[1] *De divinis officiis,* 60; Migne, P. L., vol. ccii., p. 66. See also E. von Dobschütz, art. "Legende," in the *Realencyklopaedie für Protestantische Theologie,* 3rd edition, vol. xi., p. 345.

might, therefore, in conformity with ancient usage, bestow the term legend upon all hagiographic narratives, including even those of admitted documentary value. Nevertheless, to avoid confusion in the following pages, we shall rigidly refrain from doing so, and the word legend will only be applied to stories or incidents unauthenticated by history.

Hagiographic literature has come to be written under the influence of two very distinct factors, factors to be met with, indeed, in whatever stream of literary productiveness we seek to trace to its source. There is, first, the anonymous creator called the people or, if we prefer to take the effect for the cause, the legend. Here the work is that of a mysterious and many-headed agent, uncontrolled in his methods, swift and unfettered as the imagination always is, perpetually in labour with fresh products of his fancy, but incapable of chronicling them in writing. Beside him there is the man of letters, the editor, who stands before us as one condemned to a thankless task, compelled to follow a beaten track, but giving to all he produces a deliberate and durable character. Both together have collaborated in that vast undertaking known as "The Lives of the Saints," and it is important for us to recognise the part played by each in this process of evolution, which, though the work of all time, is yet incessantly renewed.

It is our intention to restrict ourselves almost exclusively to the pious literature of the Middle Ages, and we shall seek to prove how it was elaborated by the people on the one side and the hagiographers on the other. The methods pursued both by the one and the other may appear to some people to be not yet wholly a thing of the past. It is an opinion which we ourselves are not prepared to controvert.

If, in lieu of the remainder, we substitute a series of deductions, we are merely writing the history of the battle in our own way; in fact, we ourselves then become the creators of a new legend, and we must either resign ourselves to this necessity or elect to remain in ignorance.

Every one is agreed as to the special difficulty of giving a precise account of any complicated action that cannot be taken in at a glance. It must not, however, be assumed that putting aside these exceptional cases there is nothing more easy or more common than to give a faithful description. The truth is that in daily life we are perpetually taking part in that unconscious labour from which legends are evolved, and each one of us has had occasion to testify a hundred times over how difficult it is to convey, with absolute precision, our impression of any complex incident.

To begin with, it is very rare to grasp the event in all its details, and to trace the connection between the various parts. It is still more rare for us to be in a position to distinguish the causes in such a way as to leave no possible doubt concerning the motives that have prompted the actors. Consequently we allow our instinct to fill in the gaps in our information. By a series of intuitive connections we re-establish the continuity of action, and we read our own interpretation into the forces that have brought about such and such a result. If we happen to be under the empire of passion or of any sentiment that clouds our clear view of things, if we secretly desire that any established fact should not have occurred, or that any unnoted circumstance should really have taken place, if it coincides with our wishes that the actors should have followed any special impulse, it may occur that, heedlessly, we leave one portion of the picture in the shade, or give undue prominence to another, according as our own prepossessions suggest. Unless, therefore, we submit our arguments to a rigid supervision and maintain complete control over our impressions, we are liable, to the detriment of truth, to introduce a strong subjective element into our narrative. To give an exact description of complex reality demands not only sound sense and a trained judgment but also conscious effort, and consequently requires a stimulus adequate to the object in view.

It must be admitted that apart from exceptional circumstances the average man is not endowed with the intellectual vigour necessary for such a task. The habit of analysing one's sensations and of controlling the slightest impulses of one's soul to such an extent as to be habitually on one's guard against the natural tendency to mingle what one imagines with what one knows, is the privilege of very few. Even those who, thanks to natural gifts and a superior training, rise above the average of their fellows, do not invariably make use of their special faculties.

Let me suppose that a man has been an eye-witness of some sanguinary drama. He will describe the various exciting circumstances to his friends with the most minute details, and nothing will appear to have escaped him that bears upon the criminal and his victim.

But suppose this same man subpœnaed to give evidence at the assizes, and that on his deposition, given on oath, depends the life of a fellow-creature. What a difference between the two versions of the same event! At once his narrative becomes less clear and less complete, and is far from possessing that palpitating interest that he gave to it in private. This is simply because, under such solemn circumstances, we carry to a far higher point our scrupulous exactitude, and we are no longer tempted to indulge in the petty vanity of posing as important and well-informed. Hence it is that even the most veracious and upright of men unconsciously create little legends by introducing into their narratives their own impressions, deductions and passions, and thus present the truth either embellished or disfigured according to circumstances.

These sources of error, it need scarcely be said, become multiplied with the number of intermediaries. Every one in turn understands the story in a different fashion and repeats it in his own way. Through inattention or through defective memory some one forgets to mention an important circumstance, necessary to the continuity of the history. A narrator, more observant than the rest, notes the deficiency, and by means of his imagination does his best to repair it. He invents some new detail, and suppresses another until probability and logic appear to him sufficiently safe-guarded. This result is usually only obtained at the expense of truth, for the narrator does not observe that he has substituted a very different story for the primitive version. Sometimes again the narrative may pass through the hands of a witness who does not wholly approve of it, and who will not fail to contribute markedly to its disfigurement by some imperceptible turn of thought or expression.

These things happen every day, and whether we are eye-witnesses or mere intermediaries, our limited intelligence, our carelessness, our passions, and above all perhaps our prejudices, all conspire against historical accuracy when we take it upon ourselves to become narrators.

This commonplace experience becomes much more interesting and more fraught with consequences when it is indefinitely multiplied, and when, for the intelligence and impressions of the individual we substitute the intelligence and impressions of a people or a crowd. These collective, and, in a certain sense, abstract faculties, are of a quite special nature, and their activities are subjected to laws that have been deeply studied in our own day, and to which a special branch of psychology has been assigned.[1]   Such laws as have been formulated have been verified by thousands of examples drawn from the popular literature of every country. Hagiographic literature offers a large mass of material amply confirming them.

To avoid complicating the question we shall not attempt to apportion the varying degrees of capacity of different social strata.   No task, indeed, would be more difficult, and in regard to the matters that interest us the most varied elements have to be taken into account.   In the Middle Ages the whole populace was interested in the saints.   Every one invoked them, paid them honour and loved to sing their praises.   Popular society in which the legends were elaborated was composed of many elements, and by no means excluded persons of literary pretensions.   I hasten to add that the saints gained nothing thereby.

The intellectual capacity of the multitude reveals itself on all sides as exceedingly limited, and it would be a mistake to assume that it usually submits itself to the influence of superior minds.   On the contrary, the

[1] Lazarus und Steinthal, *Zeitschrift für Völkerspsychologie und Sprachwissenschaft*, Berlin, Leipzig, i., 1860 - xix., 1889. A book by G. le Bon, *Psychologie des Foules*, Paris, 1895, treated from a very special point of view, contains, together with notable exaggerations, some useful remarks.

latter necessarily suffer loss from contact with the former, and it would be quite illogical to attribute a special value to a popular tradition because it had its origin amid surroundings in which persons of solid merit were to be met with. In a crowd superiority quickly vanishes, and the average intelligence tends to fall far below mediocrity. The best point of comparison by which we can ascertain its level is the intelligence of a child.

In truth, the number of ideas of which the popular brain is capable of receiving any impression is extremely small, and these ideas must be very simple. Equally simple are its deductions, which it arrives at by means of a small number of intuitive principles, and which are frequently little more than loosely connected conceptions or pictures.

The artless nature of popular genius betrays itself clearly in the legends it creates. Thus the number of personages and of events of which it preserves any remembrance is few indeed ; its heroes never exist side by side, but succeed each other, and the latest inherits all the greatness of his predecessors.

Antiquity has bequeathed to us many famous examples of this phenomenon of absorption. The struggles of many centuries concentrated themselves under the walls of Troy, while Solon and Lycurgus bear off the honours of a prolonged legislative evolution at Athens and in Sparta.[1] In less remote times it is Alexander,

---

[1] Concerning this and similar examples consult Wachsmuth, *Ueber die Quellen der Geschichtsfälschung (Berichte über die Verhandlungen der K. Sächsischen Gesellschaft der Wissenschaften zu Leipzig)*, Phil.-Hist. Classe, vol. viii., 1856, pp. 121-53. It is worth remembering that legends of a similar nature are growing up in our own day. "Legend has transformed the Civil Code into the principles of the Revolution expressed in two thousand articles by order of the

Cæsar and Charlemagne [1] who, in their respective lands, fire the popular imagination, and on the heads of these chosen heroes all the honours accumulate. Brilliant feats of arms which rouse enthusiasm are attributed to the national hero, public benefits are all due to him, and everything of note throughout the country is in some way connected with his name.

Were we to believe what legend tells us there is scarcely in the whole town of Alexandria a single stone that was not laid by Alexander the Great himself.[2] Since the day when Tiberius turned the rock of Capri into the scene of his debaucheries he has become, so to speak, a tutelary genius whose beneficent hand has left traces of its activity in every corner of the isle.[3]

First Consul. In this summary of history the code is no longer the outcome of centuries of effort by king and parliament, and by the citizens in their communes and corporations; there survives only the thought of the Emperor; it is the Code Napoleon," H. Leroy, *Le centenaire du Code civil* in the *Revue de Paris*, 1st October, 1903.

[1] Concerning the legend of Alexander consult P. Meyer, *Alexandre le grand dans la littérature française du moyen âge* in the *Bibliothèque française du moyen âge*, vol. iv., Paris, 1886; J. Darmesteter, *La légende d'Alexandre chez les Perses* in the *Bibliothèque de l'École des Hautes Études*, vol. 35, Paris, 1878, pp. 83-99; J. Lévi, *La légende d' Alexandre dans le Talmud* in the *Revue des Études Juives*, vol. ii., 1881, p. 203; vol. vii., p. 78; *Mélusine*, vol. v., pp. 116-18; S. S. Hoogstra, *Proza-bewerkingen van het Leven van Alexander den Groote in het Middelnederlandsch*, The Hague, 1898, pp. i.-xxiii.; Fr. Kampers, *Alexander der Grosse und die Idee des Weltimperiums in Prophetie und Sage*, Freiburg im Breisgau, 1901. Concerning the Caesar legend consult A. and G. Doutrepont, *La légende de César en Belgique* in the *IIIème Congrès des Savants Catholiques*, vol. v., Brussels, 1894, pp. 80-108. On Charlemagne, see G. Paris, *Histoire poétique de Charlemagne*, Paris, 1865; E. Müntz, *La légende de Charlemagne dans l'art au moyen âge* in *Romania*, vol. xiv., 1883 p., 320.

[2] G. Lumbroso, *L'Egitto dei Greci e dei Romani*, 2nd edition, Rome, 1895, p. 157.

[3] Maxime Du Camp, *Orient et Italie*, Paris, 1968, pp. 13, 60, 74.

It is obvious that this custom of accumulating on a single head all the glories of preceding heroes affects very markedly the true proportions of the persons concerned. The splendour of the apotheosis is sometimes such that the hero entirely loses his true physiognomy and emerges in complete disguise. Thus Virgil, having become the idol of the Neapolitans, ceased to be the inspired poet in order to be converted into the governor of the city.[1] Local tradition at Sulmona has transformed Ovid into everything that he was not: a clever magician, a rich merchant, a prophet, a preacher, a sort of paladin, and—who would believe it?—a great saint.[2]

Historic truth is put wholly out of court on these occasions, for it is an understood thing that the really popular hero plays a part in all important events; that nothing generous, noble or useful can be accomplished without the intervention of the great man who monopolises the sympathies of the populace. In the religious sphere the idol of all hearts is the saint specially venerated in the district. Here, it is St. Martin whose name crops up at every turn; there, St. Patrick.[3] The enthusiasm of the people has not failed to enlarge the sphere of their activities, including among these a number of incidents detached from their historic setting, or despoiling, for their benefit, the eclipsed heroes of an earlier stage of development.

1 This subject has been exhaustively treated by D. Comparetti, *Virgilio nel medio evo*, 2nd edition, Florence, 1896, 2 vols. 8vo.

2 A. De Nino, *Ovidio nella tradizione popolare di Sulmona*, Casalbordino, 1886, p. 1.

3 Bulliot, *La mission et le culte de St. Martin d'après les légendes et les monuments populaires dans le pays Éduen*, Autun, 1892; Shearman, *Loca Patriciana*, Dublin, 1879; W. G. Wood-Martin, *Traces of the Elder Faiths of Ireland*, London, 1902, vol. i., pp. 163, 245; vol. ii., pp. 20, 88.

Above all, do not expect the populace to distinguish
between namesakes. Great men are so rare! What
likelihood is there that there should have lived two of
the same name? It is this sort of reasoning which has
persuaded the inhabitants of Calabria that St. Louis,
on his return from the first Crusade, sojourned in several of their towns, whereas, in truth, he never set foot
in the district. The king Louis who passed through
the Neapolitan provinces with the remains of his army
of Crusaders was Louis VII. When the canonisation
of Louis IX. had cast into the shade the memory of
all his predecessors, it became quite natural to substitute him for the other Louis in the popular memory.[1]
In the same way, by the simple force of attraction, as
early as the fourth century, incidents borrowed from
the life of Cyprian of Antioch became interpolated in
that of Cyprian of Carthage.[2] It was almost inevitable
that the illustrious martyr should inherit from the
earlier and more obscure Cyprian. In the same way
Alexander the Great and Charlemagne absorbed the
achievements of all their namesakes.[3]

It may be seen from this that the populace is never
disturbed, as we are, by chronological difficulties. No
one, for instance, was startled by hearing it read out
that St. Austremonius, in the reign of the Emperor
Decius, was sent to Auvergne by St. Clement.[4] To

[1] F. Lenormant, *À travers l'Apulie et la Lucanie*, Paris, 1883, vol.
i., p. 323.

[2] Witnesses to this confusion are St. Gregory Nazianzen, Prudentius and Macarius of Magnesia. See Th. Zahn, *Cyprian von Antiochien*, Erlangen, 1882, p. 84. [This sentence and the following,
together with this footnote, are deleted in the 3d ed.]

[3] It is well known that Alexander the Great has had the credit
of the foundations of Alexander Severus, and that the name of
Charlemagne has absorbed many incidents attributed by history to
Charles Martel. P. Rajna, *Le origini dell' epopea francese*, Florence,
1884, p. 199.

[4] *Acta SS.*, November, vol. i., p. 49.

the popular mind it was perfectly natural that, in the same early days, there should have been both dukes and counts ; and why should any one have suspected that it was an anachronism to bestow the title of archdeacon on St. Stephen and St. Lawrence, who certainly were very far from being mere ordinary deacons ?

Neither was the popular mind disturbed by geography, and questions of distance scarcely existed for it.   Men listened without lifting an eyebrow to stories in which Cæsarea Philippi is confused with Cæsarea of Palestine,[1] and in which a war is referred to as breaking out between the latter town and Carthage.[2]   The caravan of seventy camels sent by Isquirinus, Prefect of Périgueux, into the desert to seek for the seventy monks who were dying of hunger, did not appear to them any less interesting because the said desert is situated on the banks of the Dordogne.[3]   I am prepared to believe that men would be more exacting concerning the topography of their native country, a knowledge of which is forced upon them by their own eyes.   But why trouble about distant scenes ?[4]

As for history, the popular intelligence conceives of it in the same spirit of naïve simplicity.   Let us see, for instance, what impression has been preserved of persecutions under the Roman Empire.   To begin with, no distinction is made between the emperors who

1 *Passio S. Procopii*, no. 27 in the *Acta SS.*, July, vol. ii., p. 564.
2 *St. Cassiodorus* in the *Mélanges Paul Fabre*, Paris, 1902, pp. 40-50.
3 *Vita S. Frontonis, auctore Gauzberto;* compare L. Duchesne, *Fastes Episcopaux de l'ancienne Gaule*, vol. ii., p. 132.
4 We have referred to the value of topographical records in hagiographic legends in the *Analecta Bollandiana*, vol. xvi., pp. 222-35, 243-44. Concerning the tenacity of the memory of the people in all that concerns the names of the places in the country they inhabit, see Père M. J. Lagrange, *La Méthode historique, surtout à propos de l'Ancien Testament*, Paris, 1903, pp. 188-92.

have ordered and those who have merely authorised proceedings against the Christians.   There is but one epithet, *impiissimus*, by which all alike are described, whether reference is made to Nero, Decius and Diocletian or to Trajan, Marcus Aurelius and Alexander Severus.   All are held to be animated by the same degree of insensate fury against Christianity, and to have no other thought but that of destroying it.   Frequently it is the emperor in person who summons the Christians before his tribunal, even though he be compelled to undertake journeys of which history has preserved no record.   It is, however, obvious that the head of the State cannot be everywhere.   This is no obstacle to his fury.   He has emissaries who scour the empire and represent him worthily.   Everywhere Christians are outlawed, hunted down and dragged before monsters of judges, who contrive to invent appalling tortures that have never been inflicted even on the worst of criminals.   Divine intervention, which prevents these refined torments from injuring the martyrs, serves to emphasise the cruelty of their persecutors, while at the same time providing an adequate and visible reason for the numbers of conversions which the rage of the executioners is unable to stem.

Such, in brief, is the picture of the age of persecutions as recorded in popular legend.   The variations in legislative enactments, and the diversity in the application of the edicts, the very marked individuality of certain of the great enemies of the Faith, the purely local character of some of the outbreaks of which the Christians were victims, do not in any sense appeal to the intelligence of the people, who much prefer a simple picture in vivid colours and strongly marked outline, to combinations of numerous and complex facts.

Need we add that historical sequence has no existence for the populace? That, without exciting suspicion, one may assign the date of a martyrdom indifferently to the reign of any one of the impious Emperors Decius, Numerian or Diocletian?[1] That the name of the judge is of no consequence, and that it is a matter of indifference whether the cruel Dacianus could or could not persecute at one and the same time in Italy and in Spain? The long list of the Popes is unfamiliar to them, and the part played by a Pope Cyriacus was not sufficient to bring under suspicion the legend of the eleven thousand virgins,[2] any more than surprise was caused by the introduction of a Pope Alexander into the story of St. Ouen.[3]

Thus robbed of their individuality, isolated in a sense from their period and their surroundings, and dragged from their natural setting, historical personages acquire, in the eyes of the people, an unreal and inconsistent character. For a vivid and clearly accentuated portrait as bequeathed to us by history, we substitute an ideal figure who is the personification of an abstraction: in place of the individual, the people know

[1 The 3d ed. adds: There are numerous examples in *Les Passions des martyrs et les genres littéraires*, p. 136-315.]

1 I may recall, among others, the martyrdom of St. Cecilia of which the date is sometimes *temporibus Alexandri imperatoris* and sometimes *Marci Aurelii et Commodi temporibus*. See *Analecta Bollandiana*, vol. xxii., pp. 86-88.

2 *Acta SS.*, October, vol. ix., pp. 100-4, 214, 276-78.

3 *Analecta Bollandiana*, vol. xx., pp. 175-76. According to the legend of SS. Chrysanthus and Daria these saints suffered martyrdom in 283 under Numerian and their acts were written by order of Pope Stephen († 257), *Acta SS.*, October, vol. xi., p. 484. As a counterpart to this anachronism one may quote the legend of St. Florian and his companions at Bologna. The martyrdom of the saints is supposed to have happened in the twenty-seventh year of Heraclius (637), and the translation of their relics during the episcopate of St. Petronius in the fifth century. See *Analecta Bollandiana*, vol. xxiii., p. 298.

only the type. Alexander personifies the conqueror ; Cæsar, the organising genius of the Roman people ; Constantine, the Empire regenerated by Christianity.

In the really popular hagiographic legends it is not St. Lawrence, but the typical martyr that is brought upon the scene, just as later St. Martin becomes the type of the missionary-bishop and miracle-worker. There is also the typical persecutor. Diocletian is the most prominent here, then certain judges who personify, so to speak, the cruelty of pagan justice. One of the most celebrated of these is the redoubtable Anulinus, who was, in reality, pro-consul of Africa during the great persecution. His name has become a synonym for executioner, and in a number of legends recourse is had to him to bring about the death of Christians at Lucca, at Milan and at Ancona, under Nero, Valerian, Gallienus and Maximianus, without counting the narratives in which his authentic exploits are recorded.[1]

It is scarcely surprising that the reading of certain hagiographic records should be monotonous work, or that there should be such remarkable resemblances between the acts of so many martyrs. While really historical documents such as the Acts of St. Polycarp and of SS. Perpetua and Felicitas and of St. Cyprian offer the most remarkable variations of detail, the *legend* of the martyrs is nothing but a mass of repetitions. This is the result of eliminating as far as possible the individual element, in order to retain only the abstract form. Every martyr, as a rule, is animated by the same sentiments, expresses the same opinions and is subject to the same trials, while the holy confessor who has earned his reward by an edifying life must needs

[1] Consult the quotations in Le Blant, *Les Actes des Martyrs,* Paris, 1882, p. 27.

have possessed all the virtues of his profession, which the hagiographer, the faithful mouthpiece of popular tradition, delights to enumerate.

Here, for example, is the portrait of St. Fursey, Abbot : " Erat enim forma præcipuus, corpore castus, mente devotus, affabilis colloquio, amabilis adspectu, prudentia præditus, temperantia clarus, interna fortitudine firmus, censura iustitiæ stabilis, longanimitate assiduus, patientia robustus, humilitate mansuetus, caritate sollicitus et ita in eo omnium virtutum decorem sapientia adornabat, ut secundum apostolum sermo illius semper in gratia sale esset conditus ".[1] Unquestionably this is a noble eulogy. But might not the same be written of every saint ?

The biographer of St. Aldegonde describes her in the following terms : " Erat namque moribus honesta, eloquio suavis, in pauperibus misericors, in lectione velox, in responsis citissima, mitis omnibus, inter nobiles humilis, iunioribus quasi æqualis, in parcitate cibi et potus ita dedita abstinentiæ ut nulla sodalium sibi æquipararetur ".[2] A few characteristic incidents revealing her admirable virtues would impress one far more than this conventional picture. But the popular mind can

1 "For he was comely to look upon, chaste of body, earnest in mind, affable of speech, gracious of presence, abounding in wisdom, a model of abstemiousness, steadfast in resolution, firm in right judgments, unwearied in longanimity, of sturdiest patience, gentle in humility, solicitous in charity, while wisdom in him so enhanced the radiance of all the virtues that his conversation, according to the Apostle, was always seasoned with wit in the grace of God" (*Acta SS.*, Jan., vol. ii, p. 37).

2 "For she was irreproachable in conduct, persuasive of speech, merciful to the poor, quick at reading, most ready in answering, gentle to all, humble among great folk, to her juniors like one of their own age, and so devoted to abnegation in abstinence of food and drink that none of her companions could be compared with her" (*Acta SS.*, Jan., vol. ii., p. 1036).

only retain a simple and general notion of sanctity. You ask for a portrait and you receive a programme.

Moreover the programme can boast of very little variety. Poverty of invention is another of the characteristics of popular intelligence. Its developments all resemble each other, and its combinations offer but little interest. As for its creative faculties, they appear condemned to sterility the moment the public has come into possession of a sufficient number of fairly interesting themes and topics to fit the situations of more ordinary occurrence.

The comparative study of folk-lore has revealed the fact that the same stories recur among all races and in all countries, that they can all be traced back to a limited number of identical themes, and that they have spread themselves over the world from a common stock.

Every one is aware that even in our own day celebrated sayings are constantly re-issued under fresh headings, that amusing anecdotes are perpetually transferred from one person to another,[1] and that, to quote but a single classical example, there is not a town without its legendary absent-minded citizen, everywhere the victim of identical misadventures.

The study of ancient authors supplies us with innumerable examples of the transmission of legendary themes. We have only to glance through the descriptions of celebrated sieges as told by the old chroniclers to discover that the effects of famine, the patriotism of the besieged, and the cunning artifices designed to deceive the enemy as to the resources of the town, are almost invariably described in identical terms.

---

[1] Some examples of this have been collected by H. Gaidoz, *Légendes Contemporaines* in *Mélusine*, vol. ix., 1898-99, pp. 77, 118, 140, 187.

Thus when the Gauls besieged Rome the soldiers were reduced to soaking the leather of their shields and sandals in order to eat it. The same fact occurred, if we are to accept the evidence of Livy, at the siege of Casilinum during the second Punic war, and again, according to Josephus, at the siege of Jerusalem. During the same siege of Rome the women sacrificed their hair to weave into ropes ; while the women of Carthage, Salonæ, Byzantium, Aquileia, Thasos and many other cities were equally capable of a devotion that may well be called heroic.[1] In the same way the chronicles of the Middle Ages are full of ingenious manœuvres invented to deceive the enemy who forthwith falls into the trap and raises the siege.[2] In order to appreciate the historic value of these curious narratives, it is sufficient to place them side by side with others of the same description.

One might vary indefinitely the examples given, and quote curious cases of quaint legends becoming acclimatised in the most incongruous localities. Strange as it may seem, the Irish have thought fit to borrow from King Midas his ass's ears,[3] with which to adorn at least two of their kings.[4]

---

1 The examples have been collected by A. Schwegler, *Römische Geschichte*, vol. iii., Tubingen, 1858, p. 260.

2 For example, a herd of fat cattle would be driven into the enemy's camp, or the besiegers would be pelted with loaves of bread, or still better with cheeses, frequently made from the milk of nursing mothers, in order to create a conviction that the town was well supplied with provisions. See G. Pitrè, *Stratagemmi leggendarii da città assediate*, new edition, Palermo, 1904, 21 pp.; also the *Archivio per lo studio delle Tradizioni popolari*, vol. xxii., 1903-04, pp. 193-211. See also *Romania*, vol. xxxiii., 1904, p. 459.

3 Ovid, *Metamorphoses*, xi., 180 and following; Hyginus, *Fabulae*, 191, 3.

4 H. D'Arbois de Jubainville in the *Revue Celtique*, vol. xxiv., 1903, p. 215.

A systematic classification of legendary themes furnished by hagiographic documents would lead to similar conclusions. Many striking episodes which an inexperienced reader would be tempted to take for original inventions are mere reminiscences or floating traditions which cling sometimes to one saint, sometimes to another.

The miraculous crucifix which appeared to St. Hubert[1] between the antlers of a stag, is in no sense the exclusive property of this saint. It may be found equally in the legend of St. Meinulf[2] and that of St. Eustace,[3] as well as in those of many others in which variations of detail render the theme less easily recognisable. Lists of saints have been compiled who all vanquished dragons,[4] but all these enumerations would have to be greatly enlarged before one could in any way hope to exhaust the subject. For myself, I see no object in doing so. It is almost always a waste of time to seek to identify the historical fact which has been responsible for the introduction of such epic incidents in the life of a saint. We might as well institute inquiries as to why a seed borne by the wind has fallen on any particular spot.

It is with reason that a critic has taken exception to a detail in the acts of SS. Sergius and Bacchus.[5] The body of the latter martyr having been flung out on the highway, was protected from dogs by birds of prey.[6] A

---

[1] *Acta SS.*, Nov., vol. i., p. 839.
[2] *Ibid.*, Oct., vol. iii., pp. 188, 212.
[3] *Ibid.*, Sept., vol. vi., p. 124; [H. Delehaye, *La légende de S. Eustache*, in *Bulletin de la classe des lettres de l'Académie Royale de Belgique*, 1919, p. 1-36.]
[4] See Ch. Cahier, *Caractéristiques des Saints*, vol. i., pp. 315-22. See also M. Meyer, *Ueber die Verwandschaft heidnischer und Christlicher Drachentödter* in the *Verhandlungen der XL, Versammlung deutscher Philologen*, Leipzig, 1890, p. 336 and following.
[5] P. Byaeus in *Acta SS.*, Oct., vol. iii., p. 838.
[6] *Ibid.*, p. 867.

similar miraculous protection was accorded to the remains of St. Vincent,[1] St. Vitus,[2] St. Florian,[3] and St.
Stanislaus of Cracow,[4] while we must not omit the
eagle summoned by Solomon to watch over the body
of David, or other similar narratives drawn from Talmudic literature.[5]   Nor, since we are on the subject of
eagles, should we forget that the miraculous bird who
spread his wings to protect St. Servatius,[6] St. Ber-
tulph,[7] St. Medard [8] and others from sun and rain is to
be met with elsewhere than in hagiographic documents.

We read in the life of St. Elizabeth of Hungary that,
before starting on the Crusades, her husband presented
her with a ring of which the precious stone possessed
the property of breaking when a calamity happened to
its donor.   This legend, introduced into her life, no
doubt on the strength of some historic incident, may
be found with slight variations in the life of St.
Honoratus of Buzançais.   It is a popular theme which
has not only been turned to account in the romance of
Flores and Blanchefleur, but in the *Arabian Nights*, in
a Kalmuk folk-tale, and in more than one Indian
story.[9]

Again, the dramatic adventure that befel the page
of St. Elizabeth of Portugal is a Christian adapta-

1 Prudentius, *Peristeph.*, v., 102 and following.
2 *Acta SS.*, Jan., vol. ii., pp. 1025-26.
3 *Ibid.*, May, vol. iv., p. 465.
4 *Ibid.*, May, vol. vii., pp. 202, 231.
5 S. Singer, *Salomon sagen in Deutschland* in *Zeitschrift für Deut-
sches Alterthum*, vol. xxxv., 1891, p. 186; *Id., Sagengeschichtliche
Parallelen aus dem Babylonischen Talmud* in *Zeitschrift des Vereins
für Volkskunde*, vol. ii., 1892, p. 301.
6 *Acta SS.*, May, vol. iii., p. 215.   7 *Ibid.*, Feb., vol. i., p. 679.
8 *Ibid.*, Jan., vol. ii., p. 87. Compare Singer, *Salomon sagen*, as
above, p. 185.
9 E. Cosquin, *Contes populaires de Lorraine*, vol. i., p. 71.

tion of a narrative that had its origin in India,[1] while the story of the crucifix dropped into the sea by St. Francis Xavier and brought to land by a crab is simply borrowed from Japanese mythology.[2]

At Valencia, in the Church of San Salvador, there is preserved a figure of Christ which drifted there miraculously by sea and up-stream; at Santa-Maria del Grao, the port of Valencia, there is another figure of Christ together with a ladder, the one used at His crucifixion, which was also carried by sea in a boat without crew or cargo. As the vessel came to a halt in mid-stream, an altercation arose between the inhabitants of the opposite banks for the possession of the sacred relics. To settle the matter, the boat was towed out to sea, where it was once more left to take what direction it pleased. Straightway it sailed up the river and became stationary close to Santa-Maria del Grao.[3]

In a similar strain Pausanias describes the coming of the statue of Hercules to Erythræ. It arrived by sea on a raft and came to a halt at the promontory of Juno called Cape Mesata because it was half-way between Erythræ and Chios. From the moment they espied the god, the inhabitants of each of the two towns did their utmost to attract it in their own direc-

---

1 E. Cosquin, *La Légende du page de Sainte Elizabeth de Portugal et le conte indien des "Bons Conseils"* in the *Revue des Questions historiques*, vol. lxxiii., 1903, pp. 3-42; *Id., La légende de Sainte Elizabeth de Portugal et les contes orientaux, ibid.*, vol. lxxiv., pp. 207-17. *Id., Etudes folkloriques*, p. 73-162; C. Formichi, *La leggenda del paggio di santa Elizabetta* in *Archivio delle tradizioni popolari*, vol. xxii., 1903, pp. 9-30.

2 Bouhours, *Vie de saint François Xavier*, vol. iii. The Japanese legend is related by A. B. Mitford, *Tales of Old Japan*, London, 1871, pp. 40-43. Attention is drawn to the loan in the *Revue des traditions populaires*, 15th August, 1890. I am indebted to M. E. Cosquin for these details.

3 See Fages, *Histoire de saint Vincent Ferrier*, vol. ii., pp. 46, 47.

tion. But the heavens decided in favour of the first. A fisherman of that town named Phormio was warned in a dream that if the women of Erythræ would sacrifice their hair in order to make a cable, they would have no difficulty in drawing in the raft. The Thracian women who inhabited the town made the sacrifice of their locks, and thus secured the miraculous statue for Erythræ. Except for the final details the two legends are identical.[1]

Nothing is more common in popular hagiography than this theme of the miraculous advent of a picture or of the body of a saint in a derelict vessel; equally common is the miracle of the ship that comes to a halt or of the oxen who refuse to go any farther, in order to indicate the spot mysteriously predestined for the guardianship of a celestial treasure, or to confirm some church in the legitimate possession of the relics of a saint.[2] We need only recall the arrival of St. James in Spain, of St. Lubentius at Dietkirchen, of St. Maternus at Rodenkirchen, of St. Emmerammus at Ratisbonne, of the girdle of the Blessed Virgin at Prato, of the Volto Santo at Lucca.[3]

These miraculous voyages of crucifixes, Madonnas and statues of saints are particularly abundant in Sicily, as has been proved by recent researches.[4] A similar

---

1 Pausanias, vii., 5, 5-8.

2 In our own country (Belgium) it is not usual to employ oxen for the transport of sacred objects. Hence, in the legend of "Le Christ des Dames Blanches" of Tirlemont, it is the Canons of Saint Germain who find themselves incapacitated from carrying their precious burden any farther. P. V. Bets, *Histoire de Tirlemont*, Louvain, 1861, vol. ii., p. 88. The same story is related of the relics of St. George by Gregory of Tours, *In gloria martyrum*, c. 101.

3 The documents have been collected by H. Usener, *Die Sintflutsagen*, Bonn, 1899, pp. 136-37.

4 G. Pitrè, *Feste patronali in Sicilia* in *Biblioteca delle tradizioni popolari Siciliane*, vol. xxi., Turin and Palermo, 1900, pp. xx.-xxii.

inquiry in other countries would probably be rewarded with equally numerous discoveries.[1] In Istria an occurrence of a similar nature is connected with the foundation of the Bishopric of Pedena by Constantine.[2]

The Greeks have not neglected to introduce into their lives of saints a theme which had proved so popular among their ancestors. The panegyrist of St. Theodore Siceotes not only made use of it, but endowed the animal with a voice in order that it might declare in explicit terms the desire of the saint to rest on the spot he had selected for himself.[3] The oxen which drew St. Cyril of Gortina to the scaffold also stopped at the chosen spot in obedience to a divine command,[4] and the reader will recall the *rôle* attributed to the camels in the history of St. Menas of Egypt.[5]

It would be an endless task to draw up a complete list of the stock incidents of hagiography. We have already been able to show from examples that some of them go back to a very remote antiquity. That is

1 Concerning the miraculous crucifix of Hoboken, near Antwerp, see P. D. Kuyl, *Hoboken en zijn wonderdadig Kruisbeeld*, Antwerp, 1866, pp. 147-56; concerning the local legend of St. Desiré (Allier) see J. Stramoy, *La légende de sainte Agathe* in *Revue des traditions populaires*, vol. xiii., p. 694; on the advent of the relics of St. Thomas at Ortona, A. de Nino, *Usi e costumi Abruzzesi*, vol. iv., Florence, 1887, p. 151. The legend of St. Rainier of Bagno, *ibid.*, pp. 162-63, may also be mentioned here. A recent work on this subject is that of M. F. de Mely, *L'image du Christ du Sancta Sanctorum et les reliques chrétiennes apportées par les flots* in *Mémoires de la Société des Antiquaires de France*, series vii., vol. iii., Paris, 1904, pp. 113-44.

2 Manzuoli, *Vite e fatti de' santi et beati dell' Istria*, Venice, 1611, pp. 107-12. [The sentence which follows was omitted in the 3d ed. *Ed.*]

3 *Analecta Bollandiana*, vol. xx., p. 269.

4 *Synaxarium ecclesiae Constantinopolitanae*, pp. 17, 750.

5 *Bibl. hag. lat.*, n. 5921.—The site of the Church of S. Auxentius in Cyprus was also indicated by the oxen which carried his relics. C. Sathas, *Vies des saints allemands de Chypre* in *Archives de l'Orient latin*, vol. ii., p. 419.

a point that cannot be too strongly insisted upon. A number of the legendary themes to be found scattered through the lives of saints, in the histories of the foundation of celebrated shrines, and in the accounts of the origin of certain miraculous pictures, are to be met with in the classics. The people of ancient times would themselves have experienced great difficulty in indicating their origin. For them, as for us, they were as leaves carried hither and thither by the wind.

The picture or letter dropped from heaven, the " acheiropœetos " or picture not made by human hand, are by no means the invention of Christian narrators. The legend of the Palladium of Troy, the statue of Pallas Athene fallen from the sky, and many other similar legends, show how common such conceptions were among the ancients.[1] Like ourselves they were familiar with holy pictures which shed tears,[2] with statues bathed in sweat in times of calamity,[3] with voices issuing from marble lips.[4]

The story of some object flung into the sea and recovered from the belly of a fish, to be met with in the lives of St. Ambrose of Cahors, St. Maurilius,[5] St. Magloire,[6] St. Kentigern [7] and many others, is nothing more than a reminiscence of the ring of Polycrates, related

---

1 See demonstration of this in E. von Dobschütz, *Christusbilder* in *Texte und Untersuchungen*, N.F., vol. iii., Leipzig, 1899.

2 "Apollo triduum et tres noctes lacrimavit," Livy, xliii., 13.

3 "Signa ad Junonis Sospitæ sudore manavere," Livy, xxiii., 31.

4 "Fortunæ item muliebris simulacrum, quod est in via Latina non semel sed bis locutum constitit, his paene verbis: Bene me matronæ vidistis riteque dedicastis," Valerius Maximus, i., 8.

5 See A. Houtin, *Les origines de l'Eglise d'Angers*, Laval, 1901, pp. 54, 55.

6 *Acta SS., Oct.*, vol. x., p. 787.

7 *Ibid.*, Jan., vol. i., p. 820.

by Herodotus.[1] The swarm of bees that alighted on
the cradle of St. Ambrose,[2] and which also visited St. Isidore,[3] had long before deposited its honey in the mouth
of Pindar[4] and in that of Plato.[5] The miracle of the
rock opening to receive St. Thecla[6] and St. Ariadne[7]
in order to snatch them from the pursuit of their persecutors is but an echo of the fable of Daphne, just as the
story of St. Barbara recalls that of Danaë confined by
her father in a brazen tower.[8]

Suetonius relates how Augustus, one day, when still
a child, imposed silence on the frogs that were croaking
near his grandfather's villa, and, it is said, he adds,
that since then frogs have never croaked on that spot.[9]
The same marvellous incident is recounted of more
than one saint : of St. Rieul, St. Antony of Padua, St.
Benno of Meissen, St. George, Bishop of Suelli, St.
Ouen, St. Hervatus, St. James of the Marches, St.
Segnorina, St. Ulphus.[10]

[1] Herodotus, *Hist.*, iii., 43. Further parallels are quoted by R.
Köhler, *Kleinere Schriften*, vol. ii., Berlin, 1900, p. 209, note 1.
[2] *Vita a Paulino*, No. 3. [3] *Acta SS.*, April, vol. i., p. 331.
[4] Pausanias, ix., 23, 2.
[5] Cicero, *De divinatione*, i., 36; Olympiodorus, *Vita Platonis*,
Westermann, p. 1.
[6] Lipsius, *Acta apostolorum apocrypha*, vol. i., p. 272.
[7] P. Franchi de' Cavalieri, *I martiri di santo Teodoto e di santa
Ariadne* in *Studi e Testi*, No. 6, Roma, 1901, p. 132. The *Acta
sanctæ Mariæ ancillæ* in *Acta SS.*, Nov., vol. i., pp. 201-6, cannot
be quoted in evidence, as they are not distinct from those of St.
Ariadne.
[8] Papebroch had already noted the borrowing; *Acta SS. Bollandiana apologeticis libris in unum volumen nunc primum contractis
vindicata*, Antwerp, 1755, p. 370.
[9] Suetonius, *Octavius*, xciv. [Antigonos, tells the same thing of
Hercules. Keller, p.l.]
[10] The hagiographic documents have been collected by Cahier,
Caractéristiques des Saints, vol. i., pp. 274-76, who did not trouble
himself about the early origin of the incident. A large number of
legends might be quoted in which other animals play an analogous
part. Thus St. Tygris caused some sparrows to keep silence who had
disturbed her at her prayers, and they never troubled her again,
Acta SS., June, vol. v., p. 74, note 9. At the request of St. Cæsarius
of Arles, the wild boars which attracted a crowd of hunters forsook

The reader will recall the vigorous language in which St. Jerome, in the early part of his life of St. Paul, summed up the horrors of the persecutions under Decius and Valerian: the martyr smeared with honey and exposed to the stings of insects, and yet another who protected himself against the snares of sensual desire by spitting out his tongue in the face of the temptress.[1] The magic of St. Jerome's style and the vivid relief of his pictures endow them with a semblance of originality to which they cannot lay claim.[2] Martyrdom from insects, which, if we may believe Sozomen, was renewed under Julian, was but another reminiscence of the classics.[3] Apuleius, among others, makes mention of it. As for the episode of the tongue, ancient writers have related the story on more than one occasion, attributing it now to the Pythagorean Timycha, now to Leæna the courtesan, and again to the philosopher Zeno of Elea.[4] St. Jerome, the recorder of this Christian adaptation of an ancient legend, did not succeed in giving it a permanent attribution. At a later date it was told of the martyr Nicetas, and Nicephorus Callistus [5] repeats it once again in connection with an ascetic who lived in the reign of Diocletian.[6]

the neighbourhood of his monastery (*Acta SS.*, August, vol. vi., p. 72, note 36). [3d ed. adds references to St. Ursin and St. Martin from *Acta SS.*, Nov., vol. iv, p. 103.]

1 These anonymous martyrs are inscribed in the Roman martyrology for 28th July. [This note in the 3d ed. reads simply *Metamorph.*, VIII, 22.]

2 [See P. Franchi de' Cavalieri, *Hagiographica*, p. 124. We do not forget the torment of Mark of Arethusa: Gregory of Nazianzus, *In Iulian.*, I, 89; Sozomène, *Hist. eccl.*, V, 10. (See p. 104 n. 1 below, ed.).]

3 *Metamorph.*, viii., 22.

4 The chief classical texts are quoted by Wachsmuth, *Berichte der k. Sächs. Gesellschaft der Wissenschaften*, Phil. Hist. Cl., vol. viii., 1856, p. 132.

5 *Acta SS.*, Sept., vol. iv., p. vii.

6 *Hist. Eccles.*, vol. vii., chap. 13.

It seems scarcely necessary to remind the reader of the legend of the Seven Sleepers. The conception of a long sleep, which occurs in the history of Epimenides, has never ceased to have currency in folk tales, and it has been repeated with endless variations.[1]

The apparent complexity of certain legends and the startling effect of certain combinations which appear highly ingenious must not deceive us, and we must not hastily draw conclusions in favour of the creative faculty of popular genius. The historic elements which do not lend themselves to simplification are merely placed in juxtaposition, and bound together by a very slender thread. The result is usually an incoherent narrative, which in most cases is distinguished by its extraordinary improbability, though on occasions the effect is not devoid of impressiveness.

The following, for example, is one version of the legend of the wood of the cross. Adam, driven from Paradise, took with him a branch of the tree of knowledge, which served him as a staff to the end of his days. This stick passed down from hand to hand to the patriarchs, and during the wars an angel hid it in a cave where it was discovered by Jethro while herding his flocks. In his old age Jethro sent a message to Moses to come and take the staff, which on the arrival of the prophet sprang miraculously towards him. Moses made use of it to hang from it the brazen serpent. Later Phineas became possessed of it and buried it in the desert. At the time of the birth of Christ the precise spot was revealed to St. Joseph, who

---

[1] H. Demoulin, *Epiménide de Crète* in the *Bibliothèque de la Faculté de Philosophie et Lettres de l'Université de Liége*, fasc. xii., Brussels, 1901, pp. 95-100, in which other versions of the sleep legend are indicated.

found the staff on the occasion of the flight into Egypt. He handed it on to his son Jacob, who gave it to the traitor Judas, and through him it came into the hands of the executioners of Jesus Christ, and from it the cross was made.[1]

It will be admitted that, reduced to these terms, the legend of the wood of the cross does not give evidence of much wealth of invention, although the root idea of the mysterious continuity of the Old and the New Testament upon which the story has been clumsily built lends it a certain dignity.

The legend of Judas's thirty pieces of silver runs on similar lines. The money was coined by the father of Abraham, and with it Abraham bought a field as a burial-place for himself and his family. Later the coins passed into the possession of the sons of Jacob, to whom they were paid over by the slave merchants who purchased Joseph. With the identical coins they paid for the corn which Joseph procured for them in Egypt. At the death of Jacob they were given in payment for the spices for his tomb, and thus passed into the land of Sheba, and there remained until they were sent with other gifts by the Queen of Sheba to Solomon's Temple. From Jerusalem the coins were transferred to Arabia, to return with the Magi. The Blessed Virgin took the money with her to Egypt, and there lost it. It was found by a shepherd, who hoarded it until, struck with leprosy, he went to Jerusalem to implore Jesus to cure him. As a thank-offering he presented the thirty pieces of silver to the Temple, and

[1] Fr. Kampers, *Mittelalterliche Sagen vom Paradiese und vom Holze des Kreuzes Christi*, Cologne, 1897, pp. 89, 90. *Cf.* W. Meyer, *Die Geschichte des Kreuzholzes vor Christus in Abhandlungen der k. Bayer. Akademie der Wissenschaften*, i. Cl., vol. xvi., 1881.

they thus became, in the hands of the chief priests, the price of Judas's betrayal. But Judas repented, and restored the price of his sin to the priests, who gave half of it to the soldiers on guard at the sepulchre and the other half to the potter for the field to be a burying-place for strangers.[1]

By a succession of similar combinations men have succeeded in identifying the stone which served as a pillow for the patriarch Jacob with that which supports the throne of the Kings of England at their coronation in Westminster Abbey.[2] One might quote many examples of such childish concatenations of historical reminiscences resulting in narratives which appear to be carefully elaborated, but which are, in reality, of puerile simplicity.

Popular imagination in its workings has not been restricted to the famous names and great events of sacred history. It has frequently given itself free scope in relation to the history of certain well-known saints, who, owing to the existence of their tombs and the veneration paid to their memories, could neither be passed over in silence nor fused into one. The recognised procedure was to group them together, to imagine links of kindred or of some common action between them, to forge a history in which each should play a

[1] See, for example, A. Graf, *Roma nella memoria e nelle immaginazioni del medio evo*, Turin, 1883, vol. ii., pp. 462-63; L. De Feis, *Le Monete del prezzo di Giuda* in *Studi Religiosi*, vol. ii., 1902, pp. 412-30, 506-21. Note also, by the way, the version of the legend of the thirty pieces of silver in Solomon of Basrah, *The Book of the Bee,* edited by E. A. W. Budge, Oxford, 1886, p. 94 and following.

[2] J. H. Rivett-Carnac, *La piedra de la coronación en la abadia de Westminster y su conexion legendaria con Santiago de Compostela* in the *Boletin de la real academia de la Historia*, vol. xl., 1902, pp. 430-38.

well-defined *rôle*, without ever stopping to inquire whether a particular saint might not be acting quite incompatible parts in two different stories. In this way, with the assistance of historical names and a topographical setting, whole cycles of purely imaginary legends have been composed.

The best-known example of this is that of the Roman martyrs of whom the legends form a series of cycles each one embracing a certain number of saints who frequently had nothing in common save the place of their sepulture.[1] Some of these legends are interesting and in places poetic; others—and they are in the majority—are trivial and meaningless. Nevertheless, if we study them as a whole, we can derive from them a picture which is not the result of design yet is none the less impressive; and if a poet had arisen to put into shape the raw material of these rude narratives, he might have drawn from them an epic poem of Christian Rome, from the foundation of the Mother and Mistress of Churches by St. Peter, through the bloody conflicts of the days of persecution, down to the final triumph under Sylvester and Constantine. Unhappily the man of genius who might have endowed us with this work of art has never arisen, and our sense of the grandeur of the subject only gives us a more vivid perception of the poverty of the legends that remain to us, and the lack of inspiration and originality in the creations of the people at large.

---

[1] *Analecta Bollandiana*, vol. xvi., pp. 2-7 and following.

II.

Predominance of sense impressions over the intelligence—Localisation
and foot-prints—Literary origin of certain of these—Iconographic
legends—Popular etymology—Miracles—The soul of the people
—Energy of expression—Exaggerated feeling—Ambitions of
individual churches—Morality of the mob—Local claims.

The brain of the multitude has been shown to be
narrow, incapable of coping with any large number
of ideas at once, or indeed with even a single idea of
any complexity, equally incapable of applying itself to
prolonged or subtle reasoning, but, on the other hand,
fully prepared to receive impressions through the
senses. The idea may fade quickly away, but the
picture remains; it is the material side of things
which attracts the populace, and it is to sensible objects
that all the people's thoughts and affections cling.   In
this respect popular intelligence scarcely exceeds the
intellectual level of a child, who, equally indifferent
to abstract concepts, turns instinctively towards that
which appeals to the senses. All the child's ideas and
reminiscences are indissolubly linked to material and
palpable objects.

Thus it is that great men live far less in the memory
of their countrymen than in the stones, rocks or buildings with which it pleases people to connect their
names. For, in the first place, the popular mind craves
for what is definite and concrete. It is not satisfied
with knowing that some celebrated personage passed
through the country. It wishes to identify the precise spot on which he stood, the tree that gave him
shelter, the house in which he lodged. Thus we have
Alexander's oak, shown in the days of Plutarch near
the Cephisus to mark the spot where he pitched his

tent at the battle of Chæronea;[1] Horace's house at Venusium, an ancient ruin shown under his name even in our own day, although no historical tradition connects it with the poet; and finally Virgil's house at Brindisi, the remains of a structure only built in the sixteenth century.[2]

In the same way the populace always feels constrained to explain the origin or the purpose of whatever impresses it and to bestow a name upon every object that excites its attention. Like a child it contents itself with the first explanation that soothes its imagination and satisfies its craving for knowledge, while reflection and the critical faculty never enlighten it concerning the insufficiency or improbability of what it invents. Thus it becomes a matter of course that people should transfer to the curious features of natural scenery or to the constructions of bygone ages, both the pictures that haunt their imagination and the celebrated names that live in their memory. It is one and the same psychological cause, which, all the world over, has bestowed well-known names on rocks of unwonted shape or natural grottoes which attract attention.

In the religious sphere the popular instinct asserts itself very emphatically in both these directions.

From this point of view nothing is more instructive than accounts of pilgrimages to celebrated shrines and more especially to the Holy Land. The earliest narratives by pious pilgrims[3] betray no trace of the

1 Plutarch, *Alexander,* ix., 2.

2 F. Lenormant, *À travers l'Apulie et la Lucanie,* vol. i., Paris, 1883, pp. 202-3. In the same way the site of Ovid's house is still shown at Sulmona. A. de Nino, *Ovidio nella tradizione popolare di Sulmona,* Casalbordino, 1886, p. 21.

3 See more especially the narratives of Antoninus, of Theodosius, and Adamnan; Geyer, *Itinera Hierosolymitana saec.,* iv.-viii., in the *Corpus script. Eccl. lat.,* vol. xxxix.

ignorance and hesitation of our most learned exegetes in topographical matters, and with glorious assurance they will point out to you the precise spot where David composed his psalms, the rock smitten by Moses, the cave that sheltered Elijah, without counting the places mentioned in the Gospels of which not one is forgotten, not even the house of the wicked Dives, or the tree into which Zaccheus climbed. To show the extent to which material things dominate the intelligence and stifle the powers of reflection, people have pretended to have seen the "corner-stone which the builders rejected," and have begged for relics "de lignis trium tabernaculorum," those three tabernacles which St. Peter, in his ecstasy, proposed to erect on the mountain of the Transfiguration.[1]

In a similar way the names of saints are frequently linked with monuments or remarkable places which appeal to the popular imagination. Thus it is quite natural that in Rome the Mamertine prison should be selected as the scene of St. Peter's imprisonment, and that men should be enabled to point out the precise spot where Simon Magus fell: *Silex ubi cecidit Simon Magus.*[2] Neither is it surprising that in Ireland so many places are connected with the memory of St. Patrick, or at Naples with that of St. Januarius, or in Touraine and the neighbourhood of Autun with St. Martin.

It is furthermore only a particular example of a universal phenomenon that people should recognise in the hollows of rocks the imprint of the feet, hands or knees of St. Peter, St. George and St. Martin, just as in other

[1] *Angilberti abbatis de ecclesia Centulensi libellus,* M. G., Scr., vol. xv., p. 176.
[2] L. Duchesne, *Le forum chrétien,* Rome, 1899, p. 17.

localities one is shown the footprints of Adam and Abraham, of Moses and Buddha.[1]   That a large number of such attributions, more especially in the case of megalithic monuments, should have been christianised, and that the Blessed Virgin and the saints should have been substituted for the heroes of heathen legends, need excite no surprise.   Whether St. Cornelius, in preference to all others, by turning the soldiers of King Adar to stone, should have created the long lines of menhirs at Carnac and Erdeven in Brittany,[2] or whether it was a fairy rather than St. Frodoberta, who dropped a lapful of stones, useless for building purposes,[3] near the lake of Maillard in the department of Seine-et-Marne, the popular tradition remains unaffected, testifying in each case that there is as yet no advance beyond the intellectual level of childhood.

It must not be forgotten that very precise identifications of locality may frequently be traced to a purely literary origin.   Thus at Verona, where Romeo and Juliet only lived in the imagination of poets,[4] travellers are shown both their palace and their tomb, while the two ruined castles perched on the neighbouring hills

1 S. Reinach, *Les monuments de pierre brute dans le langage et les croyances populaires* in the *Revue archéologique*, 3rd series, vol. xxi., p. 224.

2 S. Reinach, *loc. cit.*, p. 355.

3 *Ibid.*, p. 354.—A great number of miraculous imprints have been pointed out in Italy by various scholars who have published their notes in the *Archivio per lo studio delle Tradizioni popolari*, vol. xxii., 1903, p. 128, and the preceding years. A considerable number of these imprints are attributed to various popular saints. [Other examples are to be found in F. Lanzoni, *Le fonti della leggenda di Sant' Apollinare di Ravenna*, Bologna, 1915, p. 57.]

4 L. Frankel, *Untersuchungen zur Entwicklungsgeschichte des Stoffes von Romeo und Julia*, in *Zeitschrift für vergleichende Litteraturgeschichte*, N.F., vol. iii., 1890, p. 171-210; vol. iv, 1891, 48-91; G. Brognoligo, *La leggenda di Giulietta e Romeo* in *Giornale Linguistico*, vol. xix, 1892, p. 423-39. [There is a useful bibliography, with discussion, of the Romeo and Juliet sources in E. K. Chambers, *William Shakespeare*, Oxford, 1930, vol. i, 340 ff. *Ed.*]

have become those of the Capulets and Montagues.[1]
In Alsace are we not shown the forge which Schiller
has "immortalised" by his ballad of Fridolin, and the
castle of the Counts of Saverne, who none the less
never existed?[2] This last example proves that in
these cases tradition does not take long to germinate
and blossom. Until the old legend was turned into
verse by Schiller in 1797, Alsace had never been regarded as the home of the incident. Yet it was sufficient for the ballad to become popular for the event
to be materialised and localised in the most precise
fashion.

Of such topographical transference to suit the requirements of a legend there is no lack of examples in
hagiography. At Sofia (Sardica), near the Church of St.
Petka (Parasceve), may be seen an ancient tree-trunk
partially built into the wall and scored with many
notches. The people call it the tree of St. Therapon,
and believe that the saint suffered his martyrdom near
by. On his feast-day, 27th May, they go in pilgrimage
to the spot, and make a point of carrying away with
them some small piece of the sacred tree to which they
attribute miraculous virtues. Now, in point of fact,
St. Therapon did not die at Sardica; he was a native
of Sardis, but according to the legend a great oak-tree
sprang up from the ground that had been soaked with
his blood. This evergreen oak was said still to exist

[1] The Cappelletti and the Montecchi according to Dante are
types, and in no sense historical characters. R. Davidsohn, *Die
Feindschaft der Montecchi und Cappelletti ein Irrtum* in *Deutsche
Rundschau*, Dec., 1903, pp. 419-28. On 8th July, 1905, the "historic"
house of Juliet was purchased by the municipality of Verona. See
The Times of 10th July, 1905.

[2] W. Hertz, *Deutsche Sage im Elsass*, Stuttgart, 1872, pp. 278
and following.

and to cure every disease.[1] The confusion between
Sardis and Sardica having once established itself, it
became easy to transplant the miraculous tree.[2]

In the face of facts such as these, need we insist on
the illusory nature of the process which consists in
tracing the itinerary of a saint by means of the land-
marks established by legends? If this has sometimes
been attempted, it has not been precisely in the higher
interests of history.[3]

Popular imagination in the past has not exercised itself
solely on rough-hewn stones and buildings. Carved
figures wrongly interpreted have proved the starting-
point of a number of quaint legends.[4] A poet is represented with his foot on a large book : he must be the
most learned of men, for he can read with his feet.[5]
The two fine equestrian statues on Monte Cavallo (now
Piazza del Quirinale) in Rome gave currency during
the Middle Ages to a most curious tale. It was said that
they represented two celebrated philosophers named
Phidias and Praxiteles, who came to Rome during the
reign of Tiberius, and had the singular habit of walking

1 *Synaxarium ecclesiæ Constantinopolitanæ*, p. 711.

2 C. Jirecek, *Das christliche Element in der topographischen
Nomenclatur der Balkanländer* in the *Sitzungsberichte der kaiser-
lich. Akademie*, vol. cxxxvi., 1897, pp. 54-55. Other examples of
similar instances are to be found in this essay.

3 J. G. Bulliot et F. Thiollier, *La mission et le culte de St. Martin
d'après les légendes et les monuments populaires dans le pays
éduen*, Autun-Paris, 1892, vi., p. 483. The life of St. Radegonde has
been the object of a similar attempt. See *Analecta Bollandiana*, vol.
x., pp. 59-60.

4 C. Kinkel, *Mosaik zur Kunstgeschichte*, Berlin, 1876, devotes
a whole chapter to this question: *Sagen aus Kunstwerken entstanden*,
pp. 161-243.

5 A. de Nino, *Ovidio nella tradizione popolare di Sulmona*, p.
17.

about the city in a state of nudity, in order to inculcate the vanity of the things of this world.[1]

Every sort of invention has been forthcoming to explain the representations of saints. It was obviously the common people who created the naïve legend of the saints who carry their own heads, suggested by a prevalent iconographic type,[2] and the legend of St. Nicholas and the three children is usually traced to a similar source.[3] A symbol interpreted in a materialistic sense has built up a regular romance around an incident in the life of St. Julian,[4] and we shall see later on that the extraordinary history of St. Liberata or Uncumber merely translates into popular language the explanation of certain peculiar features in a picture.

The following is another example, drawn from hagiography. An inscription, now to be seen in the Marseilles Museum, makes mention of a certain Eusebia, Abbess of St. Quiricus, *Hic requiescit in pace Eusebia religiosa magna ancella Dei*, etc., without any indication that would lead one to assume the existence of any cultus of this admirable woman. But her body had been laid in a sarcophagus of older date adorned with the figure of the dead person for whom it had been originally intended. It was the bust of a beardless man, which, in the course of time, had become damaged and mutilated. This fact was sufficient to give rise to a legend, and it was told how St. Eusebia, abbess of a convent at Marseilles, and her forty com-

---

[1] C. L. Urlichs, *Codex urbis Romæ topographicus*, Wirceburgi, 1871, pp. 122-23.

[2] Ch. de Smedt, *Principes de la critique historique*, pp. 188-92. [This paragraph has been revised in the 3d ed. and St. Lucy adduced as an example, while the saints carrying their own heads have been omitted. The rev. fn. cites *Anal. Boll.*, vol. xxxix, p. 162.]

[3] Cahier, *Caractéristiques des Saints*, vol. i., p. 304.

[4] A. Ledru, *Le premier miracle attribué à Saint Julien* in *La province du Maine*, vol. x., 1892, pp. 177-85. *Cf. Analecta Bollandiana*, vol. xxii., p. 351.

panions cut off their noses to escape from the violence of the Saracens. "Quam traditionem confirmat generosæ illius heroinæ effigies, dimidia facie et naso præciso supra tumulum posita cum epigraphe," writes a Benedictine, quoted by M. Le Blant.[1]

Again, more than one legend owes its existence to names incorrectly understood or to resemblances of sound. To the curious examples of popular etymology collected by various learned authors,[2] we might add a large number of cases bearing specially on hagiography. We must, however, restrict ourselves to a few cursory indications.

The Church of St. Nereus and Achilleus on the Appian Way close to the Thermæ of Caracalla formerly bore the name of *Titulus de Fasciola*.[3] Opinions differ as to the meaning of the title. Some consider Fasciola to be the name of the foundress. Others regard it merely as a topographical expression of obscure origin. The erudite may hesitate: popular legend sees no cause for hesitation. The name Fasciola is a reminiscence of St. Peter. As he was passing by the spot on leaving prison he dropped the bandage that bound up his injured leg. "Tunc beatissimus Petrus," says an old writer, "dum tibiam demolitam haberet de compede ferri, cecidit ei fasciola ante Septisolium in via nova."[4] Here, indeed, we may see the naïveté of a people who

---

1 Le Blant, *Inscriptions Chrétiennes de la Gaule*, n. 545.

2 A. F. Pott, *Etymologische Legenden bei den Alten* in *Philologus*, Supplementband, vol. ii., Heft 3; O. Keller, *Lateinische Volksetymologie*, Leipzig, 1891; O. Weise, *Zur Charakteristik der Volksetymologie* in *Zeitschrift für Völkerpsychologie*, vol. xii., 1880, pp. 203-23.

3 Concerning the title of Fasciola, see De Rossi, *Bullettino di archeologia cristiana*, 1875, pp. 49-56. [Added in 3d ed.: J. P. Kirsch, *Die römischen Titelkirchen im Altertum*, Paderborn, 1918, p. 909-94.]

4 *Acta SS., Processi et Martiniani*, BHL, n. 6947.

imagine that a great man cannot even drop a handkerchief without the spot being immediately marked and remembered in order that the incident may be recorded by a monument.

The influence of sound on the popular impressions formed of certain saints is well known, and we are all aware that at times something little better than a pun decides the choice of a patron. Thus, in France, St. Clare is invoked by those who suffer from their eyes because she enables people to see *clearly ;* St. Ouen cures deafness because he enables them to hear (*ouïr*) ; St. Cloud cures boils (*clous*). Again, in certain parts of Germany St. Augustine is believed to rid people of diseases of the eye (*Auge*), and in others of a cough (*Husten*). Writers have drawn up lists of these conceits,[1] which are not solely due to popular imagination, and which learned men have amused themselves by multiplying. There is one of comparatively recent date which enjoys a surprising and regrettable popularity: St. Expeditus, thanks to his name, has been acclaimed as the advocate of urgent causes.[2]

It also happens that, under the influence of phonetic laws, the names of certain saints have become quite unrecognisable. On the Via Porto near Rome there may be seen a little country church belonging to the basilica of Santa Maria in Via Lata, known under the title of Santa Passera. Who is this saint who may be searched for in vain in the Calendar? Will it be believed that the name and the chapel are intended to recall the translation of the relics of SS. Cyrus and John, martyrs, formerly honoured at Menouthis near Alexandria?

---

1 *Mélusine,* vol. iv., pp. 505-24; vol. v., p. 152.
2 See later, chap. iii., par. 2. Compare *Analecta Bollandiana,* vol. xviii., p. 425; vol. xxv., pp. 90-98.

St. Cyrus, *ἀββὰ Κῦρος*, Abbacirus, has finally become transformed into Passera.[1] Has the metamorphosis ended there, or has the new saint acquired a legend of her own? I do not know, but even were it so I should feel no astonishment. The least that could be done was to confuse St. Passera with St. Praxedes, and sure enough the opportunity has not been missed.[2]

We have surely said enough to show how, among the people, the senses predominate over the intelligence, and how owing to the lethargy of their brains they are unable to rise to an ideal conception, but stop short at the matter, the image, the sound. It is furthermore by this spiritual feebleness that one must account for the blind attraction of the populace for the miraculous and the sensibly supernatural. The thought of the invisible guidance of Providence does not suffice; the interior working of grace offers nothing that can be grasped, and the mysterious colloquies of the soul with God must be translated into palpable results in order to produce any impression on the

1 *Abbacyrus, Abbaciro, Abbáciro, Pácero, Pácera, Passera,* such is the series of changes traced by M. Tomassetti in the *Archivio Storico Romano,* vol. xxii., p. 465. *Passera* and *Aboukir* are thus exact counterparts.—One may also quote *Sancta Fumia* on the Appian Way. This saint is no other than St. Euphemia. De Rossi, *Bullettino di archeologia cristiana,* 1869, p. 80. There is also St. Twosole, in whom it is not easy to recognise St. Oswald. J. Aubrey, *Remains of Gentilism and Judaism,* ed. J. Britten, London, 1881, p. 29.

2 Tomassetti as above, vol. xxii., p. 466. The Venetian dialect is specially rich in transformations of saints' names, very bewildering to strangers. Thus in Venice the church of *San Marcuola* is, in reality dedicated to SS. *Ermagora e Fortunato; San Trovaso* is an adaptation of S. Gervasio e Protasio; *San Zanipolo* of *S. Giovanni e Paolo; San Stae* of *S. Eustachio; San Zandegola* of *S. Giovanni decollato; San Stin* of *S. Stefanin; San Boldo* of *S. Ubaldo; San Lio* of *S. Leone,* etc. See G. Tassini, *Curiosita Veneziane,* 4th edition, Venice, 1887, p. 428 and following. [One may find other interesting examples of the phonetic transformation of saints' names in A. Longnon, *Les noms de lieu de la France,* Paris, 1920-1923, p. 400-446. 3d ed.]

4

popular mind.   The supernatural is only impressive
when it is combined with the marvellous.   Hence it is
that popular legends overflow with marvels.   Visions,
prophecies and miracles play a necessary part in the
lives of saints.

We shall not refer here to the wonders accomplished
through the intercession of the miracle-working saints
on behalf of those who visit their tombs or touch their
relics; these constitute a special category which deserves separate treatment.   But the narrative of the
acts of the saint himself is, as it were, impregnated
with the miraculous.   Even before his birth his greatness
is foreshadowed, and his cradle is enveloped in visible
signs of divine protection.   Angels guard his footsteps,
Nature obeys him, wild beasts recognise his authority.
In urgent peril he can always count on the intervention
of the celestial powers.   One might almost say that
God Himself seems to favour the very caprices of His
friends and seems to multiply miracles without any
apparent motive.   The staff of St. Gangericus (Géry)
remained upright throughout the prayers of the saint,[1]
and the same thing occurred while St. Junianus conversed with King Clothair.[2]   Various saints hung their
cloaks on a sunbeam or brought birds to life when they
were already turning on the spit.   Blessed Marianus
Scotus had no need of a candle when writing at night
as his fingers gave out the necessary light.[3]   In answer
to the prayer of St. Sebald, a peasant obtained a similar
privilege until he had found his strayed oxen.[4]   An
eagle sheltered St. Ludwin from the sun's rays with his
wings,[5] and the servant of St. Landoald brought his

---

[1] *Acta SS.*, Aug., vol. ii., p. 674.   [2] *Ibid.*, Aug., vol. iii., p. 41.
[3] *Ibid.*, Feb., vol. ii., p. 367.   [4] *Ibid.*, Aug., vol. iii., p. 772.
[5] *Ibid.*, March, vol. i., p. 319; see *ante*, p. 29.

master fire in the folds of his robe.[1] The miracle of Joshua was renewed, we learn, in the person of St. Ludwin in order to allow him to confer ordination on one and the same day at Reims and at Laon.[2] In this direction popular imagination knows no bounds, nor can it be denied that, more especially in certain surroundings, among nations of a poetic temperament, these bold and naïve fictions frequently attain to real beauty.

One must not, however, exaggerate the fertility of these hagiographic *trovatori*.* A methodical classification of the themes employed by them compels one to realise that repetitions are numerous, and that it is chiefly by means of new combinations of familiar topics that an appearance of variety is conferred on different groups of legends of the saints. Above all, we must be on our guard against the belief that from the æsthetic point of view the level of the miraculous creations of popular hagiography is, as a rule, a high one. Putting aside an occasional happy thought or a few interesting ideas worked out with some ingenuity, the material of these biographies is as a rule deplorably commonplace even where it is not beyond measure whimsical and extravagant. The imagination, over-excited by the craving for the marvellous, and possessed by a burning desire to outstrip one extraordinary narrative by another more extraordinary still, has only too frequently overstepped all bounds in a region in which an unlimited field appears to open out before the creative faculties.

The familiar miracle of the arrival of relics on a derelict vessel [3] ended by appearing tame and vulgar.

[* *trovatori*: the original in Delehaye is *trouveurs*, i.e., *trouvères*, the mediaeval poets of Northern France. *Ed.*]

1 *Acta SS.*, March, vol. iii., p .36.

2 *Ibid.*, Sept., vol. viii., p. 171.

3 See above, p. 30.

Some one, therefore, invented the idea of a heavy sarcophagus floating on the water. It was in a stone coffin
that St. Mamas landed in Cyprus,[1] as also did St.
Julian at Rimini[2] and St. Liberius at Ancona.[3] For
a babe to leap in its mother's womb like St. John the
Baptist was not enough to foreshadow the greatness
of a saint. St. Fursey spoke before his birth,[4] so
also did St. Isaac, who made his voice heard three
times in one day.[5] This miracle scarcely surpasses
that of St. Rumwold, an infant who lived but three
days after birth, but who not only repeated his profession of faith in such a way as to be understood by all
present, but also preached a long sermon to his parents
before breathing his last.[6]

In the *Acta Petri* we read not only of a child seven
months old addressing violent reproaches "in manly
tones" to Simon Magus,[7] but also of a big dog who
conversed with St. Peter by whom it was entrusted
with a message for Simon.[8] Commodianus has also
commemorated a lion who miraculously made a speech
in support of the preaching of St. Paul.[9] Such narra-

[1] Stefano Lusignano, *Raccolta di cinque discorsi intitolati corone*,
Padua, 1577, cor. iv., p. 52.

[2] *Acta SS.*, June, vol. iv., p. 139.   [3] *Ibid.*, May, vol. vi., p. 729.

[4] *Ibid.*, Jan., vol. ii., p. 45

[5] *Ibid.*, June, vol. i., p. 325. The incident of the child speaking
before its birth has not been utilised by hagiographers alone. See
Mélusine, vol. iv., pp. 228, 272-77, 297, 323, 405, 447; vol. v., pp. 36,
257; vol. vi., p. 91; vol. vii., pp. 70, 141.

[6] *Acta SS.*, Nov., vol. i., p. 605.

[7] R. A. Lipsius, *Acta apostolorum apocrypha*, vol. i., Leipzig,
1891, pp. 61, 62. In Commodianus, *Carmen apolog.*, v., 630, the
child is only five months old. *Cf.* C. Schmidt, *Die alten Petrusakten*
in *Texte und Untersuchungen*, vol. xxiv., 1903, pp. 106-7.

[8] Lipsius, *ib.*, vol. i., pp. 56-60.

[9] *Carmen apolog.*, v., pp. 57, 58. Cf. Schmidt, vol. xxiv., pp.
108-9.

tives may perhaps be mere reminiscences of Balaam's ass, unless indeed the incidents were inspired by a study of the fabulists.

These excesses lead us to speak of the passions to which the popular mind is liable, passions intense and unrestrained, and impressing everything they touch with that element of exaggeration and even of violence of which so many legends have preserved the trace. The populace can only be moved by strong emotions, and it has no idea of keeping its feelings under control. It takes no account of delicate shades, and just as it is incapable of perceiving them so it is incompetent to express them. But it makes use of energetic language to affirm its impressions and enunciate its ideas.

The following fact concerning St. Cataldus is a small example from among many. His sanctity having betrayed itself by extraordinary manifestations which appeared to be miraculous, an ecclesiastical commission was appointed to pronounce on their nature. This was too simple for literary effect. Consequently the legend relates how the Pope, followed by all the cardinals, went in procession to the house of Cataldus and visited it from cellar to garret.[1] The device reminds one of the methods of those painters whose whole talent lies in the suggestion of life and movement.

Need we add that popular admiration, not seldom ill bestowed, is always quite unmeasured ? The multitude endows its favourites with every great quality, and cannot tolerate the idea that others should appear superior to them. We may quote here, although it has no connection with the history of the saints, a legend

1 A. de Nino, *Usi e costumi abruzzesi,* vol. iv., Florence, 1887, p. 195.

that is particularly instructive from this very point of view, the legend of Saladin. The admiration and sympathy which his personal qualities and especially his moderation and humanity inspired in his prisoners gave rise to a most improbable story, but one which emphasises in a remarkable way the enthusiasm with which he was regarded. Nothing would satisfy his admirers but to connect this Mussulman prince with a French family, and to make of him a knight and next door to a Christian.[1]   Again, when popular imagination was fired by the great expeditions to the Holy Land, it seemed impossible that a warrior such as Charlemagne should not have taken part in them : accordingly from that time forth the Crusades became one of the episodes in the history of that popular hero.

Under such circumstances is it surprising that all the saints should be endowed with all the virtues, and that in a period when illustrious birth added markedly to a person's merit, a patent of nobility should invariably have been made out in their favour? But what was valued even more than noble birth was the honour of having belonged to our Saviour's immediate following. People had no hesitation in identifying the ancient patrons of churches with certain personages who are mentioned in the Gospel, or who were supposed to have taken part in some scene in the life of Christ. Thus St. Ignatius of Antioch became the child whom our Lord showed to the people when He enjoined upon them the humility and simplicity of childhood ;[2] St. Syrus of Pavia became the boy with the five loaves ;[3]   St.

---

[1] G. Paris, *La Légende de Saladin* in the *Journal des Savants*, 1893, pp. 284-99, 354-65, 428-38, 486-98.

[2] *Acta SS.*, Feb., vol. i., p. 18.

[3] Prelini, *San Siro primo vescovo di Pavia*, vol. i., Pavia, 1880, p. 312.

Martial held the towel at the washing of the feet;[1] and St. Ursinus read aloud during the Last Supper.[2]

It may readily be conceived that the legends tracing back to Christ or to St. Peter the mission of the first bishops of important dioceses were not solely inspired by a disinterested love of the saint. The passion for a noble ancestry which caused first the Romans and then the Franks to connect themselves with the heroes of the *Iliad*, discovered this fresh form of self-flattery, and the impulse once given, one church vied with another in claiming the honour of apostolic foundation.[3]

In the East these claims appear to have had their origin in a literary fraud. The forger who disguised himself as Dorotheus of Tyre drew up a list of the names of all the persons mentioned in the New Testament, and bestowed upon each one an Episcopal See. He proceeded with so much haste that he included various names that obviously had never been borne by a bishop; such as Cæsar, which he borrowed from the words of St. Paul, " All the saints salute you, especially they that are of Cæsar's household " (Phil. ii. 22), without realising that the Cæsar in question was no other than Nero.[4]

Among the churches of the West, and more especially among those of France, pretensions to apostolicity

1 *Vita S. Martialis a. Pseudo-Aureliano*, no. 2; Bourret, *Documents sur les origines chretiennes du Rouergue*, Rodez, 1887-92, p. 13.

[2 *Vita S. Ursini, in Act. SS.*, Nov., vol. iv, p. 109. 3d ed.]

3 L. Duchesne, *Les anciens recueils de légendes apostoliques* in *Compte-rendu du troisième Congrès scientifique international des Catholiques*, Brussels, vol. v., 1894, pp. 67 and following.

4 Houtin, *La controverse de l'apostolicité de l'Eglise de France*, 3rd edition, Paris, 1903. In other countries also people have taken pleasure in concocting similar legends, so flattering to national vanity. See *Analecta Bollandiana*, vol. xii., pp. 458, 462; vol. xviii., p. 402.

did not spring up with quite the same uniform impulse, and this is not the place to investigate the respective parts played by popular imagination and by literary fiction in the elaboration of these celebrated legends. What is important to note is that the inventors of these ambitious narratives could always count upon the complicity of the multitude in every enterprise that tended to flatter local sentiment.[1]

For we must not expect of people in the aggregate either keen intelligence or an enlightened morality. Taken collectively they are wholly devoid of that sense of responsibility which causes an individual to hesitate before a dishonest or irregular action. They have no scruples, and as everybody relies on his neighbour to examine the validity of the evidence brought forward, nothing is more easy in dealing with a crowd than to strike the chord of patriotism, vanity or self-interest. It matters, therefore, very little whether the interested imaginings of "apostolic" or other claims are of literary origin, or whether created by the people they have been simply disseminated by hagiographers who have become parties to the fraud by arranging and embellishing them. In either case they belong to the category of products of legendary growth, and constitute only the normal development of popular ideas and aspirations in the matter of ecclesiastical origins.

Thus freed from all trammels the ambitious designs of the people know no limit, and their audacity does not recoil before any obstacle. Neither time nor dis-

[1] A title of honour which the Greeks have been unequal to refusing to any of the holy bishops who were more or less contemporary with the Council of Nicæa was that of having sat among the "three hundred and eighteen fathers". One must therefore not be over-anxious to give credit to those biographers who confer this distinction on their heroes, *Analecta Bollandiana*, vol. xviii., p. 54.

tance will prevent them from claiming as their own special property any saint whom they may elect to honour and whose glory they may desire to see reflected upon themselves.

Every one is familiar with the legend of the great St. Catherine. Both by her birth and by her martyrdom her biographers have connected her with the town of Alexandria. This has in no way deterred the Cypriots, thanks to a series of ingenious and discreditable artifices, from annexing a saint of whom the cultus no less than the legend has always been as popular in the Greek as in the Latin Church.

Now Stephen of Lusignan declares that at Famagusta he read the Greek text of a life of St. Catherine in which one learnt, first of all, that the famous Costos, father of the saint, was not King of Egypt at all, but King of Cyprus, and in proof of this that he bestowed his name on the town of Salamis, afterwards known as Constantia. At some political crisis Diocletian transferred Costos to Alexandria and confided to him the government of Egypt. It was at this period that Catherine was born. It is well known with what care she was brought up, and how proficient she became in all the liberal arts. After the death of her father she returned to the island of Cyprus, where her uncle, learning that she had become a Christian, had her thrown into prison at Salamis—where the actual prison was shown in the time of Lusignan—and then sent her back to Egypt, where the Emperor Maxentius, despairing of her recantation, had her put to death. She suffered her martyrdom at Alexandria, which, adds the chronicler, caused it to be said that she was a native of that town.[1]

[1 The text of Lusignan is quoted by J. Hackett, *A history of the orthodox Church of Cyprus*, London, 1901, p. 395.]

It might have been supposed that the Seven Sleepers of Ephesus would have been sufficiently protected against similar attempts both by their celebrity and by the marvellous details of the legend. Nevertheless the grotto where they slept their sleep of three hundred years has been shown in the neighbourhood of Paphos.[1] Stephen of Lusignan expresses some surprise, but tries to persuade himself that the legend might refer to a different group from that of Ephesus.[2]

St. Savinus is a martyr to whom honours are known to have been paid in the sixth century[3] at Spoleto, where a basilica[4] was erected to his memory. The inhabitants of Spoleto naturally regard him as their compatriot, but he is also claimed by those of Fermo, who possess his relics, and by those of Monselice. At Monte San Savino he has been made into a bishop of the neighbouring town of Chiusi. As for the people of Faenza, they invented a sojourn of the saint within their territory, and, after his martyrdom at Spoleto, a translation of his relics. Later on they attempted to pass him off as their first bishop.[5]

[1] "Nella città di Paffò è una spelonca: la qual dicono esser delli sette dormienti. Pero, noi ritroviamo nelli leggendarii che li sette dormienti erano in Epheso, niente di meno essi cittadini di Paffo dicono ab antiquo esser chiamata quella spelonca di santi sette dormienti: et possono esser altri di quelli di Effeso." Quoted by Hackett, as above, p. 456.

[2] Concerning the localisation of the legend in the East see J. de Goeje, De legende der Zevenslapers van Efeze, Amsterdam, 1900, 25 pages. The various groups on which the title of Seven Sleepers has been conferred are discussed in the Acta SS., July, vol. vi., pp. 375-76.

[3] Gregorii I., Reg., ix., 59. M. G.; Epist., vol. ii., 3, p. 82.

[4] Paul the Deacon, Hist. Langobard., l. iv., M. G.; Scr. rer. Langob., p. 121.

[5] F. Lanzoni, La passio S. Sabini o Savini in the Römische Quartalschrift, vol. xvii., 1903, pp. 1-26.

The bonds which the people seek to establish between themselves and a favourite saint are not always as close as this. Often they are satisfied with the honour of having received him, alive or dead, within their city walls, and then all that is necessary is to imagine a journey which need in no way affect the main lines of his history. It is by means of this simple artifice that St. Nicephorus, the celebrated martyr,[1] has become a local saint in Istria,[2] and that St. Maurus has been claimed by so many towns—Rome, Fondi, Fleury, Lavello and Gallipoli, without counting Parenzo.[3]

We have now seen something of the processes of the anonymous author who creates legends. As he himself does not hold the pen, we have usually been compelled to have recourse to the hagiographer who registers his tales and discoveries. But so far we have only consulted this latter agent in those things in which he is the echo of the popular voice. In the following chapter we shall attempt to trace out what is specially his own, and to lay bare the secrets proper to his craft.

1 *Bibliotheca hagiographica latina*, n. 6085.
2 *Ibid.*, n. 6086.
3 *Analecta Bollandianna*, vol. xviii., pp. 370-80.

CHAPTER III.

THE WORK OF THE HAGIOGRAPHER.

I.

The meaning of the term "hagiographer"—Literary methods—
Moralities—Ancient ideas concerning history—Special views of
mediæval hagiographers.

THE unconscious mental processes of the people when
occupied with the manufacture of stories about the
saints leads, as we have shown, to a weakening and
obscuring of historical testimony, sometimes even to
its almost entire suppression. Have hagiographers
proved themselves more faithful guardians of historical
tradition?

Let us remember, in the first place, that we do not
propose to include under the term hagiographer every
man of letters who has occupied his pen with the lives
of saints. There are among them some who have
simply recorded what they have seen with their eyes
and touched with their hands. Their narratives constitute authentic historical memoirs no less than works of
edification. These candid witnesses, known to every
one, and accepted on all sides as furnishing the most
pure sources of hagiography, will be excluded from our
present inquiry. Neither need we occupy ourselves
here with that class of writers, possessing both literary
power and the necessary information, who have under-

taken to discharge the functions of a historian, men
like Sulpicius Severus, Hilary of Poitiers, Fortunatus,
Ennodius or Eugippius. They are the last representatives of classic antiquity, and their writings, instinct
with art and life, must not be confused with the artificial
productions of later periods, which affect at times to
be inspired by them. Again, we write with similar
respect of those conscientious biographers who, at various periods of the Middle Ages, succeeded in closely
following these models, and produced work the value
of which is in no way contested. We must reserve
our full attention for those conventional and factitious
productions composed at a distance from the events
recorded and without any tangible relation to the facts.

If we should mentally subtract from the martyrologies or lectionaries of the West and from the menologies of the Greek Church the writings which every
one is agreed in accepting as historic documents, there
will still remain a considerable collection of the Passions
of martyrs and of the lives of saints of an inferior
quality, amongst which some have been unanimously
rejected by the critics, while others are regarded with
suspicion. The authors of this residuum—for the most
part anonymous—are the hagiographers whose methods
we propose to study. The acts of the martyrs composed long after the persecutions—I wish to emphasise
this point—constitute the greater part of their literary
wares. We shall therefore occupy ourselves almost
exclusively with this class of compositions. It will be
easy to extend to other writings what we shall have
to say about these.

There is no need for drawing a distinction between
Greek and Latin authors. If from a purely literary
point of view the former usually possess an advantage,

as regards the historic sense there is nothing to choose between them, and in point of fact they constitute but a single group.

The first question that should be addressed to an author the value of whose work one wishes to estimate, concerns the class of literature that he professes to produce, for it would be manifestly unjust to condemn, on the ground of historical inaccuracy, one whose only aim was to write a work of fiction.   Certain hagiographic documents are clearly of this nature; they are parables or tales designed to bring home some religious truth or some moral principle.   The author relates as a means of teaching, and never pretends to be dealing with real facts.   Just as the ancient story-tellers brought kings and princes on the scene, so the Christian moralist would quite naturally fortify his precepts by the authority of a martyr or an ascetic.   And even when it was not a question of inculcating some truth, but merely of giving pleasure to the reader by an attractive narrative, the outlines of a saint's life at a time when lives of saints were the favourite reading of the faithful, offered an element of interest that was not to be despised.

More than one solemn lesson has been preached to the people in the guise of a hagiographic document. The celebrated *Passio S. Nicefori*[1] had no other aim, and the same may be said of the histories of Theodulus the Stylite,[2] of St. Martinianus,[3] of Boniface of Tarsus,[4]

---

[1] *Acta SS.*, Feb., vol. ii., pp. 894-95.

[2] *Ibid.*, May, vol. vi., pp. 756-65. [See H. Delehaye, *Les saints stylites*, Brussels, 1923, p. cxviii-cxix. 3d ed.]

[3] *Acta SS.*, Feb., vol. ii., p. 666; P. Rabbow, *Die Legende des Martinian* in *Wiener Studien*, 1895, pp. 253-93.

[4] Ruinart, *Act. mart. sincera*, pp. 289-91.

and of Cyprian of Antioch, the theme of which last may
be recognised in the legend of Faust.[1]   What save a
little religious romance is the oft-repeated tale of the
adventures of a pious woman hiding herself in a monastery with the name and in the garb of a man, accused
of misconduct and proved to be innocent after her
death?   The heroine is called, as the case may be,
Marina, Pelagia, Eugenia, Euphrosyne, Theodora,
Margaret or Apollinaria.[2]   It is obvious that this was
a favourite theme among pious story-tellers.   In many
cases they did not put themselves to the trouble of in-
venting, but made shift with a simple adaptation.   The
story of Œdipus in all its gloomy horror has been applied to others besides St. Gregory.[3]   Attributed in turn
to St. Albanus,[4] an imaginary personage, to St. Julian
the Hospitaller,[5] to a St. Ursius[6] and to others, it was
widely read throughout the Middle Ages as the biography of a saint.[7]   And which of us to-day is unaware that the life of the saints Barlaam and Joasaph
is merely an adaptation of the Buddha legend?[8]   In

[1] Zahn, *Cyprian von Antiochien und die deutsche Faustsage*,
Erlangen, 1882, 8°, 153 pages.

[2] See later, chap. vii. Compare *Acta SS.*, Jan., vol. i., p. 258.

[3] *Bibliotheca hagiographica latina*, n. 3649-51.

[4] *Catalogus codd. MSS. hagiogr. lat. bibl. Regiæ Bruxellensis*,
vol. ii., pp. 444-56. Compare *Analecta Bollandiana*, vol. xiv., p. 124.

[5] *Acta SS.*, Jan., vol. i i.,p. 974.

[6] *Ibid.*, May, vol. i., pp. 926-27.

[7] It is well known that this legend has also been applied to
Judas Iscariot. It may be read in the *Legenda Aurea*, chap. xlv.,
De S. Mathia Apostolo. See Creizenach, *Judas Iscarioth in Legende
und Sage des M.-A.*, 1875; V. Istrin, *Die griechische Version der
Judas Legende* in *Archiv für slavische Philologie*, vol. xx., 1898,
pp. 605-19.

[8] E. Cosquin, *La légende des saints Barlaam et Josaphat, son
origine*, in the *Revue des Questions historiques*, Oct., 1880; Kuhn,
Barlaam und Joasaph in *Abhandlungen der k. bayer. Academie*, i.
Cl., vol. xx., 1893, pp. 1-88. G. Paris, *Poèmes et légendes du moyen*

the mind of the monk John, to whom we owe it in its Christian form, it was nothing more than a pleasant and piquant narrative serving as a vehicle for religious and moral instruction.

Nevertheless, fictions of this type are not without a certain danger.   As long as they continue to be read in the spirit in which they were written, all goes well. But a moment comes, and in some cases comes very quickly, when people no longer recall the original intention of the story.   Indeed the classification of literature is not always an easy task, and we can imagine our own great-grandchildren finding themselves much embarrassed by some of our contemporary novels of a vivid and convincing realism.   In such cases, however, our ancestors suffered from no hesitations.   In their eyes all noble narratives which delighted them were history, and the heroes therein depicted were genuine saints equal in all respects to those who enjoyed traditional honours.

It also happened—though less frequently than one might be tempted to suppose—that, under favourable circumstances, these new saints quitted the literary sphere in which they had been created and really became the object of public devotion.   The fact is greatly to be deplored wherever it occurred.   Yet was it not the outcome of a natural evolution, and is it not likely to occur wherever hagiographic documents are accepted in an uncritical spirit?   In point of fact it is quite unjust on such occasions to blame the hagiographer, and he might well reproach us in our turn.   We should first ascertain what he intended to produce, and judge him only from his own standpoint.

âge, pp. 181-215. Concerning devotion to the two saints, see *Analecta Bollandiana*, vol. xxii., p. 131.

It is true that to the question of intention the hagiographer in most cases will reply that he intended to write history. Hence, in such cases it is important to ascertain what ideas he entertained concerning historical writing, and in what sense he understood the duties of a historian. It goes without saying that he did not entertain the same ideas on the subject as we do now.

When we attempt to arrive at some understanding of how the ancients themselves understood history, we are less surprised at the naïve conceptions concerning it held by men of letters in the Middle Ages. With rare exceptions—Polybius, who was never popular with the general public, might be quoted as one—classic antiquity saw but little difference between history and rhetoric. The historian holds, as it were, a place midway between the rhetorician and the poet. And when one remembers how easy a conscience rhetoricians had in matters of truth, it is not difficult to measure the distance that separates us from antiquity in our manner of judging the qualifications and duties of a historian.[1] What for us is merely accessory, for the ancients was the very essence. Then historians had regard, above all else, to literary effect; material truth troubled them less, accuracy scarce at all, and of the critical spirit they had, as a rule, no conception whatever. The main thing was to give pleasure to the reader by the interest of the narrative, the beauty of the descriptions and the brilliancy of the style.

It can easily be imagined that the Middle Ages which, in a sense, were the inheritors of the literary traditions of the ancients did not open up new paths

[1 Fine passages by the ancients on the ideal and duties of the historian are well known. . . . Study of the sources and processes should rather understand the concept that they had of historical genre and the manner of realizing it. Concerning all this see H. Peter, *Die geschichtliche Litteratur über die römische Kaiserzeit bis Theodosius I*, Leipzig, 1897, vol. i, p. 200-4; E. Norden, *Die antike Kunstprosa*, Leipzig, 1898, vol. i, p. 81 ff. 3d ed.]

in the domain of history.   Above all, their tendencies were not in the direction of criticism.   When the historian no longer desired to be restricted to the *rôle* of annalist or witness he became a compiler, one lacking discernment, and far more preoccupied with his readers' tastes than with a laborious quest after truth.   The ancients who might have been his models knew as little as he did of those complicated processes by means of which we hope to disentangle the true from the false, and to reconstruct the characteristic features of a personage or a period.   Moreover, the simple minds of these semi-barbarous scribes were lacking in the very first qualification for exercising the critical faculty in however slight a degree.   They were devoid of guile, and they never suspected that a written testimony might be false, or that a likely tale need not necessarily be true.   The confusion between history and legend was never-ending.   History, in the Middle Ages, meant everything that was told, everything that was written in books.

It goes without saying that this elementary conception of history was shared by the hagiographers. Their writings, no less than their own declarations, testify to the fact.   Nothing is more common in the prefaces to lives of saints than excuses for imperfections of form and a preoccupation concerning style.   The author frequently laments his incapacity, and professes anxiety lest he should bore his reader.   Meanwhile, he obviously ignores the many delicate problems that assail the historian, and, save in very rare instances, his only guarantee of the quality of his wares consists in commonplace protestations of sincerity which leave the reader wholly unmoved if they do not actually awaken his suspicions.

Among the many hagiographers whom we might interrogate as to the manner in which, in their day, their profession was understood, here is one—the author of the Martyrdom of St. Fortunata—who, in his opening lines, testifies to the discredit into which his predecessors and rivals had allowed the form of history which he professed to cultivate to fall. " Sanctorum martyrum passiones idcirco minoris habentur auctoritatis, quia scilicet in quibusdam illarum falsa inveniuntur mixta cum veris." [1]   The opening words are far from ordinary, and one asks oneself with a certain curiosity how the author proposes in the case of this new Passion that he has been engaged to write to give it that authoritative character which is so desirable.   He hastens to let us into his secret : " Passionem sanctissimæ virginis Fortunatæ hac ratione stilo propriæ locutionis expressi, superflua scilicet resecans, necessaria quæque subrogans, vitiata emendans, inordinata corrigens atque incomposita componens ".[2]

Thus a writer, who is quite conscious that everything is not for the best in the hagiographic world, can suggest nothing more efficacious as regards the abuses he chronicles than improved editing and an amended style.   The idea of undertaking fresh researches, of studying documents, of comparing and weighing evidence, has not even occurred to him.

In point of fact the requirements of the reading

[1] "The Passions of the holy martyrs are held to be of less authority because in some of them falsehood is found mixed up with truth." *Prologus ad Passionem S. Fortunatæ v. et m.* Mai, *Spicilegium Romanum,* vol. iv., p. 289.

[2] "My method has been to set down the Passion of the holy martyr Fortunata in my own words, cutting away what was superfluous, adding anything necessary, amending what was corrupt, correcting what was extravagant and rearranging what was disorderly."

public did not go beyond his suggestions. When the monk Theodoric arrived in Rome, the Canons of St. Peter's begged him to turn his attention to the life of Pope St. Martin, of whom they possessed a biography : "in tantum rusticano stilo prævaricata atque falsata, quæ doctas aures terrerent potius quam mulcerent".[1] It is the classic complaint of all those who would persuade an author to rewrite a biography or a martyrdom. They are shocked by the barbarity of the style. All else is indifferent to them.

The hagiographer, then, is inspired by the ideas of history current in his day. Nevertheless he writes with a special and clearly defined object, not without influence on the character of his work. For he does not relate simply in order to interest, but above all else to edify. Thus a new form of literature is created which partakes at once of the nature of biography, panegyric and moral instruction.

The inevitable pitfalls are too familiar to need recapitulation. It follows from the very purpose of his writing that the panegyrist is not bound to draw a portrait of which every detail is in precise accordance with the truth. Every one knows that he is painting an ideal picture, and that he is free to omit those aspects in which his hero appears to less advantage. In the same way the eulogy of a saint was held incompatible with the slightest suggestion of blame, and as the saints themselves were subject to human infirmities the task of the hagiographer intent on sacrificing nothing to truth presents difficulties of a somewhat delicate nature.

---

[1] "So ill-favoured and corrupt owing to its barbarous style as to horrify rather than charm learned ears." *Theodorici monachi præfatio in vitam S. Martini papæ*, Mai, vol. cit., p. 294. [On the monk Thierry, read A. Poncelet, in *Analecta Bollandiana*, vol. xxvii, p. 5-27. 3d ed.]

His fidelity, as a rule, depends largely on his state of mind. If, for instance, while pursuing his aim of edification, he can persuade himself that the sins of the saint before and even after his conversion, far from clouding his glory, actually enhance the triumph of divine grace, he is not likely to leave the more human side of his hero in the shade, and will beware of placing him on those inaccessible heights which discourage imitators. But there exists a school of hagiographers who would gladly strike out the denial of St. Peter from the Gospel, in order not to tarnish the aureola of the prince of the apostles. They submit themselves, more than we could wish, to the stern exigencies of their craft. But before we condemn them as faithless historians, we should ask ourselves whether the name of history, as we moderns understand it, should be applied to their writings at all.

Nor must we omit to bear in mind a further circumstance which assists us to grasp the attitude of the mediæval hagiographer. He was acquainted with two species of books: those in which every one was obliged to believe, *i.e.*, Holy Scripture in all its parts, and those to which no one was compelled to give credence. He was acutely conscious of the fact that his own writings belonged to the latter category, and that his readers were fully aware of it. Thus for him some books contained absolute truth, others only relative truth, and this conviction naturally gave him an easy conscience in regard to historic exactitude. Hence the feigned indignation, so frequently met with among hagiographers against all who do not give credence to their narratives. It betrays the man whose conscience is not entirely clear.

II.

We have already seen in what sense our pious
authors usually interpreted their duties while professing
to discharge the function of a historian. We have now
to examine how they exercised it, and what historical
elements we may look for in their work. Here, as
always, it is a case of solving in each individual instance
the twofold problem : What sources of information
had they at their disposal, and what use did they make
of them ?

As a general rule the hagiographer is not very eager
to inform his readers from whence he has drawn his
information. He may even display a certain affecta-
tion, not infrequently met with in classical authors, in
hiding the sources of his knowledge. At other times he
may pose as an ocular witness of facts drawn from some
written document,[1] or of incidents that he himself has
invented. For if chroniclers worthy of credence [2] have
made justifiable use of the scriptural phrase, *Quod
vidimus oculis nostris quod perspeximus* (1 John i. 1),[3]
there have also been no lack of impostors to abuse it.[4]

---

[1] An example of this may be found in an author of the Carlovin-
gian period, who when re-writing the life of St. John of Réome
(† about the year 544) by Jonas, introduces the following phrase:
*Et ne quis hoc fabulosum putet esse quod dicimus, referente viro
venerabili Agrippino diacono, ipsius Agrestii filio, cognovimus.* See
also M. G.; *Scr. rer. Merov.*, vol. iii., p. 504.

[2] *Passio Perpetuæ*, i., 5.

[3] "What we have seen with our eyes, what we have beheld."

[4] *Passio S. Andreæ*, n. 1. Bonnet, *Acta apostolorum apocrypha*,
vol. ii., 1, p. 1. *Cf. Acta Barnabæ*, n. 1; *ibid.*, vol. ii., 2, p. 292.

Others have appropriated the familiar formula of
Eusebius when he describes the persecution of Diocletian in Palestine, ὁ καθ' ἡμᾶς διωγμός,[1] and by this
means have passed themselves off as contemporaries.[2]
Above all, must we beware of authors who profess to
have discovered engraved tablets.[3]

We must assume, so numerous are the examples of
it, that the hagiographer felt justified in making use of
the literary fiction which consists in speaking in the
name of a disciple of the saint in order to give greater
weight to his narrative. We are all acquainted with
Eurippus, the pretended disciple of St. John the
Baptist;[4] with Pasicrates, the servant of St. George;[5]
Augarus, the secretary of St. Theodore;[6] Athanasius,
the stenographer of St. Catherine;[7] Nilus, the companion of St. Theodotus;[8] Theotimus, the attendant
of St. Margaret;[9] Evagrius, the disciple of St. Pancratius
of Tauromenium;[10] Florentius, the servant of SS.
Cassiodorus, Senator and Dominata;[11] Gordianus,

1 "The persecution of our own time."—*De Martyribus Palestinæ*,
3, 6, 8. See *Analecta Bollandiana*, vol. xvi., pp. 122, 127.

2 *Passio S. Sebastianæ*, n. 1. *Acta SS.*, June, vol. vi., p. 60.

3 The proceeding was already familiar to the novelists of antiquity. E. Rohde, *Der griechische Roman*, p. 271.

4 A. Vassiliev, *Anecdota Græco-Byzantina*, Moscow, 1893, p. 1.

5 *Bibliotheca hagiographica græca*, p. 47, n. 3, 6.

6 *Analecta Bollandiana*, vol. ii., p. 359.

7 Viteau, *Passion des Saints Ecatêrine et Pierre d'Alexandrie*,
Paris, 1897, p. 23.

8 *Acta SS.*, May, vol. iv., p. 149. *Also Analecta Bollandiana*, vol.
xxii., pp. 320-28.

9 *Acta SS.*, July, vol. v., pp. 31-32.

10 *Catal. codd. hag. græcorum bibliotheca Vaticanæ*, Brussels,
1899, p. 132.

11 H. Delehaye, *Saint Cassiodore* in *Mélanges Paul Fabre*, Paris,
1902, p. 44.

the servant of St. Placidus;[1] and Enoch, the witness of the doings of St. Angelo.[2] The above list might be considerably augmented.

Another device was to place history under the patronage of some well-known name. Thus the Passion of SS. Menas, Hermogenes and Eugraphus[3] is supposed to have been written by St. Athanasius; the history of the image of Camuliana is attributed to St. Gregory of Nyssa,[4] and so on.

Hence it becomes useless to interrogate the hagiographers themselves; it is their writings we have to examine, and to try to distinguish the elements of which they are composed.

The classification of historical sources suggested by Droysen can be conveniently applied to hagiography. They may be grouped in two broad categories: tradition and antiquarian remains.

In the first category we recognise primarily *written tradition*, *i.e.*, narratives, annals, chronicles, memoirs, biographies, historical inscriptions and every other kind of writing. It seems superfluous to point out that all these classes of documents, according to circumstances, have been at the disposal of hagiographers. But it would be a mistake to conclude that lack of documents would usually restrain them from undertaking the task of historians or from writing the lives of saints. We must not necessarily conclude that they themselves were fully informed because they furnish the reader with a profusion of details. We shall see later by what means they supplemented inadequate sources.

1 *Acta SS.*, Oct., vol. iii., pp. 114-38.
2 *Ibid.*, May, vol. ii., pp. 803-30.
3 *Analecta Bollandiana*, vol. xviii., p. 405.
4 E. von Dobschütz, *Christusbilder*, p. 12.

Another error, very widely spread, is to assume that in the first centuries of the Christian era authentic accounts were in existence of all the martyrs who were honoured with public worship, and to infer that the documents which clearly belong to a later date were derived from original contemporary sources.

Thanks to special circumstances the Church in Africa was, in this respect, in a privileged position. Yet even here we must not exaggerate its resources. St. Augustine, speaking of St. Stephen, whose martyrdom is related in the Acts of the Apostles, made use of these significant words: " Cum aliorum martyrum vix gesta inveniamus quæ in solemnitatibus eorum recitare possimus, huius passio in canonico libro est ".[1] It remains none the less true that the average value of hagiographic documents from Africa is very much higher than that of the materials bequeathed to us by most other Churches.

Unhappily the mistake has been made of assuming in regard to others what is in reality only true of this solitary instance. On the faith of a text which has since been appraised at its proper value, various scholars have asserted that, in the Roman Church during the years of persecution, there existed a body of notaries entrusted with the duty of collecting the acts of the martyrs, and of this supposed corporation unfair advantage has been taken to give to the narratives of the Roman Legendarium a historic authority to which they have no sort of claim.[2] It is certain that in the fourth

---

[1] "While in the case of other martyrs we can scarcely find sufficient details about them to read in public on their festivals, this saint's martyrdom is set forth in a book of the canonical Scriptures." —*Sermo,* 315, n. 1, Migne, P. L., vol. xxxviii., p. 1426.

[2] See Duchesne, *Le Liber Pontificalis,* vol. i., pp. c.-ci.

century, when Damasus placed his famous inscriptions
on the tombs of the martyrs, the people of Rome were
ignorant of the history of the greater number of them.[1]
When the necessity made itself felt of providing a
circumstantial narrative, the hagiographers had to dispense with any appeal to written tradition, for such
did not exist.

A second source of information is *oral tradition* : the
reports of contemporaries or eye-witnesses, accounts of
indirect witnesses and narratives circulating among the
people, in a word every unwritten historical or legendary report that might be used by the editor of the life
of a saint.   No doubt it has happened at times that
hagiographers have gathered precious information from
the lips of witnesses who spoke from first-hand knowledge.   But how far more often must they have been
satisfied with a tradition which had suffered from its
transmission through tortuous channels.   We have seen
in the previous chapter how an incident preserved in
the popular memory may undergo unconscious distortion and with what strange accretions the history of a
hero may sometimes be enriched.   The hagiographer
has constantly found himself confronted by legendary
narratives, the only ones with which oral tradition could
furnish him.

It is scarcely necessary to point out that it is not
always easy to determine the precise origin of legendary
data for which a hagiographer may make himself responsible.   They are as likely to have been supplied him
by literary as by oral tradition, and not infrequently he
may have drawn from his own resources what we should
at first be tempted to mistake for folk tales of spontane-

---

[1] *Analecta Bollandiana*, vol. xvi., p. 239; Dufourcq, *Les gesta des
martyrs romains*, p. 24 ff.

ous growth. After all, that which a whole people ends by saying must have been enunciated in the first place by an individual, and why should not the hagiographer who holds the pen have been the first to formulate some legendary detail? It is always with this mental reservation that we must accept oral tradition as met with in written documents.

Thirdly, *pictorial tradition* must not be neglected, for it plays an important part in hagiography. Artists, as a rule, seek their inspiration in written or oral tradition. But at the same time it may happen that both these sources enrich themselves from the creations of painters and sculptors who transform and give back to them the ideas they had previously borrowed. We know beyond a doubt that certain authors of legends were directly inspired by the frescoes or mosaics before their eyes, among others Prudentius in his description of the martyrdom of St. Hippolytus.[1] The panegyric of St. Euphemia by Asterius of Amasea is merely the description of a series of frescoes,[2] and in the panegyric of St. Theodore attributed to Gregory of Nyssa the orator draws the attention of his audience to the paintings of the basilica.[3] More than one legend, as we shall see, owes its origin to the fantasy of some artist, or to a mistaken interpretation of some iconographic detail.

Certain hagiographers have made a somewhat unexpected use of pictorial tradition. In the synaxaries of the Greek Church numbers of the biographies of illustrious saints conclude with a detailed portrait which in its precision would appear to reveal an eye-witness. When studied closely, however, it becomes obvious that these descriptions are simply borrowed from those

[1] *Peristeph.*, xi. [2] Migne, P. G., vol. xl., p. 336.
[3] *Ibid.*, vol. xlvi., p. 737.

manuals of painting from which Byzantine artists copied the features of the unchanging physiognomies of their saints.[1] For those who have not recognised their origin the portraits might possess a quite exaggerated importance.

This then is what tradition, in its various forms, can supply to the hagiographer: a more or less faithful picture of the past and certain traits of individual character. But the past has at times bequeathed to us something of itself, a building, an instrument, an authentic document. In the same way we often possess more of the saints than a mere memory; we may have their relics, their shrine, sometimes even their writings. From all these the historian draws inspiration; often indeed the hagiographer possesses no other documents than these *relics of the past*, a hallowed corpse, a tomb visited by pilgrims, a feast celebrated each year on the day of death. He knows this is insufficient to satisfy the eager curiosity of the people. If in spite of the lack of material he feels compelled to gratify popular taste we can guess what the result must be.

We have now enumerated the ordinary sources of information at the hagiographer's disposal. Let us suppose him well furnished with materials, and we will try to watch him at his work. The bent of his mind will betray itself in his choice of documents and items of information, in the interpretation he puts upon them, and in the way he wields them together.

In the first place, we must not expect a very judicious choice from our man of letters, who is forced to restrict himself and to give the preference to one authority rather than another. He has never learned how to

---

[1] See *Synaxarium ecclesiæ Constantinopolitanæ, Propylæum ad Acta SS. Novembris*, p. lxvi.

weigh evidence, and all his sources appear to him of equal value. Hence he mingles the historic element indiscriminately with legendary lore, and it is not this last which goes to the wall when space forbids a lengthy narrative.

Two hagiographic collections which first saw the light, one at the dawn of the Middle Ages, the writings of Gregory of Tours on the martys and confessors, the other the Golden Legend, at its culminating point, allow us to observe, so to speak in the very act, the methods of pious writers compelled to restrict themselves in their narrative. In both cases they had copious materials at their disposal, and deliberately neglected the sources that would have interested us the most in order to devote all their attention to the more marvellous features which betray in a marked degree their legendary character.[1]

In this they merely followed popular taste, instinctively drawn as we have seen towards everything that is miraculous and tangible, and it is perhaps to this very tendency that we must attribute the loss of the acts of a large number of saints who had enjoyed a widespread popularity. Thus, without wishing to affirm that there have ever existed written accounts of the deaths of the celebrated martyrs Theodore and Menas, whose cultus can be accurately localised, it is quite natural that the extraordinary interest displayed by the people in the fabulous tales circulated concerning them, should have encour-

---

[1] A similar preference betrays itself very clearly in the Greek life of St. Gregory the Great, which was composed, as we have attempted to show elsewhere, by means of selected extracts sent by the Greek monks of the Cœlian Hill to Constantinople, *Analecta Bollandiana,* vol. xxiii., pp. 449-54. [Several additional sentences at this point in the 3d ed. speak of the difference in the materials available to Gregory and to Voragine, the author of the *Golden Legend.*]

aged the hagiographers to neglect more and more the more sober material furnished by their acts and even to eliminate it altogether. The study of manuscripts indeed has revealed the permanent fact that between a purely historical document and a touched-up version, adorned with fantastic developments and interlarded with fables, a mediæval public rarely hesitated. It almost always happens that it is the less simple version which is preserved in the greater number of manuscripts, while often enough the primitive composition is only to be found in a single copy.[1]

The historical value of a work does not depend solely on the choice of authorities, but also on the interpretation put upon them and the treatment to which they are subjected. We might relate here, did we not fear to wander too far from our subject, what hagiographers and their assistants have occasionally been capable of deducing even from such documents as it required no special aptitude to interpret. The clearest texts may sometimes be misunderstood, and give rise to the most unexpected inferences. We must, however, restrict ourselves to one or two examples.

It is known that the Scillitan martyrs suffered death on 17th July, 180, in the beginning of the reign of the Emperor Commodus. The wording of the Acts establishes it quite clearly from the first : *Præsente bis et Condiano consulibus XVI. kal. Augustas.* The first name was wrongly understood, and some one or other mistook it for a participle. This participle was ex-

---

1 This fact is easily verified by means of the catalogues of Latin and Greek hagiographic manuscripts published by the Bollandists, both separately and in nearly all the volumes of *Analecta Bollandiana* since 1882.

changed for an equivalent, or something that was considered such : *præsidente, præstante, exsistente.* At the same time Condianus became Claudianus, then Claudius, who in his turn was identified with the consul of that name in the year 200. Now in that year there were two emperors reigning side by side. The *imperator* mentioned in the text was easily corrected into *imperatores.* There was then nothing left to do save to add the names of the emperors Severus and Caracalla. This was done without, of course, any one suspecting what a revolution this apparently justifiable correction would introduce into the chronology of the Christian persecutions. We see from the result what comes of not being able to distinguish a name from a participle ! [1]

If the name Amphibalus has been conferred on the saintly confessor to whom St. Alban of Verulam gave shelter, it is merely because Geoffrey of Monmouth mistook a chasuble for a man.[2]

In the passion of St. Fructuosus and his companions may be read the following interesting dialogue between the judge Æmilianus and the martyr : *Episcopus es ? Fructuosus episcopus dixit : Sum. Æmilianus dixit : Fuisti. Et jussit eos sua sententia vivos ardere.*[3] A copyist, failing to perceive the sarcasm of the judge, read *fustibus* in the place of *fuisti.* The word by itself having no meaning, our hagiographer supplied boldly, *Fustibus eos sternite,* thus adding a fresh

---

1 This series of alterations has been admirably exposed by M. P. Monceaux, *Histoire littéraire de l'Afrique chrétienne,* vol. i., Paris, 1901, p. 62.

2 J. Loth, *Saint Amphibalus* in the *Revue Celtique,* vol. ii., 1890, pp. 348-49.

3 "Art thou a bishop?" Fructuosus, the bishop, said: "I am". AEmilianus replied: "Thou hast been". And he sentenced them to be burned alive.

torture to the martyr in order to justify an inaccurate reading.[1]

It was possibly also a very slight error of some copyist which transformed into a miracle a quite natural incident related in the Acts of St. Marciana. A lion, let loose in the arena, sprang furiously upon her, and stood over her with its paws on her chest; then having smelt her, turned away without doing her any injury: *martyris corpus odoratus eam ultra non contigit.*[2] The author of a hymn in honour of St. Marciana has been led to confuse *odorare* with *adorare*; unless indeed he himself wished to embellish the narrative of the hagiographer by writing:—

> " Leo percurrit percitus
> Adoraturus veniens
> Non comesturus virginem." [3]

We must not omit to mention here a whole series of gross errors due to the carelessness of compilers of synaxaries or martyrologies who had summary methods of their own for dealing with any difficulties they might meet with in their editorial duties. Thus what could be more improbable than the feast of St. Babylas with the three children in competition with that other St. Babylas and his eighty-eight companions on the same date and with a more or less identical history? The origin of this duplication was an abbreviation in two letters which was mistaken for a number of two figures. A moment's reflection should have sufficed to correct the mistake. But our learned editors preferred

---

[1] *Acta SS.*, Jan., vol. ii., p. 340.
[2] *Ibid.*, Jan., vol. i., p. 569.
[3] The lion bounds forward to adore, not to devour the virgin maid. *Ibid.*, p. 570. See E. Le Blant, *Les Actes des martyrs*, p. 30.

to lengthen out the list of the saints.[1] In the same spirit they invented the three groups of SS. Cosmas and Damian, without realising the absurdities they were gaily accumulating.[2] Compared with such enormities the duplication of St. Martin, thanks to a mere question of dates, appears a venial offence.[3] It is probable that a similar origin must be assigned to the double St. Theodore of the Greeks and the Latins.[4] The two feast-days have given rise to two legends, and in this instance the man of letters would seem to have been the guilty party. For the common people, as we have seen, have their own ways of simplifying matters. They are more likely to fuse two personages together, than to create two in the place of one.

We need not revert here to the curious explanations which popular imagination has occasionally invented concerning certain carved monuments of which the meaning was obscure.[5] The hagiographers accepted such explanations with zest and embodied them in their narratives. If it was the people who created the legend of the "cephalophorous" or head-bearing saints, it was propagated by the hagiographers who bestowed upon it that special authority which the uneducated always accord to the written word.[6]

1 *Les deux Saints Babylas* in *Analecta Bolland.*, vol. xix, pp. 5-8.

2 "It should be known," say the synaxaries gravely, "that there are three groups of martyrs of the names of Cosmas and Damian, those of Arabia who were decapitated under Diocletian, those of Rome who were stoned under Carinus, and the sons of Theodota who died peacefully," *Synaxarium eccesiæ Constantinopolitanæ*, 1st July, p. 791.

3 St. Martin, Bishop of Tours, 12th November; St. Martin, Bishop of France, 12th November; *Synaxarium*, pp. 211, 217.

4 The Greeks celebrate the feast of one St. Theodore (*stratelates*) on 8th February, and another (*tiro*) on the 17th. The Latins celebrate the two saints respectively on 7th February and 9th November.

5 See above, p. 45. [In the 3d ed. there is a slight expansion of this paragraph.]

[6 M. E.-A. Stückelberg, *Die Kephalophoren*, in *Anzeiger für Schweizerische Altertumskunde*, 1916, p. 78, has drawn up a long list of saints whom legend has made cephalophorous, and the list could easily be lengthened. 3d ed.]

It has been said with truth that in all probability the Passion of St. Eleutherius [1] was partially inspired by the paintings or mosaics that adorned his sanctuary. More especially the scene in which Eleutherius, seated on a hillock, preaches to the animals grouped around him, recalls the familiar representations of Orpheus. And here a noteworthy detail presents itself. The writer asserts that the animals who listened to the saint, not being able to praise God with their voices, all lifted up the right foot. Obviously he had seen in the mosaic representations of animals walking.[1]

Our chroniclers have frequently had to pronounce on more embarrassing problems than these, and we may well ask whether their learned solutions—learning in this matter is a very relative term—are invariably worth more than the interpretations of the ignorant public. But for ourselves, who wear out our brains in attempting, and often unsuccessfully, to re-establish, with the help of the best manuscripts, the primitive readings of the Hieronymian Martyrology, why should we express surprise at the little blunders committed by our ancestors, as when they turned the eighty-third mile of a Roman road, lxxxiii mil[iario], into eighty-three martyred soldiers, lxxxiii mil[ites]? [2] One may read without much trouble in the Hieronymian Martyrology under the date of 11th June: *Romae via Aurelia miliario V. Basilidis. Tripoli Magdaletis.*[3] These are two separate entries commemorating a Roman and a Phœnician martyr. In the Middle Ages it was transformed into a single group of three, *Basilidis, Tripodis et*

[1 Pio Franchi de' Cavalieri, *I martirii di S. Teodote e di S. Ariadne*, in *Studi e Testi*, 6, p. 145; the Passion, p. 149-61.]
2 *Analecta Bollandiana*, vol. xiii., p. 164.
[3 In the 3d ed. this is given under date of 12 June.]

Magdalis, and thus a new saint was created out of the slightly disfigured name of a town.[1]

Our predecessors were also, it must be admitted, very mediocre epigraphists. They were capable of translating the classical B[onæ] M[emoriæ] by B[eati] M[artyres].[2] Sometimes in the epitaph of a bishop they would come across the word *sanctus*, which in those days was simply a title of honour corresponding to " His Holiness," or, as we should say, " His Lordship," and no one was competent to explain to them that at the period in which these inscriptions were cut the word did not bear the significance they attributed to it and which it only acquired at a later date. Mistakes of this kind have· procured the honours of an easy canonisation for more than one obscure personage.[3] But these are errors which would not always be avoided even in the age of the *Corpus inscriptionum*.

It has happened only too frequently that inscriptions

---

[1] An account of the translation of the three martyrs quoted by the priest Leo in his prologue to the Passion of SS. Rufus and Respicius has been lost, A. Mai, *Spicilegium Romanum*, vol. iv., p. 292. An ancient author asserts that the three bodies were presented by Honorius III. to the basilica of Santa Maria Transpontina, A. Mastelloni, *La Traspontina*, Naples, 1717, p. 93.

[2] See an example in G. Finazzi, *Delle iscrizioni cristiane anteriori al VII. secolo appartenenti alla chiesa di Bergamo*, Florence, 1873, pp. 16, 30, 41; A. Mazzi, *I martiri della chiesa di Bergamo*, Bergamo, 1883, p. 14. We have given other examples of a similar nature in the article on *St. Cassiodore* in *Mélanges Paul Fabre*, pp. 40-50. Some dozens of inscriptions bearing the abbreviation B. M. before the name of the deceased have supplied the learned writers of Sardinia with an equal number of martyrs. Thus, *Hic jacet B. M. Speratus* was read by them as *Hic jacet beatus martyr Speratus*, and so on. The interesting gallery of inscriptions compiled on these principles is to be seen in D. Bonfant, *Triumpho de los santos del regno de Cerdena*, En Caller, 1635, in fol.

[3] We have treated this question in *Analecta Bollandiana*, vol. xviii., pp. 407-11. [and later in the volume *Sanctus*, Brussels, 1927. 3d ed.]

have provided traps for hagiographers that appear to us now of a very obvious kind, but into which none the less they have tumbled headlong.[1] We find, for instance, the epitaph of a virgin who is described as *digna et merita*, a memorial formula in vogue at one period. Now there existed a St. Emerita whose name was recognised in the second of the two epithets. The first became quite naturally the name of another saint, Digna, the companion of Emerita, and concerning these two noble sisters the hagiographers elaborated a highly dramatic and most circumstantial history.[2] From a mistranslation of an inscription by Pope Damasus, that in honour of SS. Felix and Adauctus, there sprang a hagiographic romance of unusual improbability which assumed the existence of two martyred brothers each bearing the name of Felix.[3] It was the erroneous interpretation of another Damasian [4] inscription which gave rise to the legend of the Orientals who came to Rome in order to carry off the relics of SS. Peter and Paul. *Discipulos oriens misit* wrote Damasus, intending simply to refer to the disciples of Jesus Christ who came from the East to bring the Gospel

---

[1] It needed sometimes only a word, even less than a word, to give rise to the most extraordinary legends. In the inscription *C. Julius. L. F. Cæsar. Strabs. aed. cur. q. tr. mil. bis. X. vir agr. dand. adtr. iud. pontif.* (*C. I. L.*, vol. i., p. 278), the last two words were translated IVD(æorum) PONTIF(ex), and men referred this to the treaty of friendship between the Jews and the Romans *quod rescripserunt in tabulis æreis* (I Mach. viii. 22). Hence the precise information contained in the *Mirabilia* (see Jordan, *Topographie der Stadt Rom.*, vol. ii., pp. 470-71); *In muro S. Basilii fuit magna tabula ænea, ubi fuit scripta amicitia in loco bono et notabili, quae fuit inter Romanos et Iudæos tempore Iudæ Machabæi.* It only remains to add that the inscription in question was not engraved on a bronze but on a marble slab.

[2] *Analecta Bollandiana*, vol. xvi., pp. 30, 40.

[3] *Ibid.*, pp. 19-29.   [4] Ihm, *Damasi epigrammata*, n. 26.

to Rome. The inscription concerning St. Agnes,[1] and no doubt many others,[2] have equally been the means of revealing fresh details to the imagination of the hagiographer.[3]

An interesting example of a whole legend being suggested by the reading of an inscription is that of Abercius. His journeys were mentioned in the celebrated epitaph; the symbolic queen became the Empress Faustina, and the object of the journey the healing of a princess possessed by an evil spirit.[4] By means of various episodes which are little more than reminiscences of other legends, the hagiographer in the end put together a highly detailed narrative which met with the greatest success.[5] In spite of this no serious doubts should be entertained concerning the episcopacy of Abercius and the traditional cultus rendered to him in his native town.[6]

1 Ihm, *Damasi epigrammata,* n. 40.

2 Not long ago Father Bonavenia attempted to deduce from that of SS. Protus and Hyacinthus (Ihm, n. 49) proof that the Acts of St. Eugenia contain "un fondo di vero da atti piu antichi e sinceri". *Nuovo Bullettino di archeologia cristiana,* vol. iv., 1898, p. 80. Readers familiar with Damasian phraseology will not participate in his illusions.

3 See Pio Franchi de' Cavalieri, *S. Agnese nella tradizione e nella leggenda,* Rome, 1899, p. 35.

4 The deacon Cyriacus, in the Acts of St. Marcellus, is summoned to Rome for a similar purpose. It is a common occurrence which is to be found in the Acts of SS. Vitus, Tryphon and Potitus, and also in the lives of St. Mathurinus and of St. Naamatius, *Analecta Bollandiana,* vol. xvi., p. 76.

5 *Acta SS.,* Oct., vol. ix., pp. 485-93; L. Duchesne, *S. Abercius* in *Revue des Questions historiques,* vol. xxxiv., 1883, pp. 5-33; *Analecta Bollandiana,* vol. xvi., p. 76. A useful contribution to the criticism of the Acts of St. Abercius may be found in an article by F. C. Conybeare, *Talmudic Elements in the Acts of Abercius* in *The Academy,* 6th June, 1896, pp. 468-70.

6 *Analecta Bollandiana,* vol. xv., p. 333.

It must, alas, be confessed that the erroneous interpretation of inscriptions, of carved monuments and of
other antiquities did not give rise to legends in the
Middle Ages alone.   Before the days of De Rossi the
majority of scholars who worked in the Roman catacombs without any safe criteria by which to discern
where cultus was really paid, imagined they had discovered bodies of saints in a number of tombs before
which the pilgrims of ancient days never dreamt of
making a halt.[1]   These relics, doubtful at the best, were
eagerly sought after, and the faithful frequently refused
to be satisfied with the bare name inscribed on the
marble.   On the model of the ancient Passions many
new legends were manufactured, which, while appearing
reasonably probable, were eminently suited to satisfy
the pious curiosity of the faithful.   The best known
example of this is the case of St. Philomena, whose
insignificant epitaph has suggested the most ingenious
combinations, and has furnished the elements of a
detailed narrative including even the interrogatory of
the martyr.[2]

The inaccurate identification of geographical names
is responsible for another class of errors, of less consequence it is true, as they have not extended to creating
new objects of veneration but merely to locating them.
The reading *Caeae Antonina* in place of *Nicaeae* ap-

[1] Concerning relics from the catacombs there exists a decree of
His Holiness Leo XIII. dated 21st December, 1878. See Duchesne,
Les corps saints des Catacombes in *Bulletin critique*, vol. ii., pp.
198-202.

[2] *Analecta Bollandiana*, vol. xvii., p. 469. A recent discovery by
Signor Marucchi, *Osservazioni archeologiche sulle iscrizione di S.
Filomena*, Rome, 1904, forces one to conclude that the famous
epithet *Pax tecum Filumena* was not that of the deceased woman
(or perhaps man) found in the tomb at the time of the translation.
See *Analecta Bollandiana*, vol. xxiv., pp. 119-20.

peared to confer on the town of Cea in Spain the right
to claim St. Antonina.[1]   The inhabitants of Scilla in
Calabria imagined that the Scillitan martyrs could only
derive the name from their town.   But the people of
Squillace protested against this identification, and
claimed the Scillitans as their own fellow-citizens.
Indeed they championed these pretensions with so
much assurance that in 1740 the Congregation of Rites
authorised them to celebrate the Mass and Office of St.
Speratus and his companions.[2]   In other places great
efforts have been made to prove that St. Paul visited
the country, as may be seen from the title of a work
by Giorgi : *D. Paulus apostolus in mari quod nunc
Venetus Sinus dicitur naufragus et Militæ Dalmatensi
insulæ post naufragium hospes, sive de genuino signi-
ficatu duorum locorum in Actibus apostolorum.*[3]   These
examples, from the very fact that they are comparatively recent, make us realise all the better the methods
of mediæval hagiographers, confronted with problems
which were for them insoluble.

We have now seen the hagiographer face to face
with his historical documents.   He has made his selection and has realised how much he can draw from
them.   How has he employed his material ?

This depends of course both on his particular apti-
tudes and his personal tastes.   When it is a question of
written documents we do not hesitate to give our preference to the hagiographer who copies them most
slavishly and reproduces them with the greatest fidelity,
omitting as little as possible and adding nothing beyond

[1] *Acta SS.*, March, vol. i., p. 26.
[2] Fiore, *Della Calabria Illustrata,* Naples, 1743, vol. ii., pp. 27-28.
[3] Venetiis, 1730, in 4°.

what is strictly necessary.   Cases may be quoted in which he has been satisfied with this modest *rôle*, and we have a curious example of it in the collection of Metaphrastes.   The famous life of St. Theoctista, written by an eye-witness, was transcribed almost literally, and merely adorned with a new preface.   But as the new editor—if indeed he is worthy of the title—contented himself with giving utterance in his prologue to a few high-sounding generalities, without taking the trouble to warn the reader of his method, he succeeded in adding a new complexity to one of the most important problems in literary history, that of Metaphrastes.[1]   From the very fact that he presented himself as the author of a piece of writing filled with personal details, all these details were naturally attributed to him with the result of making him nearly half a century older than he really was.   In our own day we apply an unflattering epithet to writers who freely appropriate the wares of others, but in the Middle Ages no one resented being regarded as a plagiarist.

In most cases, as we know, the hagiographer submitted his material to a process of preparation and adaptation which conferred on it in some measure the stamp of his personality.   He would put his documents in order and dress them up in his best style, and without caring whether or not he robbed them of their documentary character, would amplify them, combine them in various ways and create a work which, if not original, was such that he was justified in passing it off under his own name.

It will be admitted that it is difficult to formulate any

1 We have referred to the matter in *La vie de St. Paul le jeune et la chronologie de Métaphraste* in the *Revue des Questions historiques,* July, 1893. [See also the bibliography cited in *Bibliotheca hagiographica graeca,* 2d ed., p. 269. The texts of the Life of St. Theoctista have now appeared in *Act. SS.,* Nov., vol. iii. p. 224-33. 3d ed.]

general precepts concerning a literature at once so vast and so varied. The use of historical sources and the methods of composition may be studied in an author or in a series of documents that are closely related,[1] but not in a collection of narratives scattered over the wide field covered by hagiographers of every nation and all periods. Nevertheless, without prejudice to them it may be said that they not infrequently embarked on that perilous course which leads to the embellishment of a tale in order that it may impress the reader more vividly. Even classical historians occasionally gave way to a mania which one would like to describe as innocent,[2] and that writers in the Middle Ages succumbed frequently to the temptation may be proved from certain cases where a comparison of texts establishes the fact beyond dispute. The following two examples are selected from comparatively recent lives of saints.[3] It is easy to imagine the degree of licence writers permitted themselves in ages of lesser culture.

When St. Bernard came to preach the Crusade in the diocese of Constance, an archer in the bodyguard of the Duke of Zähringen scoffed both at the preaching and the preacher by declaring: " He can no more work

1 The reader must be referred here to an excellent study by M. F. Lanzoni, *La Passio Sabini o Savini* in the *Römische Quartalschrift*, vol. xvii., 1903, pp. 1-26, in which the intimate relations between a whole series of Passions are brought to light: Passio Laurentii, Stephani P.; Restituti, Marii et soc.; Serapiæ et Sabinæ, Eusebii et Pontiani, Processi et Martiniani, Susannæ, Callisti, Gordiani et Epimachi, Primi et Feliciani, Viti et Crescentiæ, Marcelli P.; Petri et Marcellini, Sabini.

2 H. Peter, *Die geschichtliche Litteratur über die Römische Kaiserzeit bis Theodosius I.*, vol. ii., Leipsic, 1897, p. 292.

3 Recorded by Father E. Michael, *Geschichte des deutschen Volkes vom dreizehnten Jahrhundert bis zum Ausgang des Mittelalters*, vol. iii., Freiburg im Breisgau, 1903, pp. 392-93.

miracles than I can ". When the saint came forward to
lay his hands on the sick, the scoffer perceived him and
fell senseless to the ground, remaining unconscious for
some time. Alexander of Cologne adds: " I was quite
close to him when this occurred. . . . We called the
Abbot, and the poor man was unable to rise until
Bernard came to us, offered up a prayer and helped him
to his feet." Not one of the eye-witnesses says a
word which would suggest a resurrection from death.
And yet, a century later, Herbert, the author of a
collection of St. Bernard's miracles, Conrad, author of
the *Exordium*, and Cæsarius of Heisterbach all affirm
that the archer fell dead and that the saint restored him
to life.[1]

Every one is familiar with the beautiful incident in
the life of St. Elizabeth of Hungary when, in the very
bed she shared with her husband, she laid a miserable
leper who inspired disgust in every one, and whom no
one would tend any longer. The indignant duke
rushed into the room and dragged off the bed-clothes.
" But," in the noble words of the historian, " at that
instant God Almighty opened the eyes of his soul, and
instead of a leper he saw the figure of Christ crucified
stretched upon the bed." [2]   This admirable account by
Thierry d'Appoldia was considered too simple by later
biographers, who consequently transformed the sublime
vision of faith into a material apparition. *Tunc aperuit
Deus interiores principis oculos* wrote the historian.[3]
On the spot where the leper had slept, say the modern

[1] See G. Huffer, *Der heilige Bernard von Clairvaux*, vol. i.,
Münster, 1886, pp. 92, 182.

[2] *Bibliotheca hagiographica latina*, n. 2497.

[3] J. B. Menckenius, *Scriptores rerum germanicarum*, vol. ii., p.
1990.

hagiographers, "there lay a bleeding crucifix with out-
stretched arms".

III.

Dearth of material and methods of supplementing it—Amplification by
means of stock incidents—Acts of St. Clement of Ancyra—Compilation and adaptation—Life of St. Vincent Madelgarus—Antiquity of the process—Forgeries.

Hitherto we have almost exclusively treated of cases
in which the editor of the life of a saint follows
the lines traced for him by the materials at his disposal. It often happens that his task is less clearly
marked out. He may know the name of the saint,
sometimes even his qualification as martyr, confessor
or bishop, and the shrine dedicated to his memory.
But popular tradition may have retained nothing
further, and yet in spite of this it becomes a question
of satisfying the devout curiosity of pilgrims and pious
persons, and of supplying, from such meagre records,
matter for edifying reading. Even when writing somewhat lengthily concerning the saints Emeterius and
Chelidonius, Prudentius warns us that the necessary
documents are lacking; [1] while the author of the passion
of St. Vincent plunges into his subject with the announce-
ment : *Probabile satis est ad gloriam Vincentii martyris
quod de scriptis passionis ipsius gestis titulum invidit
inimicus.* [2] This dearth of material, which does not
appear to have checked in any degree the fertility of
his pen, is the common lot of a large number of

[1] *Peristeph.,* i., 73-78.
[2] "It is more than probable that the enemy of our race, jealous
of the glory of Vincent the Martyr, has robbed us of the title to
fame which might be found in the written record of his passion."
—*Acta SS.,* Jan., vol. ii., p. 394.

hagiographers, who, for that matter, have been equally little inconvenienced by it. As they were compelled to write, and frequently, so they themselves say, by order of their superiors, they boldly took the only course open to them, and either made a generous use of the method of development as practised in the schools, or else had recourse to borrowing.

The former method is the simplest, and has produced an abundance of colourless and insipid narratives. Endowed with more or less imagination and fluency, innumerable hagiographers have resigned themselves to the necessity of supplementing the scarcity of documents by narratives founded on probability: *omnia quæ in re præsenti accidisse credibile est*, as Quintilian says (vi. 2). Take, for example, a martyrdom. The setting of the narrative is clearly outlined. First there must come a more or less detailed account of the persecution. The Christians are being hunted out everywhere; large numbers fall into the hands of the soldiers, and amongst them the hero of the tale; he is arrested and thrown into prison. Brought before the judge he confesses his faith and suffers horrible tortures. He dies and his tomb becomes the scene of innumerable miracles.[1]

Such, more or less, is the scheme on which every editor has to work. Each part is capable of develop-

1 The process of development "in accordance with probability" has not been abandoned by hagiographers even in our own day. A saint, St. Expeditus, whose name is inscribed on the Hieronymian martyrology for the 18th or 19th of April under the rubric *Melitinæ in Armenia,* has become in accordance with this method "the valiant leader of the Thundering Legion". See Dom Bérengier, *Saint Expédit martyr en Arménie et patron des causes urgentes* in *Missions catholiques,* vol. xxviii., 1896, pp. 128-31. See also *Analecta Bollandiana,* vol. xviii., p. 425; vol. xxv., pp. 90-98.

ment on lines clearly suggested by historians who have
related similar incidents, by other legends which serve
as models and even by the analysis of the situations,
while for the most part the amplifications are full of
those exaggerations which are the prerogative of orators
anxious to make the most of what they have to say.
Thus the picture of the persecution is always painted
as black as possible ; [1] the emperor or judge usually
figures as a monster in human shape, thirsting for blood,
having no other aim than the destruction of the new
faith throughout the world. Here, then, we have the
first of our stock subjects.[2]

Readers must not let themselves be deceived even
when they think they recognise the authentic phraseology of an edict. Nothing is more easy to imitate
than the forms of an edict, just as in our own day one
might reproduce the terms of an Act of Parliament or
of a ministerial decree, and all the more easily when the
document is intended for a public the reverse of exacting in matters of phraseology.[3]

The interrogatory of the martyr is another of the
favourite themes of the hagiographer, and he depends
more especially on this portion of his narrative to assist
him in attaining the normal length of the composition.
He might, one would fancy, at least use such dialogue to

[1] The oratorical description of the persecution by St. Basil in
the panegyric on St. Gordius may serve as a model, Garnier, vol. ii.,
pp. 143-44.

[2] On all that follows see *Les Passion des martyrs et les genres
littéraires*, p. 236-315. 3d ed.]

[3] Edicts are frequent in hagiographic romances, and scholars have
sometimes been to the trouble of investigating them. See, for example, the edict in the *Passio S. Procopii* to which Mr. Goodspeed
has devoted several pages in the *American Journal of Philology*, vol.
xxiii., 1902, p. 68 ff. See also *Analecta Bollandiana*, vol. xxii., p. 409.
Signor P. Franchi de' Cavalieri, *I martirii di S. Teodoto e di S.
Ariadne*, p. 105, quotes several other examples. It should be observed that the *Passio S. Ephysii* is copied from that of St. Procopius.

bring into bolder relief the generous sentiments or the noble qualities of the martyr, as was done by the writers of antiquity, who scattered conventional discourses through their historical works just as modern writers scatter portraits. But it is very rare that from among the questions and answers one can seize any personal and characteristic trait. We find only dissertations on the absurdity of paganism and the beauty of the Christian faith, speeches of an inconceivable improbability which would be more appropriate on the lips of a pulpit orator than on those of a prisoner before a court of justice in the course of a rapid criminal procedure. The triumphant eloquence of the martyr is usually set off against the ignorance and vulgarity of the judge, unless indeed the latter displays sufficient knowledge of the Scriptures and the Christian religion to provoke some learned reply from the accused.

In many instances the hagiographer has not even taken the trouble to compose the harangue which he puts in the mouth of his hero; he has found it more convenient to transcribe a chapter or extracts from some suitable treatise,[1] a proceeding thanks to which the apology of Aristides has been preserved to us in the history of SS. Barlaam and Joasaph. To any one who has studied the authentic Acts of the martyrs it

1 There is no general work in existence bearing on this subject. There are, however, two useful works of recent date: G. Mercati, *Note di letteratura biblica e cristiana antica* in *Studi e testi*, vol. v., Rome, 1901, pp. 218-26; Bidez, *Sur diverses citations et notamment sur trois passages de Malalas retrouvés dans un texte hagiographique* in the *Byzantinische Zeitschrift*, xi., 1902, pp. 388-94. J. Fuehrer in the *Mittheilungen des k. d. archæologischen Instituts,* Roem. Abth., vol. vii., 1892, p. 159, has noted some borrowings from Clement of Alexandria by the author of the Passion of St. Philip of Heraclea (*Bibl. hag. lat.*, n. 6834). [See also E. Klostermann and E. Seeberg, *Die Apologie der hl. Katharina,* Königsberg, 1926. Cf. *Analecta Bollandiana,* vol. xlv, p. 151. 3d ed.]

is superfluous to point out how falsely such rhetoric rings, and what a difference there is between the short and touching answers of the martyrs inspired by the wisdom of the Holy Ghost, and these studied declamations which at their best recall some school display.

After the interrogatory the torture of the martyr is the subject that lends itself best to amplification. The simplicity of the final act of the tragedy in authentic chronicles, as, for example, in the martyrdom of St. Cyprian, would scarcely please our pious rhetoricians, who can conceive of no other way of establishing the heroism of the martyr than by making him undergo lengthy and refined torments. They multiply his sufferings without having to trouble themselves as to the limits of human endurance, for Divine Providence is made to intervene to prevent the saint from succumbing beneath the agony inflicted, and to allow the hagiographer to exhaust all the torments that his imagination or reminiscences from his studies may suggest.

Undoubtedly the masterpiece in this line of composition is the Passion of SS. Clement of Ancyra and Agathangelus. The scene of their torments is moved successively from a nameless town in Galicia to Rome, hence to Nicomedia, to Ancyra, to Amisos, to Tarsus, and finally back again to Ancyra. This perambulating martyrdom, diversified by the most extraordinary miracles, is prolonged for no less than twenty-eight years, during which time the following tortures are inflicted both on Clement and on his companion Agathangelus by persecutors who include in their number the Emperors Diocletian and Maximianus, and the Prefects Domitianus, Agrippinus, Curicius, Domitius, Sacerdon, Maximus, Aphrodisius, Lucius and Alexander.

To start with, Clement is hung up, his flesh torn with iron hooks, his mouth and cheeks bruised with stones ; he is bound to the wheel, beaten with sticks and horribly mutilated with knives ; his face is stabbed with stilettos, his jaws are broken and his teeth drawn while his feet are crushed in iron fetters.   Then the two martyrs together are whipped with ox thongs and suspended from a beam ; their bodies are scorched with flaring torches and they are flung to the wild beasts.   Red-hot needles are run into their fingers under their nails and they are burned in quicklime and left there two whole days, after which strips of skin are torn from them and they are once more beaten with rods.   They are stretched on iron bedsteads brought to a state of white heat, then thrown into a burning furnace ; this last torment lasts a day and a night.   After that they are again beaten with iron hooks, and a kind of harrow covered with iron points is set up and the martyrs are flung against it.   For his part Agathangelus undergoes in addition the torture of having molten lead poured upon his head ; he is dragged through the town with a mill-stone round his neck and stoned.   Clement alone has his ears pierced with red-hot needles, he is burnt with torches and he receives more blows from a stick on his mouth and head.   At last after having endured fifty strokes of the rod on several days in succession he has his head cut off at the same time as Agathangelus.[1]

It is very rare that hagiographers carry their naïveté, or perhaps we should rather say their audacity, to so high a pitch, and the accounts of the sufferings of the martyrs do not usually reach this degree of improbability.   Nevertheless, taken separately, the various

1 *Acta SS.*, Jan., vol. ii., pp. 459-60.

chapters in the Passion of St. Clement of Ancyra represent accurately enough the style of composition indulged in, and it is only when they are at the end of their own resources that the writers allow their heroes to die. After undergoing such amazing torments St. Clement simply has his head cut off, and this is such an ordinary conclusion to the most marvellous and terrible tortures, that some learned writers have seriously asked themselves how it happens that the axe and the sword have proved efficacious instruments of martyrdom when so many other methods have been of no avail. " It has been suggested that the sword being the outward sign of power in society, it is the will of God that it should not be frustrated by His providence which desires the maintenance of public order as the guarantee of a hundred other interests. But might we not also say that this happened as a Divine reprobation of the barbarous inventions to which tyrants had recourse because their hatred was not satisfied by the simple death of the Christians?"[1] While bearing in mind the relative mildness of the Roman code one cannot deny the cruelty of certain persecutors. But has the writer quoted above stated the problem fairly, and ought the question not rather to be addressed to the hagiographers, compelled in spite of everything to put a term to their rigmaroles and kill off their heroes? The natural conclusion of the drama was after all the classical punishment, death by the sword.

The composition of the life of a saint who is not a martyr is regulated by similar laws in all cases in which the author adopts the method of amplification. The narrative is necessarily less dramatic and less interesting, but it more easily admits of developments. Where

[1] Cahier, *Caractéristiques des Saints,* vol. i., p. 307.

a complete biography of a saint is desired the life divides itself into three parts. Before his birth: his nationality, his parents, his future greatness miraculously prophesied; his life: childhood, youth, the most important events in his career, his virtues, his miracles; lastly his cultus and miracles after death. In innumerable lives of saints at least one of the points in the above programme is supplied by commonplaces, and sometimes the whole biography is a mere string of them. The profession or quality of the saint is also subjected to analysis. A bishop has not the same duties as a monk, neither does an abbot practise the same virtues as a nun. Hence a diversity of episodes. In the life of a holy bishop, for instance, it is essential that he should only accept consecration under protest; for if he does not resist, it is obvious that he thinks himself worthy of the episcopal throne, and if his own opinion of himself is so indulgent, can he rightly be held up as a model of humility? If the subject of the biography is a holy monk, then clearly he must be exemplary in all the duties appertaining to his calling, and without risk of blundering one may describe his fasts and vigils and his assiduity at prayer and spiritual reading. And as it is mainly through miracles that God is pleased to make manifest the merits of His servants, one may take it for granted that the saint, whatever his condition, was in the habit of healing the blind, causing the paralytic to walk, driving out evil spirits and the like.

The methods we have just described, simple and natural as they appear, have not been wholly restricted to hagiographers anxious to fill in the gaps left by tradition. We have seen how the popular voice gladly attributes to its favourite hero the glories and virtues

of others, while many a noble deed and striking incident
has become the common property of very diverse individuals. The pious writers of the Middle Ages have
often, in their need, imitated the importations so common in legends, and have unscrupulously allowed themselves, in the interest of their saint, to pilfer narratives
that have no sort of connection with him. I am not
referring to those frequent cases in which a similarity
of names is responsible for introducing wholly extraneous matter into a biography, as, for example, when we
find in the legend of St. Fronto of Perigueux an episode
of markedly exotic hue taken from an Egyptian legend
concerning a namesake.[1] I am speaking here of importations to be accounted for neither by misconceptions
nor yet by carelessness. Sometimes it is merely a case
of commonplaces on the Christian virtues which have
been copied out word for word ; sometimes we have
incidents which at a stretch might have occurred and
have been related in identical terms, but sometimes also
we meet with examples of wholly characteristic episodes
which without any sort of apology have been imported
in their entirety from another biography.

I fully admit that one must beware of raising a cry
of plagiarism on the strength of a mere resemblance.
The most disconcerting coincidences do occasionally
occur, and I am willing to quote a noteworthy example.
If one were to read that on the same day the Church
celebrates two saints, who both died in Italy, whose
conversion in both cases was effected through the
reading of the " Lives of the Saints " ; that each founded
a religious order under one and the same title, and
that both these orders were suppressed by two popes

[1] See Duchesne, *Fastes épiscopaux de l'ancienne Gaule*, vol. ii.,
pp. 132-33.

bearing the same name, one might well feel justified in declaring on the strength of these characteristic features that a single individual had been multiplied into two, and that he must have been inscribed twice over in the martyrology under different names.   And yet there exist two saints, strictly historical and even comparatively modern, of whom all these particulars are true. St. John Colombini, who died at Siena, 31st July, 1367, was brought back to the practice of the Christian virtues by reading the " Lives of the Saints," and founded the order of the Jesuati which was suppressed by Clement IX.   St. Ignatius of Loyola who died in Rome, 31st July, 1556, was touched by grace while reading the " Lives of the Saints," which had been supplied to him in order to enliven the tedium of convalescence; he founded the order of the Jesuits, suppressed, as every one knows, by a later Clement.   If I recall the fact it is not because such coincidences can be frequent, far from it, for it would be difficult to find an analogous example to the above, which has been quoted here merely as a curiosity.[1]

The naïve hagiographers of the Middle Ages, compelled to supplement the paucity of primitive sources by more or less legitimate means, do not introduce us to any very embarrassing dilemmas.   As a rule their methods are simple, and their secrets are easily surprised.

The following, for example, shows the process by which the biographer of St. Vincent Madelgarus honoured his patron with a literary composition of adequate dimensions.[2]

In the preface he begins by transcribing the pro-

1 *Acta SS.*, July, vol. vii., pp. 333-54.
2 This life has been the object of a detailed study by Père A. Poncelet in the *Analecta Bollandiana*, vol. xii., pp. 422-40.

logue from the life of St. Erminus, to which he adds
a phrase from Sulpicius Severus; there follows a second
introduction which reproduces, word for word, St.
Gregory of Tours' preface to the life of St. Patroclus.
In order to describe the birth and early years of the
saint, he accumulates reminiscences from the life of St.
Erminus, without speaking of others from members of
St. Vincent's own family, St. Waldetrudis and St. Alde-
gond, while the history of his marriage is extracted
literally from the *Vita Leobardi* by Gregory of Tours.
Vincent's son Landric embraces the ecclesiastical state:
this is taken from the life of St. Gallus by Gregory of
Tours. The same author furnishes him with the
greater part of a vision, which fills one of the chapters
in the life of St. Leobardus. St. Vincent enters on the
religious life and trains his followers: taken from the
lives of SS. Martius and Quintianus by Gregory of
Tours. He gives himself up to prayer and penance
and practises all the religious virtues: taken from the
life of St. Bavon. Knowing himself to be on the point
of death he confides his spiritual children to his son
Landric: taken from the life of St. Ursmar. He is
buried within his monastery where he exercises his
power on behalf of the faithful who invoke him: taken
from the life of St. Bavon. A blind cleric recovers
his sight on his tomb: this miracle is appropriated in
its entirety from Gregory of Tours, who relates it of
St. Martin. We must add, moreover, to our plagiarist's
account six chapters from the life of St. Waldetrudis,
which, it is true, served him as a historic source, but
which he transcribes word for word, besides numerous
other reminiscences which it would take too long to
enumerate.

The lives of saints filled with extracts from other

lives of saints are exceedingly numerous, and some are
nothing more than a mere hagiographic anthology.   One
can imagine the perplexity of the critic on finding the
same facts related in the same words of two different
saints.   He may well ask himself what faith can be
placed in the lives of St. Hubert, St. Arnold of Metz
and St. Lambert of which several portions are shared
in common.[1]   One can guess what degree of importance he will attach to a biography such as that of St.
Remaclus, which is servilely imitated from the life of
St. Lambert.[2]

Indeed, such has been the destitution of some editors
that, not satisfied with appropriating wholesale certain
phrases of general application, or even interesting
episodes which seemed likely to prove effective in their
pages, they have been reduced to seizing whole compositions, and adapting them as best they could to their
saint, often by merely exchanging one name for another.
Thus, for example, the passion of St. Martina is literally
identical with that of St. Tatiana ; St. Castissima owns
the same acts as St. Euphrosyne, while those of St.
Caprasius are the same as those of St. Symphorian ;
the group of Florentius and Julianus possesses an identical history to that of Secundianus, Marcellianus and
Veranus, and so on, for the list of these strange dupli-
cations is far longer than one would be tempted to
suppose.   We hope some day to draw up a complete
catalogue of them.[3]

1 *Acta SS.*, Nov., vol. i., pp. 760-63.
2 G. Kurth, *Notice sur la plus ancienne biographie de saint
Remacle* in *Bulletins de la Commission royale d'histoire,* 4th series,
vol. iii., Brussels, 1876, pp. 355-68.
3 It must suffice for the moment to refer the reader to some provisional lists: *Histoire littéraire de la France,* vol. vii., p. 193;
Analecta Bollandiana, vol. xvi., p. 496.

Another variety of the species of composition we have been characterising is that of the narratives in which the author has contented himself with introducing a new personage while still retaining the original hero and all the story belonging to him. I might recall the example of St. Florian, honoured at Bologna, who, in order that he might be provided with a history, has been introduced into the Passion of the sixty martyrs of Eleutheropolis,[1] and also that of St. Florentius of Mont Glonne, whom one is surprised to meet in the company of St. Florian of Lorsch.[2]

If Latin hagiographers have had frequent recourse to the convenient process of adaptation, the Greeks have not deprived themselves of the same resource, as may be proved by comparing the history of St. Barbara with that of Irene and Cyriæna,[3] and the life of St. Onesimus with that of St. Alexis.[4] Not long ago further parallel cases were unearthed in Syrian hagiography: the life of Mar Mikha scarcely differs from that of Mar Benjamin,[5] while the history of St. Azazaïl is a mere adaptation of that of St. Pancratius of Rome.[6]

[1] *Analecta Bollandiana*, vol. xxiii., pp. 292-95.

[2] *Acta SS.*, Sept., vol. vi., pp. 428-30. See also Krusch, in *M. G.*, *Script. rer. merov.*, vol. iii., p. 67.

[3] *Acta SS.*, Nov., vol. i., p. 210.

[4] *Synaxarium ecclesiæ Constantinopolitanæ*, p. 820.

[5] The life of Mar Mikha was published by Bedjan, *Acta martyrum et sanctorum*, vol. iii., pp. 513-32; that of Mar Benjamin by V. Scheil, *La vie de Mar Benjamin* in the *Zeitschrift für Assyriologie*, vol. xii., 1897, pp. 62-96. It was M. C. Brockelmann, *Zum Leben des Mar Benjamin, ibid.*, pp. 270-71, who pointed out this interesting example of a monk who appropriates the legend of a neighbouring monastery and does not hesitate to dedicate his plagiarism to the Patriarch Symeon.

[6] F. Macler, *Histoire de Saint Azazaïl* in the *Bibliothèque de l'Ecole des Hautes Études*, fasc. 141. See also *Analecta Bollandiana*, vol. xxiii., pp. 93-95.

The process appears so puerile and summary that one is tempted to assume that it can only have been carried out in the darkest epochs of the Middle Ages, and one can scarcely resist the temptation to locate this wretched plagiarism among barbarous surroundings in which literary culture was practically unknown. Unhappily we must remember that as early as the fourth century in Italy, and indeed in Rome, we come across deliberate adaptations of foreign legends to fit national saints. The passion of St. Lawrence, even in its minor details, is borrowed from that of the martyrs of Phrygia as related by Socrates and Sozomen, while the martyrdom of St. Cassian scarcely differs from that of St. Mark of Arethusa.[1] The martyrdom of St. Eutychius as related by Pope Damasus[2] is simply a reproduction of that of St. Lucian,[3] and the Damasian version of the death of St. Agnes possesses undeniable resemblances to that of St. Eulalia.[4] It is not as yet plagiarism in its crudest form, not the almost word for word transcription of the original. But already legend has come to be regarded as no-man's land. It belongs, in a quite unexpected sense, to the " common of saints," and transfers are effected on a somewhat liberal scale.

It is not solely in hagiographic literature that editors of saints' lives have sought the material for their compilations. Thus the legend of St. Vidian, a local martyr

1 See *Analecta Bollandiana*, vol. xix., pp. 452-53. The torture of St. Mark of Arethusa is testified to by St. Gregory Nazianzen, *In Julian*, i., as M. Pio Franchi has pointed out, *Nuove Note agiografiche* in *Studi e Testi*, vol. ix., p. 68. We may observe by the way that after St. Cassian, St. Artemas of Pozzuoli inherited the Passion of St. Mark of Arethusa, *Acta SS.*, Jan., vol. ii., p. 617. [This sentence is modified in the 3d ed., and that revision is included as a special note at the end of this chapter, on. p. 106.]

2 Ihm, *Damasi epigrammata*, n. 27.

3 P. Franchi, as above, p. 58, n. 2.

4 *Id.*, *Santa Agnese nella tradizione e nella leggenda*, Rome, 1899, p. 20.

honoured at Martres-Tolosanes might easily be con-
founded with the epic legend of Vivian, nephew to
William of Orange, which is related in two metrical
romances, the *Enfances Vivien* and *Aliscans*;[1] the
legend of St. Dymphna is an adaptation of a popular
tale,[2] as is that of St. Olive which has been popularised
in Italy, not by the Church, but by the stage.[3]

The writings we have been describing undoubtedly
constitute literary frauds which one feels inclined to condemn with great severity. I should not, however, venture, at least as a general rule, to class them as forgeries,
or to regard the authors of these substitutions as more
guilty than those who naïvely believed themselves entitled to supplement the silence of tradition by narratives mainly supplied by their own imaginations. They
were reduced to the extremity of imitating the sculptors
who changed the statue of a consul into that of a saint
by supplying a new head, or by placing in his hand a
cross, a key, a lily or some other symbolical object.

We must freely confess, however, that hagiographic
literature has been disgraced by a certain number of
forgers whose naïveté can scarce avail as their excuse.
There have been audacious fabrications, the product of
falsehood and ambition which for long misled credul-
ous minds and unsuspecting critics; among these we

---

[1] A. Thomas, *Viviens d'Aliscans et la légende de saint Vidian* in
the *Études romanes dédiées a Gaston Paris,* Paris, 1891, pp. 121-35;
L. Saltet, *Saint Vidian de Martres-Tolosanes et la légende de Vivien
des chansons de geste* in the *Bulletin de littérature ecclésiastique,*
Feb. 1902, pp. 44-56. Dom Lobineau, *Les vies des saints de Bretagne,*
Rennes, 1725, p. 25, is of opinion that the author of the life of St.
Colledoc had no "other materials to work with than the romance
of Lancelot du Lac and a bold and fertile imagination".

[2] See above, p. 9.

[3] Al. d'Ancona, *Origini del teatro italiano,* 2nd edition, Turin,
1891, vol. i., pp. 436-37.

CHAPTER IV.

THE CLASSIFICATION OF HAGIOGRAPHIC TEXTS.

Defective System—Classification according to Subjects—According to Categories of Saints—System Adopted. Historical Point of View—Division into six classes—Application of System to Ruinart's *Acta sincera*—The "Supplements" of Le Blant.

It may be useful at this stage to summarise the preceding pages while attempting to draw up a system of classification by means of which it will be possible to arrange in groups the majority of what may be called hagiographic documents.

We may leave out of account purely external divisions founded on the subject of the narrative such as Passions, Biographies, Translations, Miracles, or even on the literary form, as Metrical, or Rhymed Lives and so on. This mechanical kind of classification scarcely affords any indication of the historical value of the documents. Thus it would be a mistake to conclude from the circumstance of a hagiographer writing in verse, that he has necessarily profited by the licence that we are agreed in according to poets. Mediæval poets are often as ingenious in turning their original text into hexameters as they are lacking in inspiration and poetic invention.[1]

---

[1] A curious example of this may be seen in the *Versus domni Bertharii abbatis de miraculis almi Patris Benedicti* (M.G., *Poet. Lat. aevi carol.*, vol. iii., pp. 394-98), in which book ii. of the Dialogues of St. Gregory is turned into verse, chapter by chapter.

Another system of classification, and at first sight more logical, would consist in grouping the documents under the various categories of saints.   In point of fact, hagiographic literature treats of a large and varied assortment of personages who do not all possess equally valid claims on public veneration.   There are, in the first place, those whose cultus has been canonically established by the Church and has received the sanction of centuries.   St. Lawrence in the Church of Rome, St. Cyprian in that of Africa, and St. Martin in that of Gaul, belong incontestably to this class, and we possess the Acts of each one of them.

Next to them come those real personages devotion to whom was in the first instance irregularly established, whatever consecration it may have acquired through length of usage.   We have already pointed out that the word "sanctus" did not always possess the very precise significance that it bears to-day, and that it has been the means of conferring the honours of a tardy canonisation on more than one bishop, known only for his orthodoxy.[1]   It may be remembered that all the pious personages of whom St. Gregory the Great recalled the virtues in his Dialogues ultimately took their places among the saints of the Latin Church,[2] just as the hermits of whom Theodoret wrote the biography suddenly found themselves during their very life-time incorporated in the annals of the Greek Church through some caprice of the hagiographers.[3]   It has even happened that worthy individuals on whom their contemporaries had never conferred the aureole of sanctity, have been raised to the ranks of the martyrs or the

---

[1] *Analecta Bollandiana,* vol. xviii., pp. 406-11. [The subject has been taken up with great development in our work *Sanctus,* Brussels, 1927.]

[2] *Civiltà Cattolica,* series xv., vol. vi., 1894, pp. 292-305, 653-69.

[3] *Analecta Bollandiana,* vol. xiv., pp. 420-21.

Blessed as the result of some special circumstances. Such a one is Cassiodorus, who became, no one quite knows how, a martyr of the early centuries.[1] And how frequently has not the discovery of a tomb or of a group of bodies whose identity could not be definitely established given rise to some local devotion which has often enjoyed a lengthy popularity? The greater number of these saints, unauthentic in varying degrees, have none the less found hagiographers ready to do honour to them.

The long lists of the saints furnish us with yet a third category, relatively few in number, but not on that account to be neglected : the imaginary personages to whom a real existence has ultimately been attributed. Some of them have a purely literary origin. We have already referred to various heroes of romance and of hagiographic tales transformed into historical personages and gradually becoming a nucleus of devotion. The reader will remember the *chanson de geste* of Amis and Amile who were killed by Ogier the Dane near Mortara in the Montferrat district. Their history was transformed into a saint's life and they were honoured with a chapel at Novara, Milan, and possibly other places.[2] The poem of Flores and Blanchefleur would have given birth to a St. Rosana—whose life was even printed—had not the Roman authorities intervened.[3] Other fictitious saints owed their origin to some iconographic accident, as, for example, the celebrated St. Liberata or Wilgefortis (called in English St. Uncumber) who was represented as a bearded

---

1 See above, pp. 21 and 71.
2 *Acta SS.*, Oct., vol. vi., pp. 124-26.
3 Al. d'Ancona, *Origini del teatro italiano*, 2nd edition, vol. i., p. 437; vol. ii., p. 60. See also H. Reusch, *Der Index der verbotenen Bücher*, vol. ii., 1, 1885, p. 227.

woman nailed to a cross, and whose legend was inspired by one of those draped crucifixes of which
the *Volto Santo* of Lucca offers the best-known example.[1]

We need not insist very strongly on the inconveni-
ences of a classification of hagiographic documents in
strict accordance with these various categories of saints.
It is obvious that there need be no intimate relation between the subject of a narrative and its historical value.
Thus it happens that saints as celebrated and as well-
authenticated as St. Lawrence and St. Agnes are chiefly
known to us by legendary Acts, while, on the other hand,
various saints of the second category are provided with
quite fairly authenic title-deeds.   This common and most
regrettable anomaly suggests a number of embarrassing
problems that cannot always be solved.   When historical records are lacking it is often possible to supplement
their silence by the help of other documents, and to
establish the fact of a traditional veneration by martyrologies, itineraries, monuments, etc.[2]   When this
means of identification fails it becomes impossible to
decide in which of the three categories we should place
a saint whose name legend has handed down to us.
Thus if, in the case of St. Sebastian, we had nothing
but his Acts on which to base our judgment, we might
feel concerning him the same hesitation as about St.
Martina, who appears to have been unknown to anti-

---

1 *Acta SS.*, July, vol. v., pp. 50-70; A. Lutolf, *Sanct Kümmerniss
und die Kümmernisse der Schweizer* in *Geschichtsfreund*, vol. xix.,
1863, pp. 183-205; G. Schnürer, *Die Kümmernisbilder als Kopien
des Volto Santo von Lucca* in the *Jahresbericht der Görres-Gesell-
schaft*, 1901, pp. 43-50; *Id.*, *Der Kultus des Volto Santo und der
hl. Wilgefortis in Freiburg* in the *Freiburger Geschichtsblaetter*,
vol. ix, 1902, pp. 74-105; *Id.*, *Ueber Alter und Herkunft des Volto
Santo von Lucca*, in *Römische Quartalschrift*, vol. xxxiv, 1926, p.
271-306. Cf. *Analecta Bollandiana*, vol. xxii, p. 482; vol. xxiii, p. 128.

[2 Midway on this page, Delehaye "opened up" this paragraph to
discuss the documentation of the lives of St. George and St.
Theodore; much of this material is drawn from his own work, *Les
légendes grecques des saints militaires. Ed.*]

quity.[1] Nor is it likely that we shall ever obtain decisive evidence for placing St. Catherine or St. Barbara in either the first or the second category of the saints.

Under these circumstances we must have recourse to the one and only principle which allows of a strict classification of the Acts of the martyrs and of hagiographic documents in general; they must be classed by the degree of truth and historic value they possess. The following results have been arrived at by the application of this principle as far as the main divisions are concerned.

1. The *official reports* of the interrogatories of martyrs are entitled in theory to the first place in importance. The existence of records of this nature deposited in the archives of the proconsul has been attested by more than one witness. The question is whether any of these *procès-verbaux* have been preserved.

It might be objected that such official records do not come within the scope of any category of hagiographic documents, and that, strictly speaking, we ought not to take them into consideration. Such a protest would, however, be quite superfluous, for it does not require prolonged investigation to ascertain that no *procès-verbal* of the times of persecution has come down to us in a separate and unadulterated form; the documents which are honoured with the title of Proconsular Acts are, at best, compositions intended for the edification of the faithful, in which the official text of the interrogatory, scrupulously respected, forms the main portion of the narrative. Thus it happens that the most celebrated of all these documents, which has

1 Pio Franchi de' Cavalieri, *S. Martina* in the *Römische Quartal-schrift*, vol. xvii., 1903, pp. 222-36.

been held up to us as the most perfect model of Proconsular Acts, the *Passio Cypriani*, is, in reality, a
composite record in which one must distinguish three
separate documents strung together by a few phrases
of their latest editor : first, the official text of an early
interrogatory in 257, as the result of which Cyprian
was sent into exile ; then the official report of the
arrest and the second interrogatory in 258 ; finally the
account of the martyrdom. In the Passion of the
Scillitan martyrs the hand of the hagiographer is less
visible. One hears only the words of the martyrs and
their persecutor, and one is present at the carrying out
of the sentence. Was the interrogatory copied in the
proconsular office, or did some Christian in the audience
take it down in shorthand? It would be difficult to
decide this point, but it is safe to affirm that the editor
has introduced nothing of his own into the phrases he
places on the lips of the martyrs.

These authentic interrogatories are always quite admirable, and even after so many centuries the emotions
they excite have lost nothing of their intensity. If
anything could spoil the impression they produce it
would be the clumsy imitations which are to be found
far too frequently in the passionaries. In the dramatic
scenes devised by hagiographers to emphasise the
heroism of his sacrifice, the martyr poses as though he
were on the stage, and gives utterance to academic
orations. In point of fact nothing is easier than to
recognise authentic " consular acts ". But we have
reluctantly to admit that very few are in existence.

2. A second category of authentic Acts comprises
the *accounts of eye-witnesses*, and others worthy of
confidence, or of well-informed contemporaries record-
ing the testimonies of other eye-witnesses. In these

narratives, which are of a literary character, considerable space is accorded to the subjective element, an element which is entirely absent from the purely official Acts. It follows that we may carry the analysis farther and subdivide this category under three headings :—

(*a*) Documents in which the witness alone speaks in his own name.

(*b*) Those in which a contemporary author restricts himself to chronicling the testimony of others.

(*c*) Those in which personal observation is added to the testimony, as in several chapters of Eusebius's *Martyrs of Palestine*, and in the life of Cyprian by the Deacon Pontius. But all these varieties have this in common, that they express directly, without the intervention of any written source, an oral and contemporary testimony.

3. The third category is composed of Acts *of which the principal source is a written document* belonging to one or other of the preceding categories. It includes every degree of remodelling from simple editorial corrections as regards the arrangement of the composition and details of development, up to the free recasting of the original which a fresh editor quarries from, amplifies, turns inside out, or even on occasion interpolates. In this way we possess seven different versions of the Passion of the Scillitan martyrs, and the historical records that have come down to us only in an amended form are extremely numerous. A certain number of the lives which compose the menology of Metaphrastes belong to the category of adaptations which have for their sole source an historic document that the editor has abridged or paraphrased, according to his own sweet will. We may naturally include in this class redactions at second or third hand, in other words,

those produced by authors at work not on an original document but on a composition which has already been recast.

4. The fourth category consists of Acts of which the source is not a written document, but the fantastic combination of a few real events in a framework of pure imagination, in other words, *historical romances*. This class is very numerous, and in particular we must include in it the whole series of cycles of the Roman *Legendarium*. In these compositions which consist frequently of a tissue of literary reminiscences, popular traditions and fictitious situations, the historic element is almost always reduced to an infinitesimal quantity. The name of the saint, the existence of his shrine, and the date of his feast are in many cases all that can be safely inferred from a species of composition in which fantasy has a free field.

Although their authors do not as a rule sin from excess of imagination, I would add to the above class those Acts which are simple adaptations. As a general rule the historic residue in these plagiarised compositions is of about the same value as that of the laboriously compiled romances of which mention has just been made; for the minimum of adaptation demanded to transform the history of one saint into that of another is necessarily concerned with his name, his feast and his shrine.

5. After the historical romances dealing with real personages, come the *imaginative romances*, in which the hero himself is the creation of the poet. The Passion of St. Nicephorus and the history of Barlaam and Joasaph are types of this class.

6. It is only proper to place in a separate category all *forgeries* properly so called, that is to say, all hagio-

graphic legends composed with the object of deceiving the reader. It is not always easy to ascertain the real author of the fraud, and it must frequently happen that the editor has merely registered a version which circulated before his day; in that case the work must be classified under one of the previous headings.[1]

We might refrain here from entering into fuller explanations, and might leave to the reader the task of applying the principles enunciated to the numerous examples before him. It would indeed require endless investigations, and the combined efforts of many workers to arrive at a strict classification, under the various headings enumerated, of all the hagiographic legends that have come down to us. We can, however, scarcely dispense ourselves from passing in rapid review, a justly celebrated collection which for a long period, in the eyes of most scholars, expressed the latest word in hagiographic criticism, and thanks to which the line of demarcation between fable and history had been drawn once and for all : we refer to Dom Ruinart's *Acta sincera.*

This fine work well-conceived, if somewhat summarily carried out, has rendered the greatest service, and it would be a grave injustice on our part to attempt to depreciate it. It is, however, only right to say that it fails to come up to modern requirements. Every one is to-day agreed in demanding better authenticated texts according to strict philological methods. The necessity for a process of weeding out, or to speak

---

1 M. A. Harnack, *Die Chronologie der altchristlichen Litteratur bis Eusebius,* vol. ii., Leipzig, 1904, pp. 464-65, quotes our classification with approval. He proposes to add a seventh category, that of a class of dummy Acts drawn up solely upon the model of celebrated Passions. From the historic standpoint which we have adopted this group would be included in our fourth category.

more precisely, for a re-classification of the documents selected by Ruinart seems not to be so keenly felt.

Let us admit also that, from our modern standpoint, the title of *Acta sincera* lends itself easily to misconceptions. I feel no difficulty in allowing that all the Acts collected by the learned Benedictine are "sincere" in the sense that he set himself to exclude from his collection all the fabrications of forgers. But his selections are not all sincere in the sense that we can accept them as pure historic sources without any alloy of fiction or fantasy. Prudentius, like many other poets, is sincere, but who would ever dream of accepting his poems as though they were an historic text? The candid and loyal soul of St. John Chrysostom is reflected in his panegyrics no less than in his homilies, but ought we therefore to neglect to take into account the oratorical temperament and must we give to his sermons the same value as to a legal report? Clearly not. But what every one would freely admit in regard to a poem or an oratorical passage is too often forgotten when we are dealing with narratives by unknown authors, of which the historic value can only be determined by internal criteria.

It has been customary to place all Ruinart's texts on the same level, and, taking them in the mass, to attribute to them an absolute authority. It would be easy to quote a whole series of writings on the history of the primitive Church, or on various points of discipline in which the *Acta sincera* are cited promiscuously without any one having realised the necessity of some sifting process with a view to the special use that was to be made of them. Save for the recent revision by Harnack,[1] it may be said that the lists of authentic records

---

1 *Die Chronologie*, vol. ii., pp. 463-82. See also *Analecta Bollandiana*, vol. xxiii., pp. 476-80. [We may also refer to the chapter 'Les Passion historiques,' in *Les Passion des martyrs et les genres littéraires*, p. 11-182.]

drawn up of late years give evidence of very little serious labour. Except for a few insignificant corrections they are simply the reproduction of Ruinart's tables.[1] It has not been sufficiently noted that the learned Benedictine had somewhat vague ideas concerning the classification of hagiographic texts. Nowhere does he lay down any criteria for distinguishing between them, and his solitary rule appears to have been to give concerning every martyr the most ancient and most respectable record he could find.

The *Acta sincera* are composed of one hundred and seventeen documents [2] of a very unequal value which it is manifestly impossible to subject to a uniform critical examination, and which, therefore, must be considered in groups.

Concerning a small number of saints (Irenæus, Alexander Bishop of Jerusalem, Priscus, Malchus and Alexander, Mamas, Soteris) Ruinart has been compelled to restrict himself to putting together a few scattered fragments with which to make compilations of the kind entitled by the Bollandists *Sylloge.*

In the case of others he has availed himself of authors, whether historians, orators or poets, whose writings are sufficiently well known and whose credibility is recognised. Thus he quotes Eusebius for Jacob, Bishop of Jerusalem, Simeon, Bishop of Jerusalem, Ptolemæus and Lucius, Apollonius, Leonides and companions, Dionysius, Alexandrinus, Maximus, the martyrs under Diocletian, the Palestinian martyrs and Romanus. He

---

1 Preuschen in Harnack, *Geschichte der altchristlichen Litteratur bis Eusebius,* vol. i., pp. 807-34; G. Krüger, *Geschichte der altchristlichen Litteratur in den ersten drei Jahrhunderten,* pp. 237-45; *Dictionnaire de théologie Catholique,* vol. i., pp. 320-34; *Dictionnaire d'archéologie chrétienne et de liturgie,* vol. i., pp. 409-10.

2 The *Acta Firmi et Rustici* were added by the Verona editor.

quotes Prudentius for Hippolytus, Laurentius, Romanus, Vincentius, Eulalia, Agnes, the martyrs of Saragossa, Quirinus and Cassianus; St. John Chrysostom for Domnina and companions, Lucianus, Pelagia, Drosis and Julianus; St. Gregory of Nyssa for Theodorus, martyr; St. Basil for Barlaam,[1] Gordius, Julitta and the Forty Martyrs; St. Asterius of Amasea for Euphemia and Phocas; St. Ambrose for Laurentius, Vitalis and Agricola, Agnes, Theodora and Didymus; Rufinus for Apollonius and Theodorus, confessor; Paulinus of Nola for Felix; Socrates for Macedonius and companions; Sozomen for Eusebius and companions and Basil of Ancyra; Theodoret for Cyrillus and companions, Juventinus and Maximinus; Palladius for Potamiæna; St. Augustine for the twenty African martyrs; and finally St. Vigilius for Sisinnius and companions.

There remain the separate Passions to the number of seventy-four, upon which the future efforts of criticism will have to be directed. Already a certain number of these have been definitely classed. Others have received provisional recognition, while it is to be feared that not a few will have to remain in the limbo to which critics have been forced to relegate them from lack of information by which to judge of their merits or demerits.

Scholars are generally agreed in giving the place of honour—corresponding to the two first categories in our classification—to certain celebrated documents of which unhappily the list is far from long: Polycarp, Justinus, the Martyrs of Lyons, the Scillitan Martyrs,[2] Perpetua[3]

---

[1] The attribution to St. Basil is erroneous. See *Analecta Bollandiana,* vol. xxii., p. 132.

[2] The recension given by Ruinart, *Bibl. hag. lat.,* n. 7531, ought to be replaced by *Bibl. hag. lat.,* n. 7527.

[3 See p. 24 above.]

Cyprianus, Fructuosus, Jacob and Marianus, Maxi-milianus, Marcellus and Cassianus Tingitanus.* If one puts the setting out of the question, and simply retains the Epistle of Ignatius to the Romans which belongs to them it is evident that the Acts of St. Ignatius of Antioch should be classed among the pearls of the collection.[1] Nor must we forget the Passion of St. Procopius of which the great importance was not at first discerned, as it was not recognised as being a fragment of the book of the martyrs of Palestine,[2] an authentic work by Eusebius.

Let us pass at once to the other extreme. The *Passio Nicephori* and the *Passio Bonifatii* belong to the category of imaginative romance. We may add to them the Acts of Didymus and Theodora[3] of Genesius the Comedian, as well as the Acts of Theodotus of Ancyra of which the kernel is a tale related by Herodotus,[4] while the existence of the hero of the narrative is not vouched for by any historical document.[5]

The historical romance category, that is to say the fourth variety of hagiographic texts, is by no means slenderly represented in Ruinart. No one will resent our placing on the list Symphorosa, Felicitas and her seven sons, Afra, Cyricus and Julitta, Petrus Bal-

---

[* This last name is omitted in 3d ed. and the following reference added for Marcellus: *Analecta Bollandiana*, vol. xli, p. 257-87. Then the following sentence is inserted: It is necessary to add Felix, relieved of the serious interpolations which have made him suspect — *ibid.*, vol. xxxix, p. 241-76 — Pionius, Montanus and Lucius, Sabas Gothus — See our *Saints de Thrace et de Mésie*, p. 288-91 — Phileas and Philoromus — See our *Martyrs d'Egypte*, p. 161-68.]

1 Vain efforts have been made to rehabilitate the Ignatian Acts in their entirety. See *Analecta Bollandiana*, vol. xvii., p. 362; vol. xix., p. 38.

2 *Analecta Bollandiana*, vol. xvi., p. 115.

3 To be compared with the Acts of Alexander and Antonina, *Acta SS.*, May, vol. i., pp. 744-46.

4 Concerning this tale see A. Schiefner, *De quelques versions orientales du conte du trésor de Rhampsinite* in the *Bulletin de l'Académie de Saint-Pétersbourg*, vol. xiv., 1869, pp. 299-316.

5 *Analecta Bollandiana*, vol. xxii., pp. 320-28; vol. xxiii., p. 478.

samus, Vincentius, Firmus and Rusticus, Lucianus and Marianus. I can see no sufficient reason for according a higher place to the Martyrs of Agaunum, to Donatianus and Rogatianus, Victor, Tarachus and Probus, Ferreolus, Arcadius or to Leo and Paregorius.*

The remaining documents of the collection must remain for the time being in the third category, *i.e.*, among the Passions which have as their principal source an historic document of the first or the second rank. Is it necessary to add that this class subdivides itself into numerous varieties determined both by the quality of the primitive document and the capacity of the editor ? Nor must it be forgotten that in the case of the majority of these documents critics have not yet been able to arrive at a unanimous conclusion, owing to their not having been submitted to any searching study ; let us add that some of them, by reason of their mixed character, lend themselves with difficulty to a strict classification.

The most important of the contents of the third class are undoubtedly the Passions of Pionius, Montanus and Lucius, Maximus and Crispina.† Possibly it may be thought that they have not been placed in sufficiently good company. I do not think it would be justifiable to show them greater honour. It is scarcely possible to hesitate as to adding to them the following Passions: Achatius, Petrus, Andreas and his companions, Felix,[1] Saturninus, Dativus and his companions, Agape and Chionia,[2] Irenæus, Pollio, Euplus,

[* To this list the 3d ed. adds Trypho and Respicius. In the preceding sentence the name of *Afra* was deleted in the 3d ed.]

[† The first three names deleted in 3d ed.]

[1] The Acts of St. Felix no longer exist in their primitive form. The portion concerning the journey to Italy is an interpolation. See *Analecta Bollandiana*, vol. xvi., pp. 27-28; vol. xxii., p. 460.

[2] P. Franchi, *Nuove note agiografiche* in *Studi e Testi*, vol. ix., pp. 3-19. [The list is considerably changed in the 3d ed.]

Philippus,[1] Phileas and Philoromus,[2] Quirinus, Julius, Marcianus and Nicander [3] and Sabas Gothus.[4]

To these may be added the following Acts which have been much less studied : Epipodius and Alexander, Trypho and Respicius, Cyrillus, Claudius, Astorius and his companions, Serenus, Faustus and Januarius, Genesius Arelatensis, Patricius Bishop of Prusa, and the Egyptian martyrs. It is not impossible that a thorough study of their origin and composition might result in the deposition of some of them from the rank that has so far been assigned to them.[5]

The Acts concerning the Persian martyrs (Symeon, Pherbute, Sadoth and Bademus) constitute a separate group which might be included in the class under discussion.[6] Previous to the publication of their various recensions (so far unprinted) both in Armenian and Syriac it would be premature to pronounce on the original form and consequently also on the documentary value of these narratives.

One can scarcely discuss Dom Ruinart's collection without mentioning the enterprise of Le Blant, to whom

[1] J. Fuehrer in the *Mittheilungen des k. deutschen archæologischen Instituts,* Roman section, vol. vii., 1892, pp. 158-65; Harnack, *Die Chronologie,* p. 478.

[2] C. Schmidt in *Fragmente einer Schrift des Märtyrerbischofs Petrus von Alexandrien* in *Texte und Untersuchungen,* N.F., vol. v., p. 22, rejects these Acts. The judgment of Harnack in *Die Chronologie* is far more favourable.

[3] P. Franchi in *Nuovo bullettino di archeologia cristiana,* vol. x., 1904, pp. 22-26.

[4] *Analecta Bollandiana,* vol. xxiii., pp. 96-98. [This is one of the names not included in the 3d ed. list, which concludes with this statement: The *Acta disputationis* of Achatius remain an enigma — *Les Passions des martyrs,* p. 344-364.]

[5] P. Franchi in *Nuovo bullettino,* vol. x., p. 17. [From this list of names the 3d ed. deletes those of Trypho and Respicius.]

[6] J. Labourt, *Le Christianisme dans l'empire perse sous la dynastie sassanide,* 224-632, Paris, 1904, pp. 63-82; H. Delehaye, *Les versions grecques des actes des martyrs persans sous Sapor II.,* Paris, 1905, pp. 5-19.

we owe a "Supplement to the *Acta Sincera*".[1]   This
learned scholar did not propose in any sense to enlarge
Ruinart's volume by introducing into it historical texts
that the erudite Benedictine had overlooked, or that
had been brought to light by recent discoveries.   He
tried to show that various narratives not included in
the *Acta sincera* " have retained—although re-cast and
added to in varying degrees—certain genuine portions
derived from original documents".[2]   He calls these
"interpolated Acts," possessing a certain value as containing fragments of the truth,[3] and the following is the
method by which he proposes to identify them: " A
systematic collating of these pieces with the information
furnished by civil and criminal law, with the text of
the most authentic Acts and with the data solidly established by witnesses from the past, such is, in my
opinion, a clear means of establishing the degree of
credibility to which hagiographic narratives may be
entitled; such is the method I propose to follow in
seeking out those grains of truth scattered through
certain documents which, in accordance with the
opinion of Tillemont cannot be wholly rejected even
though they may offer some disquieting features".[4]

I admire as highly as any one the vast erudition of
Le Blant and the exemplary patience with which he
has pursued the vestiges of antiquity, often so hard to
recognise, through a mass of insipid literature.   Yet it
must needs be said that the very conception under-
lying his work has been a false one, and likely to mis-

---

1 *Les Actes des martyrs. Supplément aux Acta sincera de Dom
Ruinart.* Extrait des *Mémoires de l'Académie des Inscriptions et
Belles lettres,* vol. xxx., 2nd part, Paris, 1882.
2 *Les persécuteurs et les martyrs aux premiers siècles de notre
ère,* Paris, 1893, p. 1.
3 *Les Actes des martyrs,* p. 5.   4 *Ibid.,* p. 4.

lead investigators. For, in point of fact, in order that an interpolated or paraphrased narrative should possess any value it must be derived from some historical source the pedigree of which can be clearly ascertained. Purely literary accretions may go back very far without imparting the least credit to the stock on which they are grafted. In all ages centos from Virgil have been composed. Observe to what conclusions one might be drawn if one wished to make capital out of the antiquity of their various parts. From the correct legal phraseology to be met with in certain Passions we may sometimes, no doubt, conclude that the author lived at a time when the ancient formulæ had not yet fallen into disuse, but more often it would be truer to infer that he had studied a classical model which had supplied him with felicitious expressions and technical phrases. It would be entirely a mistake to deduce from this solitary fact that he had worked on a historic record, and that his narrative was derived from a contemporary chronicle of events.

In point of fact Le Blant has frequently succeeded in discovering in documents of a debased period or devoid of historic value details which reveal a condition of things going back to classical antiquity ; but he has been mistaken in concluding that " these writings have preserved, in more points than one, features of the lost originals ".[1] If we followed him on these lines, we ought to infer from certain superficial indications that the Acts of St. Agnes, St. Agatha, St. Urban, SS. Cosmas and Damian, St. Cecilia, etc., as we possess them to-day, are all versions of earlier Acts which have undergone, as he expresses it, "des retouches évidentes".[2]

[1] *Les Actes des martyrs,* p. 127.
[2] *Les persecuteurs et les martyrs,* p. 1.

I might quote more than one contemporary of our own, who in his novels has affected the knowledge of a specialist in certain technical details. Will posterity be forced to conclude that his stories possess a foundation of truth and that he has merely made a free use of original documents?

No doubt Le Blant has done good service by showing "that frequently the information furnished by secondary texts is in agreement with that supplied by classic documents,"[1] but he was mistaken in supposing that "if these latter had not come into our hands we should have obtained much useful information from the rest concerning the principal features in the history of the persecutions". On the contrary, it must be obvious to all that if we had not the check provided by the classic texts, we should have no means of discerning the really primitive elements in documents without intrinsic value, and that we should be building up the history of the persecutions upon a foundation of sand.

This, however, is no reason for giving up the idea of supplementing Ruinart, after having taken much away from him. But, as we have seen, the first thing to be done is to realise clearly the place to be given to every document in the hierarchy of hagiographic records. The new Ruinart which we should like to compile would only contain the historical records belonging to the first three categories set out at the beginning of this chapter.

[1] *Les Actes des martyrs.* p. 279.

CHAPTER V.

THE "DOSSIER" OF A SAINT.

Documents concerning St. Procopius of Cæsarea—Account given by
  Eusebius — Monuments testifying to the cultus — The three
  legends of St. Procopius—Analysis of the three legends—The
  Synaxaries—Latin Acts of St. Procopius—Adaptations to St.
  Ephysius and to St. John of Alexandria—Conclusions.

It is often an arduous task to establish the claims of a
saint of the first centuries to the honours of public worship. Where historical documents are not entirely
lacking they have sometimes undergone such marked
modifications under the combined efforts of legend and
legend writers that one can only make use of them with
extreme caution. Nor is it all plain sailing when, by
rare good fortune, the cause of a saint is founded on a
comparatively well-furnished record. One must know
how to classify the documents, to interpret them at
their proper value, to weigh evidence, and to establish
the degree of credibility to which each witness is entitled. It is a long and infinitely delicate task in which
the inexperienced critic, unfamiliar with hagiography,
meets with many a disappointment.

A providential accident has preserved for us an ex-
ceptionally complete series of documents concerning a
saint of the persecution under Diocletian. Contemporary records, narratives derived from them and revised
more than once, entries in the martyrologies, historical

proofs of the existence of a local cultus, the distant echoes of legend, everything that tradition is in the habit of distributing with niggardly hand between several saints is here united round a single name. The saint in question is St. Procopius, the "great martyr," honoured by the Greek Church on 8th July, and inscribed on the same date in the Roman Martyrology. In following step by step the traces of his cultus in literary monuments we shall arrive at an exact appreciation of the value of the documents concerning him. It will then be easy to extend to analogous cases the conclusions to which this examination will have led us.[1]

St. Procopius is the first of those martyrs of Palestine, of whom Eusebius, at once historian and eye-witness of the great persecution, has related the valiant resistance and the intrepid calmness in the face of death. Two versions have come down to us of Eusebius's tractate. The shortest and best known is usually read between the eighth and ninth book of the *Ecclesiastical History*. The other, more developed, has only come down to us in its entirety in a Syriac translation. Of the Greek text there only remain fragments and abstracts. The chapter concerning Procopius in the longer recension has not been found, like other chapters of the same work, in the Greek menologies. But the Latin Passionaries have preserved this fragment of Eusebius's book, the only fragment, so far as is known, to penetrate to the West. The following are the words in which the Bishop of Cæsarea relates the history of Procopius and his martyrdom.[2]

" The first of the martyrs of Palestine was Procopius,

---

[1] Concerning all this see *Analecta Bollandiana*, vol. xvi., pp. 113-22.

[2] *Bibl. hag. lat.*, n. 6949.

a man filled with Divine grace, who, before his martyrdom, had ordered his life so well that from childhood
he had been vowed to chastity and to the practice of
all the virtues.   He had reduced his body until he had
given it so to speak the appearance of a corpse, but
his soul drew from the Word of God so great a vigour
that the body itself was refreshed by it.   He lived on
bread and water, and only ate food every two or three
days; sometimes he prolonged his fast during a whole
week.   Meditation on the Divine Word so filled his
being that he remained absorbed in it day and night
without any sense of fatigue.   Filled with goodness
and gentleness, regarding himself as the least of men,
he edified every one by his discourses.[1]   The word of
God was his sole study, and of profane sciences he had
but a mediocre knowledge.   Born at Elia, he had
taken up his residence at Scythopolis where he filled
three ecclesiastical functions.   He was reader and in-
terpreter in the Syriac language, and cast out evil
spirits by the imposition of hands.

"Sent with companions from Scythopolis to Cæsarea
he had scarcely passed the city gates when he was
conducted into the presence of the governor, and even
before he had had a taste of chains or prison walls he
was at once urged by the judge Flavian to sacrifice to
the gods.   But he, in a strong voice, proclaimed that
there are not several gods, but one alone, the creator
and author of all things.   This answer made a vivid
impression on the judge.   Finding nothing to say in
reply, he tried to persuade Procopius at least to sacrifice
to the Emperors.   But the martyr of God despised his
entreaties.   'Listen,' he said, 'to this verse of Homer:

[1] The condition of the text renders the sentence very difficult to
translate. We can only give the general sense of the passage.

It is not good to have several masters ; let there be one single chief, one single king.'

Οὐκ ἀγαθὸν πολυκοιρανίη · εἷς κοίρανος ἔστω
εἷς βασιλεύς.[1]

At these words, as though he had uttered imprecations against the emperors, the judge ordered him to be led to the place of execution. They cut off his head, and he passed happily to eternal life by the shortest road, on the 7th of the month of Desius, the day that the Latins call the nones of July, in the first year of our persecution. This was the first martyrdom that took place at Cæsarea."

Comment would but weaken the impression made by this noble and sober narrative, and, in our own day, no one would dream of putting it into a better style, as the process was called in the Middle Ages. We shall see directly the sort of success it achieved.

It was not long before St. Procopius was in the enjoyment of all the honours accorded to martyrs. It is perhaps scarcely right to quote in evidence the inscription of his name in the Eastern martyrology, which has come down to us in the pseudo-Hieronymian compilation. He figures on 8th July, under the formula, *In Cæsarea Cappadociæ, Procopi.* The value of this evidence is not actually lessened by the erroneous reference to Cæsarea in Cappadocia, instead of to Cæsarea in Palestine. This is a mistake which runs through the Hieronymian martyrology and was wholly attributable to the editor. But the Oriental annals depended, in the case of the Palestine martyrs, on Eusebius's book. They do not therefore in themselves testify to the existence of a living cultus.

Happily, so far as St. Procopius is concerned, we

[1] *Iliad,* ii., 204.

have other proofs establishing the antiquity of the
honours rendered him.   Pilgrims journeyed to Cæsarea
to venerate his holy remains,[1] over which they erected
a basilica.   In 484 it was restored by the Emperor
Zeno.[2]   Scythopolis, the home of the martyr, also set
up a shrine in his honour the existence of which was
attested in the sixth century.[3]   Devotion to St. Procopius must soon have become popular and have spread
far beyond the boundaries of Palestine.   In proof of
this we find the blossoming of legends which early developed around the memory of the martyr of Cæsarea,
and of which we shall attempt to trace out the principal
phases.

There are in existence a whole series of different
versions, for the most part unpublished, of the legend
of St. Procopius, for the detailed study of which there
is no room here.   On some other occasion we propose
to discuss from a technical point of view and to classify
the various texts in their relations to one another.
But the following are the results to which this work of
classification has led us.

Three main versions of the legend must be distinguished.   The first, and the most ancient, is represented by the text of the Paris manuscript, 1470,[4] and
by a Latin Passion which has come down to us in a
manuscript belonging to Monte Cassino.[5]   The Latin
version presupposes a Greek version varying somewhat from the one that we still possess.   We shall,
however, restrict ourselves to a study of this latter, as

1 *Antonini Itinerarium,* 46, Geyer, p. 190.
2 *Chronicon paschale,* ed. Paris, p. 327.
3 Cyrilli Scythopolitani, *Vita S. Sabæ,* c. 75, Cotelier, p. 349.
4 *Catalogus codicum hagiographicorum græcorum bibliothecæ
nationalis Parisiensis,* p. 149. [publ. in *Les légendes grecques des
saints militaires,* p. 214-27.]
5 *Bibl. hag. lat.,* n. 6950.

from our immediate point of view the divergences are of no importance. The group thus composed of the two texts will henceforth be referred to as the *first legend* of St. Procopius.

The *second legend* is to be met with in a large number of manuscripts, in various more or less developed versions. M. A. Papadopoulos-Kerameus has published the one which is most widely spread, printed from a manuscript in the convent of Vatopedi on Mount Athos.[1] Unhappily this particular copy is abridged, and in order to analyse the legend we have made use of the Greek manuscript Paris, 897.

The title of *third legend* will be reserved for the group consisting of two closely allied versions of which one has been published in Greek by the Bollandists,[2] and the other in Latin by Lipomani,[3] and after him by Surius.[4]

We need not at this point take into consideration the various panegyrics of the saint, which are usually derived from one or other of the preceding categories.

We shall begin by summarising the first legend of St. Procopius. As far as bulk is concerned, it is seven or eight times as long as Eusebius's narrative: of its literary qualities the reader must judge for himself.

The narrative opens with an imaginary edict by Diocletian, a violent attack upon the faithful. The persecution breaks out, and the judge, Flavianus, a monster of cruelty, arrives at Cæsarea. The Blessed Procopius was a native of Elia and performed the functions of lector and exorcist. His ministry met

---

[1] Ἀνάλεκτα ἱεροσολυμιτικῆς σταχυολογίας, vol. v., St. Petersburg, 1898, pp. 1-27.

[2] *Acta SS.*, July, vol. ii., pp. 556-76.

[3] *Tomus sextus vitarum sanctorum patrum*, Rome, 1558, ff. 107-15v.

[4] *De probatis sanctorum vitis*, for 8th July.

with so much success that the attention of Flavianus
was quite naturally drawn to him. Accordingly Flavianus summons him to his presence.

The judge is seated on the judgment-seat when
Blessed Procopius is led in. As soon as he appears
the people are unable to restrain their fury and roar like
wild beasts : " There is the man who despises our gods,
and tramples under foot the decree of the emperor".
Flavianus, inspired by the devil, asks the martyr :
" What is your name ? " The martyr replies : " I am
a Christian. My name is Procopius." The judge :
" Are you alone ignorant of the divine commands of the
Emperor, in accordance with which those who refuse
to sacrifice to the gods must themselves be tortured
and put to death ? I cannot express my astonishment
at seeing you, at your mature age, acting with such
madness. How can you teach others, when you your-
self have lost your senses ? How dare you pretend
that God was born of a woman and was crucified !
Who would not scoff at such an invention ? I warn
you, therefore, to forsake this foolish error and to
sacrifice to the gods and respectfully adore the image
of the emperor, if you do not wish to suffer death. It
is to be hoped that the tortures undergone by those
who have preceded you may teach you a little sense."

This harangue by Flavianus is followed by a long
speech from the martyr, who exhorts him to recognise
God the Creator. Among the arguments he brings
forward are the views of the philosophers, Hermes
Trismegistus, Homer, Plato, Aristotle, Socrates, Galen
and Scamandrus, who all proclaimed the unity of God.
After various arguments in favour of Christianity the
orator is interrupted by the judge who mingles threats
with his exhortations.

The martyr replies, but this time with less calm, nor is he sparing of insults. The invectives fade away into a lengthy dissertation, after which the judge orders the tortures to be begun. The martyr is strung up, his body is scraped, his wounds are made more painful by being covered with salt and rubbed with a rough hair-cloth. The executioners tear the flesh on his face with iron hooks till he is past recognition, and they break his bones.

Then the judge commands a certain person named Archelaus to cut the martyr's head off, but the man's hands are suddenly paralysed and he falls down dead.

The exasperated Flavianus sends Procopius to prison, loaded with chains. There the martyr recites a long prayer. Christ appears to him in the guise of an angel and heals his wounds. Three days later there is a second interrogatory, in the course of which Flavianus reproaches him for having had recourse to magic in order to kill Archelaus and to efface the scars of his own wounds. Then he orders him to be hung up and whipped with thongs of ox hide; the executioners apply burning coal to his back and reopen all his wounds by driving red-hot nails into his flesh. The saint does not cease speaking and overwhelms the judge with reproaches and insults, to which the judge replies by fresh tortures. The dialogue continues while more red-hot skewers are driven into the martyr's flesh. At length Flavianus invents a fresh ordeal. He orders a little altar to be set up. The martyr is made to stretch out his hand filled with burning coal, and incense is flung upon it. "If you throw the burning incense on the altar," declares Flavianus, "you will have sacrificed to the gods." Procopius remains resolute and his hand never moves. He weeps, but it is not his own sufferings that draws tears from his eyes, but the obstinacy of Flavianus. Thunderstruck, Flavianus at length pronounces sentence of death. The Blessed Procopius is led outside the town to be executed. He begs for an hour's reprieve, and offers up a lengthy prayer, after which he submits to the fatal blow. The Christians carry off his body and give it decent sepulture.

Here we are indeed far removed from the discreet simplicity of Eusebius and the pious enthusiasm which pervades his narrative. The *Passio Procopii*, that we have summarised, is a piece of cold and clumsy rhetoric, relying for its effect on long speeches supplemented by commonplace sentiments and descriptions of tortures.

It cannot be pretended that the hagiographer was compelled to write in this way for lack of information concerning the saint. He had in his hands, not the mere summary by Eusebius contained in the *Ecclesiastical History*, but his developed text. It was there he learned that Procopius was a native of Elia, that he lived a holy life, that he performed ecclesiastical functions—as he omits all reference to Scythopolis, the assumption is that it was at Jerusalem—that the judge was named Flavianus, that the martyr died by the sword. Everything that he adds is pure invention, as, for example, the episode of Archelaus miraculously struck down at the moment when he is about to decapitate the saint, the vision enjoyed by the martyr in prison, the instant healing of his wounds, and finally the scene of the incense which is borrowed from the life of St. Barlaam.[1]

It is not easy, beneath these borrowed plumes, to

1 *Analecta Bollandiana*, vol. xxii., pp. 134-45.

recognise the martyr commended by Eusebius, the simple-minded Christian nourished on Holy Scripture, an entire stranger to rhetorical methods and dialectical subtlety. True, we still have the lector, the exorcist and the ascetic. In later legends the transformation is carried much farther. In them the austere figure of the clerk of Scythopolis is wholly lost, and we have in his place a mail-clad warrior, his sword by his side and his lance at rest.

We must now summarise the second legend, notably longer than its predecessor.

Diocletian initiated a terrible persecution against the Christians, despatching edicts to all parts. The contents of the copy sent to Elia are given. The emperor himself goes to Egypt where he defeats the usurper Achilles, and thence he proceeds to Antioch where he receives from the senate a sort of profession of idolatrous faith.

Now there lived at Jerusalem, at that time called Elia, a noble lady named Theodosia who had a son named Neanias, a pagan like herself. His mother brought him to Antioch in order to recommend him to the kind notice of the emperor. The latter, captivated by his good looks and by his zeal on behalf of the heathen deities, forthwith created him Duke of Alexandria, and before he started to take up his new appointment urged upon him to seek out the Christians and to punish them severely. And in order to convince him of the folly of the Christians, Diocletian gave him a summary of the life of Christ with commentaries of his own.

Thus Neanias takes his departure, like a second Saul, breathing hatred and vengeance. But he too was to tread the road to Damascus. As he was leaving

Apamea, an earthquake accompanied by lightning made itself felt, and a voice from a cloud was heard: "Whither goest thou, Neanias?" At the same time a crystal cross became visible, and he heard the words: "I am Jesus crucified, the Son of God". Neanias makes various protestations, but the voice continues, "Thou shalt be to me a vessel of election," and again, "By this sign thou shalt conquer".

The converted Neanias journeys with his soldiers to Scythopolis, and there commissions a certain Mark to make him a gold and silver cross similar to the one seen in his vision. As soon as it was completed three figures appeared upon it with the names in Hebrew, Emanuel, Michael and Gabriel. With the help of this miraculous cross Neanias put to flight a body of Agarenians, killing 6,000 of them. He then returned home to his mother and broke up all the family idols, distributing the precious metal among the poor. His terrified mother denounces her son to Diocletian, and he consoles her by giving her permission to select a new son for herself from among the senators. At the same time he despatches a letter to the governor named Oulcion, charging him to examine Neanias and put him to death with torture should he persist in his impiety. Neanias learns the contents of the emperor's letter, tears it into a thousand fragments, and declares himself a Christian. The governor orders him to be put in chains and escorted to Cæsarea.

Oulcion presides at the trial and condemns Neanias to be hung up and his flesh torn with iron hooks. When the executioners are exhausted and all the martyr's bones are exposed, he is led back to prison. There he is visited by angels, and favoured by a vision of Christ who baptises him, changes his name to Procopius and heals all his wounds.

The next day there is a fresh interrogatory. The governor attributes the healing of the martyr to the power of the gods. Procopius immediately requests to be taken to the temple. The impious judge and the people imagine that the constancy of the martyr has given way and that he is about to sacrifice to the gods. He is therefore conducted to the temple with much pomp. But far from denying his Christian faith, Neanias breaks the idols in pieces by the virtue of the sign of the cross.

Here two long episodes occur. The first is that of the conversion of the soldiers, who go to visit Procopius in prison. The martyr persuades his jailer to allow him to conduct them to the bishop Leontius who baptises them, after which the martyr returns to prison. He confirms the new converts in their faith, and later they are martyred before his eyes.

As a counterpart to this narrative concerning the soldiers we next have the history of twelve matrons of senatorial rank who, in their turn, embrace the Christian religion and die after enduring inexpressible tortures. Theodosia, the mother of Procopius, is so touched by the spectacle of their constancy that she too is converted and suffers death with them.

Not long afterwards the governor Oulcion contracts a malignant fever and dies, and Flavianus takes his place at Cæsarea. The martyr is summoned before his tribunal, and there follow almost all the scenes described in the earlier legend.

Is it necessary to bring evidence to prove that this version is of later date than that which we have entitled the first legend? It is clear that this longer story is derived from it and marks a definite step in the legendary development. Neither the setting nor the rhetoric of the first legend went so far as to alter the physiognomy of the martyr in any essential details. It preserved at least the memory of his ecclesiastical functions.   In the later version the lector and exorcist disappears entirely, and we have in his stead a young heathen soldier and magistrate miraculously converted to Christianity.   His name was originally Neanias, and it required nothing less than a vision to impose the name Procopius upon him.

This detail alone should suffice to betray the methods of the hagiographer.   He has joined together two histories, that of Neanias which took place under the governorship of Oulcion and that of Procopius with Flavianus as judge.

What is the origin of the Neanias legend?   It is impossible to say, nor is it necessary to investigate further before relegating it among compositions of the purest fantasy.   It is a medley of stock incidents and reminiscences.   The conversion of St. Paul, the vision of Constantine, the Acts of St. Polycarp and many other narratives which it were tedious to recall further, have furnished the compiler of this history with the main incidents.   The introduction of Neanias into the legend has completed the metamorphosis of St. Procopius.   Save for his name, nothing remains of him, and of Eusebius's narrative one can recall only vague reminiscences seen in the names of Elia, Scythopolis, Cæsarea and Flavianus.

The second legend is of great antiquity.   It was current in the eighth century, and inspired sufficient confidence to be produced before the Fathers of the second council of Nicæa.[1]   The episode of the miraculous cross was quoted as evidence in favour of the

[1] Hardouin, *Concilia,* vol. iv., pp. 229-32.

veneration of images, as may be read in the Acts of the Council.

In its third disguise the legend has enjoyed a notoriety no less widespread. It was incorporated in the collection of Metaphrastes, and with the other documents was reproduced in a large number of copies.[1]

There are even in existence two versions of this recension, of which the one that would appear to be the earlier in point of date has not yet been printed. We can, however, gather a sufficient idea of it from the translation published by Lipomani.[2] The second provides the text of the *Acta Sanctorum*. These two versions of the third legend are not sufficiently distinct to require separate treatment here. Without any inconvenience we may pass over the details peculiar to each and restrict ourselves to the features they possess in common.

Let us admit at once that between the second and third legend there are no essential differences. The succession of incidents is the same in both cases, nor has the new editor thought it necessary to tone down the absurdities of his model. His efforts appear to have been concentrated upon the style, and all the conventions of old-fashioned rhetoric are pretentiously displayed throughout the pages in which the Passion of St. Procopius is supposed to be related in a more attractive form. I will quote only a single instance in illustration of the methods of a school of hagiographers which has enjoyed much popularity.

Each time the editor comes across an historical or geographical name he uses it as a text on which to build up an erudite little dissertation into which he

1 *Analecta Bollandiana*, vol. xvi., pp. 311-29.
2 See above, p. 130.

drags all the reminiscences that the name recalls to his mind. Thus, when he relates that Diocletian arrived at Antioch, it reminds him that at Daphne, near the town, there was a celebrated sanctuary of Apollo. He therefore hastens to add that the Emperor went there to make solemn sacrifice to the God. Nor was it possible for him to forget that Antioch played an illustrious part in the history of the primitive Church, and that it was there the disciples of the new faith first received the title of Christians. The writer has no idea of passing the fact over in silence.[1]

A few lines farther on the question arises as to the native town of Theodosia, the mother of Procopius. In all earlier texts the town had been said to be Elia. This is how the new editor deals with the theme: "Theodosia occupied a leading position in the city. This city had previously borne the names of Jerusalem and of Sion. But after it had been taken by the Romans as a punishment for its crime towards Christ, Hadrian, who then wielded the imperial sceptre, renamed it Elia."[2]

The mention of Cæsarea furnishes yet further occasion for a display of erudition. Unfortunately in this instance the editor's learning is at fault, for he confuses Cæsarea Paneas or Philippi with Cæsarea Stratonica in Palestine, and he flounders in his error. "The judge commanded that the saint should be conducted to Cæsarea, where he was busy with the construction of a temple. We refer to that town of Cæsarea which we are accustomed to call of Philip, and which was formerly called Tower of Straton. The Phœnicians named it Paneas, a title derived from the neighbouring

---

[1] *Acta SS.*, July, vol. ii., p. 55, n. 5, 6.
[2] *Ibid.*, n. 7.

mountain range Paneos.   And as we have recalled that town, we should reproach ourselves were we to pass over in silence an interesting story that has reference to it " . . . and he proceeds to relate, in the words of Eusebius,[1] the well-known legend of the sculptured group representing, according to tradition, Christ and the woman who suffered from an issue of blood.[2]

We need not proceed further with the accumulation of proofs of the pedantry of our author.   It has not diminished the popularity of his narrative.   It is of this third legend that there still exists the greatest number of copies, and it served definitely to instal St. Procopius for all future ages in the character of a warrior martyr.

The inevitable result of transforming Procopius lector into Procopius soldier has been to duplicate the individual.   In certain synaxaries one may read, under the date 8th July, the passion of the great martyr Procopius, that is to say the officer of the second and third legend, followed by the commemoration of Procopius, exorcist, martyred at Cæsarea.[3]   This latter is further celebrated on 22nd November, and on that occasion a slightly abbreviated version of Eusebius's account is read.[4]

In some copies the commemoration of St. Procopius is repeated on the following day, 23rd November. But there he no longer bears his own name " Procopius of Palestine," but is styled Procopius "who suffered in Persia ".[5]

Whence comes this qualification ?   We know of no

1 *Hist. Eccl.*, viii., 18.
2 *Acta SS.*, July, vol. ii., pp. 563-64, n. 27-29.
3 *Synaxarium ecclesiæ Constantinopolitanæ*, pp. 805, 808.
4 *Synaxarium ecclesiæ Constantinopolitanæ*, p. 245.
5 *Ibid.*, pp. 247, 249.

Persian martyr of the name of Procopius. It is obvious that we are here in the presence of a blunder, but it is impossible to ascertain its origin in any very precise way, and we can but chronicle another of the many aberrations of the compilers of synaxaries. Those who are in the habit of handling this class of volume will entertain no doubt whatever that it is the one and only St. Procopius who is made to figure in these various disguises.[1]

The synaxaries of recent date and the menæa which have borrowed their historical sections, only inscribe St. Procopius the officer, and add commemorations of his mother Theodosia, of the twelve matrons put to death with her, and of the officers Antiochus and Nicostratus, who, according to the legend, were in command of the soldiers converted by Procopius.

The Latins[2] have also studied the Acts of St. Procopius, and we have seen that the original narrative of Eusebius has been preserved as a separate document in their passionaries alone. From it is derived the very exact commemoration contained in the historic Latin martyrologies.[3] We have explained further that the

[1] The Vatican MS. 679 contains an ἐγκώμιον εἰς τὸν ὅσιον μάρτυρα Προκόπιον τὸν Πέρσην, of which the author is Hesychius, a priest of Jerusalem. There is nothing in this document by which one may distinguish Procopius the Persian from Procopius of Cæsarea. See *Analecta Bollandiana,* vol. xxiv., pp. 473-82.

[2] I will not discuss here the cultus of St. Procopius in Slavonic countries. The literary monuments all have their origin in Greek sources. The others are of comparatively recent date. Concerning the cultus of the saint in Servia see C. Jirecek, *Das Christliche Element in der topographischen Nomenclatur der Balkanländer in* the *Sitzungsberichte der kaiserlichen Akademie der Wissenschaften,* vol. cxxxvi., 1897, n. xi., pp. 36-37.

[3] The following is the text of Adon: "In Palæstina natalis sancti Procopii martyris, qui ab Scythopoli ductus Cæsaream, ad primam responsionum eius confidentiam, irato judice Fabiano (*read* Flaviano) capite cæsus est". The same account occurs in Usuard, *Ed.* Sollerius, pp. 388-89.

first legend of St. Procopius was probably known to the West through a Latin version made in Southern Italy. The portion of the second legend that was read at the Council of Nicæa was translated by Anastasius the librarian. But it is almost certain that a complete translation must also have existed.

We are justified in inferring this from a study of the Latin adaptations of the Acts of St. Procopius. For the illustrious martyr has not been spared a single one of the indignities to which clumsy hagiographers have subjected those saints on whom they have bestowed special attention. Not satisfied with composing on his behalf a history in which facts are completely travestied, and the character of the saint perverted, they have further transformed his history into a sort of *passe-partout*, a specimen biography which has been made to fit the lives of various obscure saints concerning whom all information is lacking.

The second legend of St. Procopius served in the first place to furnish Acts for St. Ephysius of Cagliari.[1] Apart from a few petty incidents clumsily tacked on to the text, and a few names of places designed to connect the saint with Sardinia, the story such as we know it has scarcely been revised, and in particular nothing has been done to give it a greater appearance of probability.

There is of course no question of a mission to Alexandria in the legend of Ephysius, but the name of the city has become that of the mother of the martyr who, in the original legend, was called Theodosia. Both are equally described as noble ladies of Elia and as having for husband a Christian named Christopher. Like Procopius,

---

[1] *Analecta Bollandiani,* vol. iii., pp. 362-77.

Ephysius is taken to Antioch by his mother and introduced to Diocletian, who entrusts him with the duty of persecuting the Christians, not indeed of Egypt, but of Italy. The vision occurs at a place called Vrittania, and it is at Gaeta that a silversmith named John supplies him with a crucifix. By the power of the sign of the cross Ephysius scatters the Saracens and then sets sail for Sardinia. He lands at Arborea, and in a short time makes himself master of the whole island. It is from Cagliari that he writes to Diocletian and to his mother to announce his conversion.

The emperor despatches to him one of his officers named Julicus, who, on Ephysius's refusal to apostatise, subjects him to cruel tortures. Like Oulcion in the original legend, Julicus is shortly struck down by a fatal fever. His place is taken by Flavianus, whose acquaintance we have already made. This savage judge does not forget to inflict on the martyr the ordeal of St. Barlaam, after which he condemns him to have his head cut off. The sentence is carried out *apud Caralitanam civitatem in loco qui dicitur Nuras.*

The history ends with a short narrative concerning a St. Juvenalis, Archbishop of Cagliari, an entirely unknown personage,[1] and with the following declaration, which however does not enable us to believe for a moment in the good faith of the biographer : *Cuius passionem ego presbyter Marcus, dum a principio usque ad finem oculis meis vidissem, oratu ipsius beati martyris Ephysi fideliter veraciterque descripsi præsentibus atque posteris profuturam.*[2]

[1 *Acta SS.*, May, vol. vi., 732. 3d ed.]

2 "And seeing that I, Mark, the priest, had beheld his passion with my own eyes from the beginning unto the end, at the request of the blessed martyr Ephysius himself, I have faithfully and truly recounted it in the hope that it will be profitable alike to our contemporaries and to posterity." [*Analecta Bollandiana*, vol. iii., p. 377. 3d ed.]

At Venice, in the church of St. Daniel, there is preserved the body of a St. John, martyr (*sancti Johannis ducis Alexandrini martyris*), which was brought there from Constantinople in 1215.[1] For this unknown martyr some history some needed, and no better plan was forthcoming than that of despoiling St. Procopius for his benefit, and applying to him the legend in all its details and in its most complete and fabulous form. In this case also the martyr was called Neanias in his pre-Christian days and his mother was born at Elia, while it was the Emperor Maximian who entrusted to him the duty of exterminating the faïthful of Alexandria. The two prefects who successively summoned him before their tribunal bore the names of Oulcion and Flavianus; the conversion of the soldiers, of the twelve matrons and of the mother of the martyr all recur. Leontius, instead of being Bishop of Cæsarea, figures on this occasion as Bishop of Alexandria, and it is in the latter city that John meets with his death.[2]

It is now time to summarise the preceding pages. Thanks to the testimony of Eusebius, the existence of the martyr St. Procopius is fully established together with the main outlines of his life and the manner of his death. Of itself this narrative would not be sufficient to establish the fact of a traditional cultus, and the same is true, as has been already explained, of the inclusion of the saint in the Hieronymian Martyrology. The existence, however, of the shrines at Cæsarea and at Scythopolis supply an incontrovertible proof of veneration.

[1] Flaminius Cornelius, *Ecclesiæ Venetæ antiquis monumentis . . . illustratæ,* vol. iv., Venice, 1749, pp. 170-71.
[2] *Acta SS.,* May, vol. iv., pp. 304-7.

The narrative of Eusebius was rapidly supplanted by legends throughout the East. It has left no trace in the Greek menologies in which the place which one would have liked to see assigned to it on 8th July is invariably filled by one or other of the legendary forms. Of the three legends with which we are familiar it is the most historical version that has enjoyed the least popularity.

One may say briefly that throughout the Middle Ages St. Procopius was venerated in the character attributed to him by the second legend. Even in our own day he still belongs to the category of warrior saints. It is important to remember that the type is one common to a number of well-known heroes—George, Theodore, Mercurius, Menas, Demetrius and others— and that the only literary monuments in which we can inform ourselves concerning most of them are documents of the same class as those which constitute the legend of Procopius.[1] Let us now see how much of them the historian must reject or retain.

The historic residue is this: a Christian named Procopius, a native of Jerusalem, was martyred under Diocletian by order of the judge Flavianus, and suffered death by the sword. We have the good fortune to be able to verify these details, and to confirm their accuracy, thanks to the single historical source which acquaints us with the personality of St. Procopius, and which a providential accident has preserved for us. On the other hand, the comparison of our legend with Eusebius's book establishes without a doubt that all the other details are a pure invention.

Thus the names of the saint's parents, his state of life, his qualities, his life and adventures, the tortures he endured, his imprisonment, the conversions he

[1 See our *Légendes grecques des saints militaires*, p. 1-119. 3d ed.]

brought about, his miracles, the visions with which he was favoured, all these are mere fabrications. Not only must the impossible Oulcion be expunged from the list of Roman magistrates, but we must exclude from the Greek liturgical books the names of Theodosia, of the twelve matrons and of the two officers as being the simple inventions of hagiographers.

And yet the legends we have been dissecting had their origin in a historical work of the first quality.[1] Such are the results hagiographers are capable of producing when they have good documents to work upon. In what terms shall we qualify their productions when, in the absence of all guidance, they have felt justified in giving free rein to their imaginations?

In the *dossier* of St. Procopius, therefore, the legend fills the lowest place, and if we had no other document to add to it we should find ourselves reduced even when dealing with so illustrious a martyr to a series of notes of interrogation. The certitude at which we may arrive of the historical existence of a saint and the legitimacy of his cultus, in no sense depends on the popularity of his legend. A few lines written by a contemporary, the text of a martyrology based on the liturgical traditions of a Church, or a basilica dating from ancient times, these are elements of far greater value to the student, and one is thankful to be able to affirm that they are not wholly lacking in the credentials of some very celebrated saints, whose credit has been seriously compromised by the clumsy tactics of their biographers.

Such testimony is not to be found, alas, among the documentary evidence concerning St. Ephysius of Cagliari or St. John of Alexandria. The very exist-

[1] *Acta SS.*, July, vol. ii., p. 576.

ence of the former and the antiquity of the cultus paid
to him are only guaranteed, as we have seen, by a title
which is patently spurious. Saintship on this insecure
basis is unhappily by no means without precedent in
the annals of Sardinian hagiography.

As for the martyr John, it appears that his body was
stolen from the chapel of a monastery in Constantinople as little known as the saint himself.[1] His incompetent biographer has only succeeded in accentuating
our suspicions concerning his identity.

1 Flaminius Cornelius, *Ecclesiæ Venetæ*, vol. iv., p. 171.

CHAPTER VI.

PAGAN SURVIVALS AND REMINISCENCES.

I.

Rites and symbols common to Christianity and to ancient religions—
Suspicious Practices—Incubation—Collections of Miracles—
Literary borrowings from pagan sources—Unavoidable analogies
—Superstitions.

THE subject on which we are about to enter is fertile
in surprises, and, let us confess at once, in regrettable
confusions. It has borne, and still bears, the brunt of
an over-ingenious criticism, eager to connect certain
religious phenomena which come specially within the
range of hagiography with certain pagan beliefs and
practices. By means of a subtle exegesis, frequently
based on a very wide learning, students try to discern
beneath the surface of Christian legend remains of the
older mythologies and links with an earlier worship;
they point out, between rival religions, analogies or
similitudes which they maintain can only be explained
by the fact of their having been borrowed.

There are men indeed who do not hesitate to assert
that in the struggle between Christianity and idolatry
victory was not always on the side where it has been
assumed to be, and, as might be supposed, it is the
cultus of the saints that supplies arguments in support
of this paradox.

It were unfair to try and discredit the study of rites or of comparative religion by insisting unduly on the exaggerations of those who have sinned in these matters by over-refinement or by superficiality. The problem before us, in spite of the obscurity in which it is involved, is worthy of serious examination.

A material but wholly external link between the new religion and the old consists in the common possession of a certain number of rites and symbols which we are accustomed to regard as our own special property, and which we are consequently surprised to discern existing in polytheism and bearing much the same meaning.

In point of fact it would be very surprising if, when seeking to propagate her doctrines in the midst of Græco-Roman civilisation, the Church had adopted for her intercourse with the people a wholly unknown language, and had systematically repudiated everything that until then had served to give expression to religious feeling.

Within the limit imposed by the conventions of race and culture, the method of interpreting the emotions of the heart cannot be indefinitely varied, and it was natural that the new religion should end by appropriating to itself a whole ritual which only required to be sanely interpreted to become the language of the Christian soul aspiring to the one True God. All external signs which did not implicitly involve the recognition of polytheism would find grace in the eyes of the Church, and if on the one hand she showed no undue haste in adapting them officially to her use, on the other hand she did not protest when they made their appearance as a means of expressing the religious instincts of the people. Certain attitudes of prayer and reverence, the

use of incense and of lamps burning night and day in
the sanctuary, the offering of ex-votos as a testimony
to benefits received, are such natural expressions of
piety and gratitude towards a divine power, that it
would be strange if their equivalents were not met with
in all religions.

It is therefore an uncritical proceeding to fall back on
the hypothesis of a direct borrowing, when human nature,
acting under the influence of religious feeling, affords
an adequate explanation.[1]   Nevertheless I know there
are persons who in our places of pilgrimage cannot
watch the faithful mounting the steps of the shrine on
their knees, without reflecting that the Emperor Claudius
ascended the steps of the Capitol in the same manner.[2]
Others are quick to recall that renowned fresco in
the Naples museum in which one may see a priest of
Isis standing before the *cella* of the temple and pre-

[1] The prayer of Demetrius, given by Seneca in *De Providentiu,*
v., 5-6, offers one of the most curious examples in illustration of
this. The following are the terms in which the philosopher expresses
the conformity of his will to that of the gods: "Hoc unum de vobis,
di immortales, queri possum, quod non ante mihi voluntatem vestram
notam fecistis. Prior enim ad ista venissem, ad quæ nunc vocatus
adsum. Vultis liberos sumere? vobis illos sustuli. Vultis aliquam
partem corporis? sumite. Non magnam rem promitto; cito totum
relinquam. Vultis spiritum? Quidni? nullam moram faciam, quo
minus recipiatis quod dedistis. A volente feretis, quicquid petieritis.
Quid ergo est? maluissem offerre quam tradere. Quid opus fuit
auferre? accipere potuistis. Sed ne nunc quidem auferetis, quia nihil
eripitur nisi retinenti. Nihil cogor nihil patior invitus, nec servio Deo
sed adsentior, eo quidem magis quod scio omnia certa et in æternum
dicta lege decurrere." If the reader will compare this prayer with
the *Suscipe* of St. Ignatius, the eloquent outpouring which closes
the volume of Spiritual Exercises, he will be surprised at the resemblance between the two. Yet it is scarcely temerarious of me to
affirm that in the moment of composing it St. Ignatius was in no
way inspired by the recent reading of Seneca.
[2] Dion Cassius, lx., 23.

senting to the adoration of the congregation a form of pyx containing water from the sacred Nile.[1] With but little alteration this scene might be made to represent an exposition of relics or a benediction in accordance with our existing rites. Cicero tells us that at Agrigentum there was a much-venerated statue of Hercules of which the mouth and chin were worn away by the many worshippers who pressed their lips to it. The bronze foot of the statue of St. Peter in Rome has not withstood any better the kisses of the faithful.[2]

Yet modern Christians have undoubtedly learnt nothing from the Sicilian contemporaries of Verres, any more than the pilgrims dragging themselves on their knees in the fulfilment of a vow, or a Catholic priest blessing his congregation with a reliquary are carrying out rites inherited from the Romans under the Empire. What is true is that the same thought, under analogous circumstances has found expression after an interval of centuries in identical actions and attitudes. Concerning this point it appears to me that no further discussion is called for.

It must however be confessed that there are certain rites of a markedly pagan character sometimes brought to our notice, the origin of which is distinctly open to suspicion. The curious ceremony which consists in dipping the images of saints into water, too obviously recalls the sacred bath of the mother of the gods [3] for it to be possible that there is no connection between the two. In the same way, it has been thought the Church preserved for many centuries a survival of the

1 C. A. Böttiger, *Isis-vesper* in *Kleine Schriften,* vol. ii., Dresden, 1838, pp. 210-30.
2 Verr., iv., 43.   3 Ovid, *Fasti,* iv., 337-46.

rite of incubation, a superstitious usage widely practised
in the sanctuaries of Æsculapius, Amphiaraus and
Serapis.   In its essential features it consisted in sleeping in the temple, after due preparation and certain
prescribed ceremonies, with the object of being favoured
in a dream by an apparition of the divinity, and ob-
taining either a revelation as to the future or the healing of some disease.

We possess very full information concerning incubation, thanks mainly to the inscriptions at Epidaurus.[1]
The object aimed at was the dream in which the god
revealed himself and bestowed health, or, more frequently, indicated the treatment to be followed.   The
somewhat complicated ritual which usually served as
preparation was only a condition for propitiating the
divinity.

Among the documents which have been collected on
the subject of Christian incubation [2] a first place must
be accorded to the miracles of SS. Cosmas and Damian
and SS. Cyrus and John.   It would be difficult to deny
that a number of their features do recall incubation as
it was practised in the temples of Æsculapius.   The
saints appear to the patients during their sleep and either
cure them or prescribe remedies.   Nevertheless, there
is nothing to show that at these Christian shrines the
practice of incubation was systematically organised as
it was at Epidaurus, or that we have in fact anything
more here than isolated occurrences.

Without wishing to contest the fact of the survival,
in certain basilicas, of a rite that undoubtedly had its

1 Collitz-Bechtel, *Sammlung der griechischen Dialekt-Inschriften*,
n. 3339-41; P. Cavvadias Τὸ ἱερὸν τοῦ Ἀσκληπιοῦ ἐν Ἐπιδαύρῳ, Athens,
1900, pp. 256-67. [A. Defrasse- H. Lechat, *Epidaure*, Paris, 1895.
3d ed.]

2 L. Deubner, *De incubatione capita quatuor*, Leipzig, 1900, 138
pages. [3d ed. has added about two pages of discussions of incubation, with particular reference to practises in the Orient, largely
drawn from his *Les recueils antiques de miracles des saints*, Brussels,
1925.]

superstitious side, we must not lose sight of the very
special character of the documents which give us information concerning it.   It is an admitted fact that
the larger collections of miracles bequeathed to us by
the Middle Ages are compilations in which the most
varied materials are mixed up at random, and which
in consequence can only be used with the utmost
circumspection.

Greek hagiographic literature is notably less rich
than the Latin in collections of this kind.   But the
examples it does contain greatly surpass all others in
their grotesque and improbable features, and there can
be no doubt that a close study of their origins would
lead to the identification of a number of pagan reminiscences and even of formal adaptations.

One of the most celebrated collections is that of the
miracles of St. Menas, attributed to Timothy of Alexandria.[1]   Tillemont who was only acquainted with an
incomplete edition of the work containing but five miracles,[2] declared that "the first is altogether extraordinary, the second rather less so, the third and fourth not
bad, and the fifth in the highest degree scandalous".
Tillemont was not the first person to be scandalised, and
editors of the Menæa [3] felt they could not admit the
narrative in question without notable modifications.
The fundamental idea of this imaginary miracle, putting
aside the burlesque treatment, is anything but Christian.
The story bears as its title, *The Paralytic and the Dumb
Woman*, and it tells how the saint ordered a paralytic to
share the couch of a dumb woman, and it was as the

---

[1] Published by J. Pomjalovskij, *Vie de St. Pàisios le grand* (in
Russian), St. Petersburg, 1900, pp. 62-89.

[2] *Mémoires pour servir a l'histoire ecclésiastique*, vol. v., p. 760.

[3] At the date 11th November.

result of this order, under the influence of surprise and emotion, that the one recovered the use of his limbs and the other her powers of speech.

This anecdote recalls too vividly certain comic cures attributed to Æsculapius, not to have some connection with the ἰάματα of the god. What proves moreover that it has no personal connection with St. Menas, is that the story is to be found with identical details in the volume of miracles of SS. Cosmas and Damian.[1]   As for those who resent the idea of any literary interdependence between Christian miracles and the official records of the marvellous cures wrought through the invocation of Æsculapius, it is necessary to remind them of several well-authenticated examples of identical miracles in the one and in the other which must be derived from one and the same source.   The miracle of the broken goblet, attributed to St. Lawrence by Gregory of Tours,[2] may be read in a closely similar form on one of the stelæ at Epidaurus.[3]   The marvellous history of the decapitated head, related on the same stelæ, is an adaptation of a still more ancient narrative;[4] it also has been taken over by Christian chroniclers in spite of its obviously grotesque character.[5]

The editors of volumes of miracles have freely availed themselves of both borrowing and adaptation, and it will only be after a thorough inquiry into the sources

1 Wangnereckius-Dehnius, *Syntagmatis historici de tribus sanctorum Cosmæ et Damiani nomine paribus partes duæ*, Vienna, 1660, pp. 481-83.

2 *In gloria martyrum*, c. xxx.

3 Collitz-Bechtel, *Sammlung der griechischen Dialekt-Inschriften*, n. 3339. *Le miracle du vase brisé* in *Archiv für Religions-wissenschaft*, ser. viii. (1905), pp. 305-9.

4 See O. Crusius in *Mélusine*, vol. v., p. 203.

5 P. Perdrizet in the *Revue des études anciennes*, vol. ii., 1900, pp. 78-79; also in *Mélusine*, vol. v., pp. 97-100.

from which these miracle books are derived that they can be made use of as historical documents. As far as investigations have gone at present, it is impossible to ascertain what really belongs to them, and it is consequently only with prudent reservations that they can be quoted in evidence of the custom we are discussing.

It is therefore very difficult to decide to what extent incubation, as it appears to have been practised in certain basilicas, continued to retain all the characteristics of pagan incubation, nor do we know whether the Church ever formally sanctioned the rite in certain places, while attempting to give it a Christian character. It is however quite certain that the extent of its diffusion throughout the Christian world has been greatly exaggerated. In point of fact the majority of examples that are quoted have no more real connection with incubation than the story of Redemptus, Bishop of Ferentino, related by St. Gregory as follows :—

" Quadam die dum parochias suas ex more circuiret, pervenit ad ecclesiam beati Eutychii martyris. Advesperascente autem die, stratum fieri sibi juxta sepulcrum martyris voluit, atque ibi post laborem quievit. Cum nocte media, ut asserebat, nec dormiebat, nec perfecte vigilare poterat, sed depressus, ut solet, somno, gravabatur quodam pondere vigilans animus ; atque ante eum idem beatus martyr Eutychius adstitit, dicens: Redemte, vigilas ? cui respondit : Vigilo. Qui ait : Finis venit universæ carnis, finis venit universæ carnis, finis venit universæ carnis. Post quam trinam vocem visio martyris, quæ mentis eius oculis apparebat, evanuit." [1]

[1] "On a certain day as he was making the round of his diocese he came to the church of blessed Eutychius, the martyr. As night was coming on, he had a bed made for himself beside the martyr's tomb, and there after his labour he lay down to rest. Towards midnight, so he declared, he was neither asleep nor yet could keep fully awake,

Note that the bishop, without expecting any vision, merely had his couch prepared in the basilica of the martyr. There was neither rite nor religious observance involved. Save for the apparition, which was quite accidental, the incident was one which might still occur in missionary lands. Bishop and priest are frequently compelled to pass the night in the humble little chapels of the villages they pass through on their apostolic journeys. In other instances we hear of sick persons who refuse to quit the tomb of the saint until they are cured. They fall asleep and the cure comes to them, with or without a vision, while they are sleeping. In all these instances there are certain details in common with those of incubation, but the ceremonial as a whole and the institution itself are not found.

In general the study of superstitious practices of which the existence has been proved at certain shrines dedicated to very popular saints, should be carried on with far greater discernment and a more critical spirit than is generally to be met with among folk-lorists who have undertaken the duty of collecting documents for the historian. The accuracy of their information is often more apparent than real, and not a few among them possess a quite remarkable gift for establishing far-fetched resemblances.

Thus there is the ancient rite which consisted in passing through some aperture—a stone with a hole

but his active mind oppressed with drowsiness, as often happens, seemed to be crushed by some heavy weight. When lo! the said blessed martyr Eutychius stood before him, saying, 'Redemptus, sleepest thou?' To whom he answered, 'I am awake'. Whereupon he said, 'The end of all flesh has come, the end of all flesh has come, the end of all flesh has come'. After which triple utterance, the appearance of the martyr which had been perceptible to his mental vision vanished." *Dial.*, iii., 38. [There has been some re-ordering of the paragraphs in the 3d ed.]

in it or the hollow of a tree—in order to be cured of certain diseases. Folk-lorists may be excused for discovering reminiscences of the custom in certain churches in which the tomb of the saint is raised from the ground in such a way as to allow of pilgrims passing beneath, as for example at Gheel in Campine where lunatics make the round of the choir by passing beneath the archway above which stands the shrine of St. Dymphna. It must, however, be admitted that even if it exists at all, the connection between such rites is extremely remote, and that there is a wide distinction between a vain observance the efficacy of which depended upon a pierced stone, and a practice mainly founded on a belief in the virtue of relics.[1]

But folk-lorists have gone much further than this, and have been determined to discover examples of the suspected practice here, there and everywhere, even in the first ages of Christianity and beneath the roof of our most venerable basilicas. St. Peter's in Rome itself has not escaped. This is how Gregory of Tours described the tomb of the apostle in a celebrated chapter.[2] " Hoc enim sepulcrum sub altare collocatum valde rarum habetur. Sed qui orare desiderat, reseratis cancellis, quibus locus ille ambitur, accedit super sepulcrum, et sic fenestella parvula patefacta immisso introrsum capite, quæ necessitas promit efflagitat." [3]

Archæologists are too familiar with the " fenestella confessionis " (the window or orifice of the " confession ") for it to be necessary to explain its purpose :

[1] H. Gaidoz, *Un vieux rite médical*, Paris, 1892, 85 pages.
[2] *In gloria martyrum*, xxvii.
[3] "For this tomb placed beneath the altar is considered to be a very rare thing. But he who desires to pray, opening the grating with which the spot is enclosed, comes right over the tomb, and when the little orifice is exposed to view, inserting his head he makes such petitions as his needs suggest."

its position was affected by the arrangement of its surroundings and the shape of the "confession," and in no sense whatever by any superstitious custom. The sepulchre of St. Venerandus at Clermont,[1] which also had its "fenestella," has been quoted with equally little reason; with still less, the tomb of St. Martin which Gregory of Tours touched with his aching tongue "per lignum cancelli".[2] Far from recalling pagan rites, these acts of devotion at the shrine of a saint inspired by a desire to approach as closely as possible to the relics, are distinctly redolent of the spirit of primitive Christianity.

Nevertheless we are far from denying the survival, among Christian nations, of a certain number of customs of which the origin is extremely remote, and which are in direct opposition to Christian beliefs or Christian ethics. The greater number of the superstitions against which the Church has perpetually made war with changeful tactics and varying degrees of success, are an inheritance from our pagan ancestors.[3] As a general rule they have no direct relation with public worship, and their accidental association with established religious practices or even their connection with the name of a saint confers on them no sort of authorisation. The incident of the Count of Toulouse, who suddenly left Montpellier in 1212, terror-stricken at having seen St. Martin's bird flying on his left hand,[4]

1 *In Gloria confessorum*, xxxvi.
2 "Through the bars of the grating." *De virtutibus S. Martini*, iv., 2.—All these examples are quoted by Gaidoz, *op. cit.*, pp. 36-37.
3 See, for example, Weinhold's studies on the vestiges of ritual nudity in various superstitious practices, *Zum heidnischen Ritus* in the *Abhandlungen der k. Akademie der Wissenschaften zu Berlin*, 1896, i., pp. 1-50.
4 Pierre de Vaux-Cernay, *Hist. Albigensium*, n. 47; Bouquet, vol. xix., p. 43: "Viderat enim quandam avem quam indigenæ vocant avem sancti Martini, ad sinistram volantem, et perterritus fuit valde.

has no reference either to hagiography or to the history of religions, but is connected with the history of superstitions just as definitely as the "sinistra cornix" of Moeris in Virgil. The same may be said of all astrological practices [1] and incantation formulas,[2] in which one would be surprised at meeting with the names of saints, did we not know that absurdity and incoherence is the characteristic note of all manifestations of popular credulity. This aspect of the question, however, need not detain us for the moment. What does interest us is to know in what instances and to what extent hagiographic monuments reveal the existence of an actual link between polytheism and any public and normal manifestation of Christian piety.

Ipse enim more Sarracenorum, in volatu et cantu avium et ceteris auguriis spem habebat."

[1] In a collection of portents published by D. Bassi and E. Martini, *Catalogus codicum astrologorum græcorum, Codd. Ital.*, Brussels, 1903, pp. 158-69, one may find the following invocations recommended: Stephen, Thecla, Michael, Parasceve, George, Irene, Cosmas and Damian, Catherine, Demetrius, Anastasia, the Holy Cross, Anne, the Blessed Virgin, Nicholas, Barbara, Pantaleone and Gregory. They would appear to be the saints whose names had been given to the stars from which the portents were derived.

[2] In Egypt the names of the Seven Sleepers of Ephesus and the forty martyrs of Sebaste have more than once been found inserted in magic formulas. R. Pietschmann, *Les inscriptions coptes de Farâs* in the *Recueil de travaux relatifs à la philologie et à l'archeologie egyptiennes et assyriennes*, vol. xxi., 1899, pp. 175-76. See also W. Pleyte and P. A. Boeser, *Manuscrits coptes du musée d'antiquites des PaysBas*, Leyden, 1897, pp. 441-86.

II.

THE debate at this point has to be transferred to a
vast arena, for it is the veneration of saints itself which
is denounced as being a prolongation of idolatrous
paganism.   The critics admit that, in its first beginnings, the religion of Christ was pure and undefiled,
and rejected everything that could obscure the conception of the one True God.   But when the faithful ceased
to be an elect few, and when the Church was, so to
speak, invaded by the populace, she was forced to relax
her severity, give way before the instincts of the mob,
and make concessions to the polytheistic ideas that were
still stirring in the brain of the people.

By the introduction of the cultus of the saints, the
Church opened the door to a clearly marked current of
paganism.   There is no essential difference, so it is
affirmed, between the saints of the Church and the
heroes of Greek polytheism.   Beyond question the two
cults resemble each other in their manifestations,
but they are also identical in their spirit, and we are
clearly here in the presence of a pagan survival.[1]   Such
is the thesis that is developed by the folklorists with
much self-complacency.

We cannot neglect the details of the parallel.   Nothing could be more instructive, if only that it enables

---

1 "Christianorum quoque religio habebat atque habet suos sem-
ideos, suos heroas; sanctos scilicet martyresque." L. Deubner, *De
Incubatione*, p. 57: "Die Heiligen der christlichen Kirchen vor
allem die der griechischen Kirche, stellen die gerade Fortentwick-
lung des griechischen Heroenkults dar. Die Heilige sind die Heroen
der Antike." G. Wobbermin, *Religionsgeschichtliche Studien*, Berlin,
1896, p. 18. See also E. Maass, *Orpheus*, Munich, 1895, p. 244.

us to appreciate the exact value of certain hagiographic legends.[1]

Among the Greeks, heroes are mortals made superior to the vulgar herd by the gifts they have received from the gods. Privileged beings, holding a position midway between divine and human nature, they can lay claim to some portion of the power of the immortals, and they are enabled to intervene effectually in human affairs.

These heroes, the mortal sons of some divinity, great warriors, benefactors of humanity or founders of nations, were specially honoured in the city with which they were connected either by birth or by their exploits. They became its protectors and patrons. Every country, indeed every town, had its heroes to whom monuments were erected and whom the people invoked in their prayers.

The centre of devotion to a hero was his tomb, which was sometimes erected in the middle of the agora, the cerftre of public life. In most cases it was sheltered by a building, a sort of chapel known as ἡρῷον. A great number of tombs of heroes adorned the celebrated temples, just as the tombs of saints are honoured in Christian churches.[2]

When the actual body of the hero could not be venerated a cenotaph was erected to his memory. But no means were neglected to secure the veritable re-

[1]Concerning hero-worship see F. A. Ukert, *Ueber Dämonen, Heroen und Genien* in the *Abhandlungen der k. sächsischen Gesellschaft der Wissenschaften*, vol. i., pp. 138-219; Preller, *Griechische Mythologie*, vol. ii.; W. Schmidt, *Der Atticismus*, vol. iv., Stuttgardt, 1896, p. 572, and above all F. Deneken, *Heros*, in Roscher, *Lexikon der griechischen und römischen Mythologie*, vol. i., col. 2441-589. [P. Foucart, *Le Culte des héros chez les Grecs*, in *Mémoires de l'Institut*, vol. xlii, 1922, p. 1-166. Added in 3d ed.]

[2] On this special point see K. Th. Pyl, *Die griechischen Rundbauten*, Greifswald, 1861, p. 67 ff.

mains, for the people had faith in the power of a hero's bones and ashes, and when the precious object which was to serve as a protection to the city could be discovered, it was seized upon and conveyed thither with the greatest pomp and with ceremonies which undoubtedly recall the translation of Christian relics.[1]

The most celebrated account of one of these pagan translations is that of the transference of the remains of Theseus to Athens,[2] under the archonship of Apsephion (B.C. 469). The hero rested in the island of Scyros, but the spot of his interment was carefully kept secret by the inhabitants. An oracle arrived in the first instance from Delphi, recommending the Athenians to go and take possession of the bones of Theseus and cherish them in their own city with all the honour that was due to them. Cimon, son of Miltiades, proceeded to lead an expedition against Scyros, took possession of the island and instituted a search for the tomb. A further prodigy revealed the exact spot : he was simply to dig at the place that an eagle would point out to him with beak and talon. In the coffin was found the skeleton of a tall man with spear and sword. Cimon carried his precious burden on board his trireme, and the remains of the hero made a triumphal entry into Athens amid sacrifices and every demonstration of joy. He was laid to rest in the centre of the town near the site of the gymnasium, and the tomb of the hero, who, in his life-time had been kind and helpful to the humble, became an inviolable refuge for slaves and other needy persons anxious to escape from the exactions of the mighty. A great sacrifice in his honour was established on the eighth of the

1 Lobeck, *Aglaophamus*, p. 280; Rohde, *Psyche*, vol. i., pp. 161-63.
2 Plutarch, *Theseus*, 36; *Cimon*, 8.

month of Pyanepsion in memory of his return from Crete, but he was also commemorated on the eighth of other months.

This page of Plutarch might be adapted, with but few alterations, to more than one mediæval translation of relics. In the majority of cases these solemn journeys of relics are preceded in the same way by heavenly warnings; miraculous incidents accompany the discovery of the sacred remains; the people provide a brilliant and enthusiastic welcome; magnificent shrines are erected for their reception, and their presence is regarded as a protection to the country; finally an annual feast-day is inaugurated in honour of the happy event.

Nor was this an isolated case. The translations of the ashes of heroes were of frequent occurrence in Greece.[1] Thebes recovers from Ilion the bones of Hector, and presents to Athens those of Œdipus, to Lebadea those of Arcesilaus, and to Megara those of Aigialeus. Rarely are these disinterments ventured upon without an authorisation or command from some oracle. In spite of these divine interventions it is frequently necessary to have recourse to cunning in order to gain possession of a sacred tomb, and the incident of Lichas possessing himself of the body of Orestes[2] forms a curious counterpart to certain expeditions in search of the relics of a saint.

Not infrequently also it happened, as in the Middle Ages, that a new cultus sprang up at some fresh discovery of human bones. Whenever these were of

[1] Pausanias is our leading authority on this point. The most important documents have been quoted by Rohde, *Psyche,* vol. i., p. 161, and by Deneken previously cited.

[2] Herodotus, i., 67, 68.

large size they were assumed to be the skeleton of a hero, and sometimes an oracle would be consulted as to his name. Thus it was that the Syrians learnt from the god of Claros that the body of a giant found in the dry bed of the Orontes was that of a hero of the same name, of Indian origin.[1]

It is not only in the honours paid to the mortal remains of heroes that we may trace an analogy between pagan practices and devotion to relics. Just as, in our own churches, objects that have belonged to saints or that recall their memory in some special way are exposed for the veneration of the faithful, so in the temples visitors would be shown divers curiosities whose connection with a god or hero would command their respect. In Rome were to be seen the bones of a whale found at Joppa which were said to be those of the monster to which Andromeda was exposed. In other places might be seen the cithara of Paris, the lyre of Orpheus, the ships of Agamemnon and Æneas. And as the eager credulity of travellers rendered the *neocoroi* and the *periegetai* as ingenious as our modern vergers and *ciceroni*, in the end no relic was too improbable for them to profess to exhibit : Leda's egg, the white sow with her thirty little ones sacrificed by Æneas on the site of Alba, the anvil which Jupiter suspended to Juno's feet, and the remains of the clay out of which Prometheus had created man.[2]

No single detail will be lacking from the parallel when we have pointed out that, like ourselves, the ancients were not without experience of duplicated

---

1 Pausanias, viii., 29, 4.
2 The documents have been collected by Lobeck, *Aglaophamus*, p. 52. Ukert, *op. cit.*, pp. 202-4; Friedländer, *Sittengeschichte*, vol. ii., chap. i., *Die Reisen*.

relics, and were surprised to discover at Memphis the hair which Isis had torn out in her despair at the death of Osiris and which they had already been shown at Coptos. More remarkable still the tombs of certain heroes were to be found on more than one spot. Thus that of Æneas was pointed out not only at Berecyntus in Phrygia, but also at Ænea in Macedonia, and on the shores of the Numicius near Lavinium.[1]

Would it not appear as though the critics had established their case now that we have had to admit the existence among the Greeks of a cultus which in every detail recalls that paid to our saints, a cultus with relics, translations, inventions, apparitions and spurious or even forged relics. Can further parallels be needed to prove that the veneration of saints is merely a pagan survival?

The theory is plausible, and yet it will not stand for a second before the judgment of history. The cultus of the saints is not an outcome of hero-worship, but of reverence for the martyrs; and the honours paid to the martyrs from the outset by the early Christians, men who had known the baptism of blood, are a direct consequence of the high dignity of those witnesses to Christ as proclaimed by our Lord Himself. From the veneration with which their mortal remains were treated and from the confidence of Christians in their intercession arose the cultus of relics, with its varied manifestations, with, alas, its too natural exaggerations,—indeed, we may frankly say, with its excesses, excesses which have occasionally compromised the memory of those to whom it was intended to pay honour.[2]

It seems scarcely necessary to insist that hero-worship among the Greeks never possessed the same

---

[1] J. A. Hild, *La légende d'Enée* in the *Revue de l'histoire des religions*, vol. vi., 1882, p. 67.

[2 See *Les origines du culte des martyrs*. p. 1-119. 3rd ed.]

theological foundation and was never expressed in the same exact definitions which always place an infinite distance between God and man favoured by God. But it had an analogous starting-point and developed under the influence of general ideas which are not without some affinity with those which urged swarms of the faithful towards the tombs of the martyrs. Hence it necessarily arrived at practically identical consequences, and the history of these two cults represents a logical and parallel development without however any interdependence. It was not necessary to remember the gods and the heroes in order to turn in perfect confidence to the martyrs, to beg of them the healing of the sick, to place perilous journeys and difficult undertakings under their protection or to bestow on them visible proofs of gratitude for benefits received. Moreover it was certain to come about that the tomb of a martyr should be regarded not only as an honour but as a safeguard to the town that possessed it, and that the patron saint should receive all those honorary titles which in earlier days had fallen to protecting heroes: Sosipolis, Sosipatris, Philopolis and the like.[1]

In the same way, there is no real reason for supposing that the earliest narratives of the finding of relics, whatever may be the analogy of the facts or the similitude

---

[1] Upon these grounds M. Gelzer maintains that St. Demetrius came to replace the tutelary god of Thessalonica. His words are these: "Der Typus einer solchen Paganisierung des Christentums ist nun vor allem der heilige Demetrius. Er ist gleichsam die Personifikation oder die Fleischwerdung des antiken griechischen Polisgedankens. Wie Apollon und Herakles führt er den Beinamen Sosipolis." *Die Genesis der Byzantinischen Themenverfassung* in the *Abhandlungen der kgl. sächsischen Gesellschaft der Wissenschaften,* vol. xviii, 1899, n. 5, p. 54.

of the details, were inspired by the records of pagan translations. These narratives, of which the earliest date from the fourth century, were neither forgeries nor imitations. They are the natural outcome of an identical state of mind under similar circumstances.

We must, however, guard against exaggeration. If we are told that the ideas disseminated through society by hero-worship predisposed the mind to a ready acceptance of the *rôle* of saints in the Christian dispensation and of their value as intercessors before God, I see no reason whatever for contesting the statement. The markedly rapid development of the cultus of saints and martyrs may well be explained by the fact that the human mind was already prepared to accept it. In point of fact, ancient ecclesiastical writers made no sort of difficulty about admitting the existence of analogies between the cultus of martyrs and that of heroes. Indeed, Theodoret made use of the fact as the starting-point of his controversy with the pagans. Although other people should take exception to our practices, he declares, you should be the last to complain, you who possess heroes and demi-gods and deified men.[1]

As for certain exaggerations which from time to time have made their appearance to the detriment of the religious spirit, I see no reason whatever for connecting them with unconscious reversions to paganism. We have already pointed out sufficiently the popular tendency towards material and tangible things to account for these aberrations, which need to be continually kept in check, and which are to be found more especially in countries where passions are strong and imaginations keen. A statue or the body of a saint which appeals to a man's eyes, impresses him far more vividly than

[1] *Græc. affect. curatio*, viii., Schulze, vol. iv., pp. 902-3.

mysteries which appeal only to his faith. I should not therefore regard the manifestations of Neapolitan piety as mere paganism,[1] though I am far indeed from proposing them as a model to be imitated.

III.

Pagan survivals in worship—Holy places—Christian transformations —Adaptation of names—A method for ascertaining primitive titles—Sacred sources.

We believe we have sufficiently demonstrated by examples that too much value must not be attributed to exterior resemblances or fortuitous coincidences when any question arises regarding the continuity that may have existed between certain Christian practices and the Græco-Roman faith, not to mention other religions. The matter has to be investigated somewhat more closely, and wherever, in hagiographic matters, there is question of going back to the origins of a traditional cultus, three essential elements must be studied: the place, the date, and the legend. We will examine briefly the various questions connected with these points.

It was only after the complete triumph of Christianity that it became possible to establish her sanctuaries on the very sites of ancient temples that were either disused or had been wrecked. The Christians had not awaited the final abandonment of pagan monuments to erect magnificent buildings in accordance with the

[1] The work by Th. Trede, *Das Heidentum in der Römischen Kirche,* 4 vols., Gotha, 1889-91, is not only very wearisome to read, but is the outcome of a very superficial study. The author is intimately acquainted with the Neapolitans, but his prejudices, which he is never able to set aside, show that he is quite incapable of understanding the character of the people and their exuberant devotion. Throughout the work he makes no allowances for them.

requirements of their liturgy. In many cases they attacked the ancient religion on its own ground and contested its pre-eminence.

We are fairly well instructed concerning the methods adopted by the Church to combat superstitions attached to certain localities. In most cases she did so by erecting a basilica or a chapel, and by fostering there a new cultus of her own in order to distract popular attention, and to supply Christian nourishment to the religious instincts of the people.

We know, for example, how Cæsar Gallus (351) caused the body of the martyr Babylas to be conveyed to Daphne, which was at that time both a centre of idolatry and a scene of debauchery, and how in order to house it he commanded a church to be built in the immediate vicinity of the temple of Apollo of which the oracle was forthwith reduced to silence. Julian, enraged at receiving no reply from it, caused the relics of the martyr to be returned to Antioch.[1]

In the time of St. Cyril there was a little town named Menouthis near Canopus, about twelve miles east of Alexandria, celebrated for its oracle which the heathens came in crowds to consult and by which even Christians were sometimes led away.[2] It is true there was a Christian church at Menouthis dedicated to the apostles that had been built by Theophilus of Alexandria, but the den of superstition attracted greater crowds than the house of God. Cyril put a stop to these idolatrous gatherings by causing the bodies of SS. Cyrus and John which until then had lain in the Church of St.

[1] The documents on this point have been collected by Tillemont, *Mémoires*, vol. iii., p. 405.
[2] *Acta SS.*, Jan., vol. ii., p. 1083; *Deubner, De incubatione*, pp. 80-98. [See *Analecta Bollandiana*, vol. xxx, p. 448-450, 3d ed.]

Mark at Alexandria, to be transported in solemn state to Menouthis.   Such were the beginnings of one of the most famous shrines of Christian Egypt.

Gregory of Tours relates[1] how, in the Gévaudan district, there was a large lake on a mountain named Helanus, to which, as he says, the country folk made some sort of libation, by flinging stuffs, cakes and various objects into the water.   Every year the people would arrive with waggons, bringing food and drink with them, slaughtering cattle and giving themselves up for three whole days to feasting.   The fourth day, just as they were starting for home, they were always caught in a violent storm.   The Bishop of Javols arrived on the scene and exhorted the crowd to abstain from evil practices, threatening them with divine wrath. But his preaching was in vain.   Then, under the inspiration of God, he built a church in honour of St. Hilary of Poitiers on the shores of the lake, transported thither certain relics of the saint and began his exhortations anew.   This time he was more successful, the lake was abandoned and the objects that formerly had been flung into its waters were offered to the basilica. Moreover the storms ceased to rage at the time of the festival, which henceforward was consecrated to God[2] as the dedication feast.

In this particular instance we see that the Church did not take possession of the sacred spot, but that she

1 *In gloria confessorum*, ii. [*Helanus* becomes *Helarius* in the 3d ed.]

2 We have less reliable information concerning the substitution that took place on the Mons Garganus. But it has long been admitted that the legend of the sanctuary contains echoes of the oracle of Calchas so celebrated on this spot. See, for example, F. Lenormant, *À travers l'Apulie et la Lucanie*, vol. i., Paris, 1883, p. 61; G. Gothein, *Die Culturentwicklung Süd-Italiens*, Breslau, 1886, pp. 67-75.

ruined it by competition. When once the temples were definitely forsaken she was too wise to abandon to secular usages sites that had frequently been selected with great discrimination, and she consecrated them to the one true God whenever circumstances rendered such a course possible.

The history of the liquidation of the property of vanquished paganism has been related many times, and it has been possible to draw up long lists of churches erected upon the foundations of heathen temples, or built with their very stones, or indeed simply installed in the ancient edifice.[1] The classic examples of this latter category are the Pantheon in Rome and the Parthenon at Athens.

In the case of many other less illustrious temples replaced at a later date by Christian churches the memory of their primitive destination has been less carefully preserved. Certain learned men have invented an ingenious theory in order to supplement, in many instances, the silence of history. Because it has sometimes been possible to note an analogy between the Christian title of the transformed temple and its earlier title, they have felt justified in attributing to the Church a systematic Christianisation of pagan sanctuaries supposed to be based upon a very accommodating consideration for new converts. In order to permit them the illusion of not having wholly broken with the past, the new churches were placed under the patronage of saints

---

[1] Marangoni, *Delle cose gentilesche e profane trasportate ad uso e adornamento delle chiese,* Rome, 1744, pp. 256-87; L. Petit de Julleville, *Recherches sur l'emplacement et le vocable des églises chrétiennes en Grèc* in the *Archives des Missions scientifiques,* second series, vol. v., Paris, 1868, pp. 469-533; P. Allard, *L'art paien sous les empereurs chrétiens,* Paris, 1874, pp. 259-98.

who, by their name or legend, recalled the divinity
who had previously been honoured on the same spot.

Thus, at Eleusis we find a church of St. Demetrius
on the site of a temple of Demeter : it is the name
of the goddess but slightly modified.   It is true that
there was also a church of St. George, but it was again
Demeter, the goddess of agriculture, who was disguised
under the name of the "holy agriculturist," Γεώργιος.[1]
In other places St. George has taken the place of
Theseus or Hercules, but on those occasions it is as the
vanquisher of wild beasts that he is substituted for the
victor over the Minotaur or the destroyer of the Ler-
nean hydra.[2]   Thus, whether the analogy be phonetic
or symbolic the archæologists make capital out of it,
and find little difficulty in pointing out some resemblance
between the new patrons and the old.

It is somewhat more difficult to prove that these
resemblances have been generally sought after, and the
proof should certainly be forthcoming whenever it is
proposed to link the name of the saint with that of the
deity he displaced.   It is clear that most valuable topographical indications might be collected by this process.[3]
But its efficacy is entirely illusory, and if certain critics
have put it to strange uses, others have regarded it
with well-merited suspicion.

In those instances in which we have historical proof
of the action of the Church, favouring the cultus of a
saint in order to uproot some superstitious practice, we
have no reason to suspect any link between either the
name or the legend of the saint and those of the pagan
divinity he supplanted.   Remember the martyr-bishop

[1] Petit de Julleville, *op. cit.*, pp. 492, 493.

[2] *Ibid.*, pp. 504, 505.

[3 A few examples are offered in the 3d ed. — Helarius, Cyril of
Alexandria and St. Cyr, bishop Babylas at Antioch — with the
warning that "from a small number of examples one may not conclude a system." This revised section largely subsumes the following paragraph, "In those instances . . . a sacred lake," which does
not appear in the 3d ed.]

Babylas opposed to Apollo; Cyrus and John, the one a soldier, the other a monk, brought to Menouthis to combat the oracle of the goddess; and Hilary of Poitiers, confessor and pontiff, enticing the populace from the shores of a sacred lake.

I am far from denying that here and there popular devotion may occasionally have become tinged with the still vivid memories of ancient superstitions and that they have often profoundly modified the physiognomy of certain saints; that, for example, SS. Cyrus and John have ended by becoming types of healing saints, or disinterested physicians, like Cosmas and Damian, or that this latter group—of which the origin and true history will probably always evade research —have assumed in popular imagination a new and definite character as kindly genii eager to help humanity in imitation of the Dioscuri.[1] But, as far as facts are concerned, nothing authorises one to affirm that the Church has systematically encouraged these transpositions of names leaving the thing unaltered, and indeed it is most improbable that in early days she should have lent herself to such dangerous equivocations.

A few examples are necessary to put the reader on his guard concerning this seductive theory to which we have referred. Thus there is St. Elias, dedicated to whom there exist in Greece a large number of chapels built on the summit of hills and mountains. Some

---

[1] Pagans were in the habit of noting the resemblance as may be seen from various texts of the miracles of SS. Cosmas and Damian. They have been collected by Deubner, *De incubatione*, p. 77. Dr. R. Harris who has searched all hagiographic literature for replicas of Castor and Pollux has strangely overlooked Cosmas and Damian. [The omission, however, has been supplied in his later book, *The Cult of the Heavenly Twins*, Cambridge, 1906, pp. 96-104.]

writers have admitted that Elias usually takes the place of his namesake Helios, the god of the sun.[1] The assimilation is specious, but it is not borne out by the facts. It is not on the heights of Greece that the shrines of Helios were the most numerous. Moreover, sun-worship became almost completely absorbed in Apollo-worship, a fact which upsets the play upon words that is supposed to account for the numerous chapels erected to St. Elias. The history of the prophet as it is related in the Bible, his being carried up to heaven in a chariot of fire, his apparition at the side of Christ in the Transfiguration, "made of him the natural patron of high places".[2] It is probable enough that the invocation of St. Elias has taken the place in many instances of some pagan divinity, but there is nothing to prove that the divinity in question was Helios.

Moreover in order to draw conclusions from these titles they ought at least to be primitive and to belong to a time anterior to the moment when the dedication of the sanctuary was altered. But in point of fact several of those quoted are of more recent date.

At Athens, for example, the church of St. Paraskeve occupies the site of the Pompeion, a building dedicated to the organisation of religious processions,[3] as Pausanias tells us: ἐς παρασκευήν ἐστι τῶν πομπῶν.[4] Is it not obvious that there must be some connection between St. Παρασκευή, the titular saint of the church,

[1] C. Wachsmuth, *Das alte Griechenland im neuen,* Bonn, 1864, p. 23; Petit de Julleville, *op. cit.,* pp. 505-6.

[2] F. Lenormant, *Monographie de la voie sacrée Éleusinienne,* Paris, 1864, p. 452.

[3] Petit de Julleville, *op. cit.,* pp. 488, 514; A. Mommsen, *Athenæ christianæ,* p. 89.

[4] Pausanias, i., ii., 4.

and the preparation, παρασκευή, of processions which took place on the same spot? And yet we are in a position to affirm, without fear of error, that no such connection exists, and that we are in the presence of a simple coincidence the importance of which has been exaggerated by certain archæologists.

In point of fact St. Paraskeve can only have bestowed her name upon the chapel at a comparatively recent date, for she was unknown to the ancients, and liturgical documents of the tenth and eleventh centuries prove that her cultus, and still more her popularity, were posterior to that period. Need we add that even had her memory been held in honour from the most remote times, no one would have dreamt of bestowing her name on the little edifice to which Pausanias refers. If the author makes use of the word παρασκευή in this connection it was certainly not the name by which the building in question was known to the people.

It may be observed that various scholars, starting from a vague resemblance between names combined with certain topographical data, have built up regular romances on the strength of some hagiographic text. Among these productions we may class the attempt of a mythologist[1] to prove that St. Donatus took the place of Pluto, or, what comes to the same thing, of Aidoneus, King of the Molossi, whose name, every one is ready to admit, bears a resemblance to " Aios Donatos ". I should be the first to concede that we possess no really authentic records concerning St. Donatus, and moreover that various scraps of mythological lore have been made use of in order to supply him with a

[1] E. de Gubernatis, *Aidoneo e San Donato, studio di mitologia epirotica* in the *Rivista Europea*, an. v., 1874, vol. ii., pp. 425-38.

biography.   But the erudite fiction which seeks to
identify him with the god of the infernal regions merits
as little consideration as the traditional narrative.

At the back of more than one learned disquisition
on the origins of devotion to the saints one may discern the idea that the great martyrs and thaumaturgists of the ancient world, more especially those who
were early regarded as the patrons of cities, were the
direct inheritors of some tutelary deity whose altars
attracted the multitude.   The concourse of pilgrims
could thus be easily explained by the renown attached
to the spot.   The wave of popular devotion would
merely have been slightly deflected from its earlier
course, abandoning the temple of the idol in order to
flow past the Christian basilica.[1]

The instances, previously quoted, of a species of
Christian "canalisation" of the irresistible stream of
religious emotion, are by no means rare in history.
Occasionally even, we are willing to admit, the phenomenon may have been spontaneously produced, without any intervention from the leaders of the Church.
But all this does not justify us in formulating a general
law which, if true, would have a very important bearing
on the study of comparative religions.   It would not be
difficult, with the assistance of texts and documents, to
quote the name of some god or pagan hero specially
honoured in each of the Greek towns which later were
to become the centres of Christian pilgrimages.   This
only amounts to saying that one local cult replaced

---

[1] Exception might be taken on more than one point to the ideas
on this subject expressed in his posthumous volume by E. Lucius,
recently published by G. Anrich, *Die Anfänge des Heiligenkults in
der christlichen Kirche*, Tübingen, 1904. See *Analecta Bollandiana*,
vol. xxiv., p. 487.

another just as one may note everywhere that one religion succeeded to another. But it does not follow that there was any bond of connection between the two.

On the Capitoline hill in Rome there was a temple dedicated to the lord of heaven, who there received through many centuries the incense of kings and people. In later centuries pilgrims from the whole world flocked to Rome to the tomb of the prince of the apostles. Yet would any one seriously suggest that St. Peter is the direct heir of Jupiter Capitolinus?

A chapter of popular hagiography connected with the christianisation of centres of superstition by the introduction of the cultus of the saints is suggested by the passage from Gregory of Tours already quoted. We refer to water-worship, which was all the more difficult to uproot as the object of it could neither be destroyed nor removed at will. The number of wells placed under the patronage of some saint is very considerable. Certain devoted students of local history have drawn from the fact conclusions which cannot all be equally commended for accuracy and definiteness.[1] It would be a wearisome undertaking to attempt a synthesis of this mass of material, incongruous and ill-classified as it is. We shall not embark upon the task, although we cannot refrain from inquiring whether the majority of

[1] It would be difficult to draw up anything like a complete bibliography on this subject, and we do not propose to undertake the task. References to it may be found in A. Bertrand, *La religion des Gaulois*, Paris, 1897, pp. 191-212; *Bulletin archéologique du comité des travaux historiques*, 1897, pp. 150-60; 1898, pp. lxv.-lxvi. Consult also the important work by R. C. Hope, *Holy Wells: Their legends and Superstitions*, in The *Antiquary*, vol. xxi., 1890, pp. 23-31, and the following volumes; also the book by the same author, *Legendary Lore of the Holy Wells of England*, London, 1893, 222 pages.

the wells to which the names of saints are attached are in any sense witnesses to the struggle of the Church against paganism.

This is clearly not the case. It would be extremely difficult to prove that all these springs were the objects, in remote times, of superstitious worship, and it is obviously false to assert that the memory of a saint could only be connected with them by an act of ecclesiastical authority. As we have already shown, the common people never miss an opportunity of baptising the noteworthy spots in their locality, and quite naturally they bestow upon them any name that happens to occupy their minds. A well dedicated to St. Martin is not necessarily a holy well; it merely testifies to the popularity of St. Martin. One must therefore distinguish carefully between the wells which only attract attention by their name, and those which have been a centre of devotion or superstition. To this second category belong all those to which the heathen were in the habit of offering their prayers and their gifts.

IV.

Dates of festivals—Alteration of object—Difficulty of proving coincidences—A method for ascertaining dates of pagan festivals—Examples.

An important element in seeking to establish the first beginnings of a cultus is the correspondence of dates. Celebrations which attract a large concourse of people are necessarily fixed for specified days. Every one will agree that there is nothing more difficult to alter than the date of a fair or pilgrimage; in nothing does the tenacity of popular custom display itself more forcibly than in the faithful observance of festivals.

One may be perfectly certain that if a Christian people has retained anything whatever of a pagan festival it will certainly be the date.

Generally speaking, it may be said that when it was simply a question of affording some compensation to converts compelled to renounce all pagan rejoicings, they were invited to keep the feasts of the martyrs which were celebrated on the anniversary of their death. In this way St. Gregory Thaumaturgus organised annual reunions for his people in honour of the martyrs, and thus facilitated the transition from worldly pleasures to purely spiritual joys.[1]

It was far otherwise where the bishops had to combat some definitely idolatrous festival and to uproot some celebration of immemorial antiquity. When, as must frequently have happened, it was impossible for them to prevent the people coming together, the only thing for them to do was to change the purpose of the gathering, and thus sanctify the day.[2] The Bishop of Javols would never have triumphed over the superstitions that were rife in his diocese, had he been content to celebrate the feast of St. Hilary on the shores of Lake Helanus on the day appointed by the liturgy. What

---

[1] *Vita S. Gregorii Thaumat.*, Migne, P. G., vol. xlvi., p. 954.

[2 On the island of Malta at the end of the sixteenth century, a feast in honour of St. John the Baptist was celebrated, the ceremony of which had plainly showed pagan aspects. R. Wünsch, *Das Frühlingsfest der Insel Malta*, Leipzig, 1902, there saw the feast of the return of spring, christianized at an unknown period. He had reason; but I cannot follow him when he pretends to recognize in the procession of 12 March (pp. 68-70) a following of that custom already long abolished. And I like less his ideas on the ceremony of Good Friday at Athens, which for him recalls the feasts of Adonis; and not at all the minute paralleling of St. John the Baptist and Adonis which is not essential to his thesis. 3d ed.]

he did do was to celebrate it on the day of the heathen festival: *in hac solemnitate quae dei erat*, says Gregory of Tours.[1]   Hence the coincidence of the dates becomes an element of the first importance for those who are anxious to establish any bond of continuity between the pagan and the Christian feast-day.

But if all are agreed as to the importance of this class of proof, they are far from agreement as to the difficulty of demonstration.   Precise details are indispensable and it may well be asked whether the subject is of a nature to afford it.   The differences between the various calendars, the difficulty of bringing them into agreement, the multiplicity of feasts in honour of the same divinity, the liturgical divergencies in various localities, all complicate the problem of the date to such an extent as to render the assimilation almost always illusory.

Where it is merely a question of establishing a parallel between some Christian solemnity and a festival of the Roman calendar the problem is simple enough and one can arrive at definite conclusions. Thus it may freely be admitted that the greater Litanies of St. Mark's Day are a Christian continuation of the Robigalia observed on 25th April.[2]   The date, taken in conjunction with the similarity of the rite, and the identity of the object of the festival, leaves no place for reasonable doubt.

But the solution in other cases is often far less easy to arrive at.   The number of pagan festivals being very considerable, the chances of a purely fortuitous coincidence are proportionately great, and it seems

---

[1] See above, p. 170.
[2] Anrich, *Mysterienwesen*, Leipzig, 1894, p. 231; Duchesne, *Christian Worship* (Eng. tr.), pp. 261-62.

probable that the *natalis invicti*, which was celebrated on 25th December, had no influence on the choice of that day as the Feast of the Nativity of our Lord. The selection of the date would appear to have been the result of a calculation having as its basis 25th March, that being presumed to be the date of the death of Christ.[1] This last theory, which makes the cycle of the feasts of the infancy of our Lord depend upon Easter, certainly the older celebration, is more probable than the other, which rests only on an ingenious identification of date.

People have also professed to see in the Feast of the Purification a Christianised version of the Lupercalia. In point of fact this last was kept not on the 2nd of February but on the 15th.[2]

Coincidences are far more difficult to establish when it becomes a question of comparing our own calendar with that of the Greeks or Asiatics, and with very varying systems of festivals. Thus we find that the festival of the gods and the heroes was celebrated at Athens not only on a special date but on the corresponding date of each month.[3] These repeated commemorations increase very materially the possibilities of a coincidence, and it becomes obvious that we must

[1] Duchesne, *op. cit.*, pp. 247-54; Thurston, *Amer. Eccles. Rev.*, Dec. 1898, pp. 561-576. [See also an article by P. H. Grisar, *Relazione tra alcune feste cristiane antiche e alcune usanze pagane*, in *Civiltà cattolica*, ser. xvii, vol. xii, p. 450-8. 3d ed.]

[2] Marquardt, *Le culte chez les Romains*, vol. ii., pp. 179-83. A. Dufourcq in *Études sur les Gesta martyrum*, Paris, 1900, p. 207, asks himself whether the date of the feast of St. Hippolytus, 13th August, has not been fixed by that of the pagan festival *Dianæ in Aventino* (Marquardt, *op. cit.*, vol. ii., p. 373). The link he suggests between the two feasts is of the slenderest, and 13th August in undoubtedly the date of the death of St. Hippolytus. [After the Marquardt citation the 3d ed. adds: Cf. D. DeBruyne, in *Revue Bénédictine*, vol. xxxiv, p. 18-26.]

[3] Chr. Petersen, *Ueber die Geburtstagsfeier bei den Griechen*, Leipzig, 1857, pp. 313-14. See also A. Mommsen, *Feste der Stadt Athen*, Leipzig, 1898, pp. 1-5.

not hastily jump at conclusions because two feasts happen to fall on the same day.

We have already pointed out how inconclusive is the reasoning which professes to recognise, in the Christian titles of certain ancient shrines, the primitive name of the tutelary divinity of the same place. It is equally dangerous to attempt to deduce the unknown date of a pagan festival from Christian data presumed to have some sort of connection with it.[1]   The efforts already made in this direction have always appeared to me, if their authors will forgive my saying so, particularly unfortunate, in spite of the remarkable ingenuity of which they give evidence.   The following is a recent example.   A series of deductions, drawn from the survival of the worship of the Dioscuri, would seem to point to the existence from the very earliest times of a monthly festival in honour of the two heroes, which would fall, in accordance with common usage, on the corresponding date of each month, either the 18th or the 19th.   The following is the argument by which we arrive at this unexpected discovery.[2]

We start with the assertion that a whole series of saints are merely Castor and Pollux in a Christian disguise ; then the dates of their feasts are collocated in the following fashion :—

[1] M. H. Usener is of a different opinion. This is how he expresses himself: "Die christlichen Heiligen die an die Stellen von Göttern gesetzt worden sind, gestatten uns in ihrem Gedenktag die Zeit des ursprünglichen Götterfestes mit Sicherheit zu erkennen und dadurch das Wesen des Festes und der Gottheit zu ermitteln," *Archiv für Religionswissenschaft,* vol. vii., 1904, p. 14.

[2] J. Rendel-Harris, *The Dioscuri in the Christian Legends,* London, 1903, p. 62. The same author has recently published on this subject a new work which is scarcely an improvement on its predecessor: *The Cult of the Heavenly Twins,* Cambridge, 1906. See H. Thurston, S.J., in *The Month,* cviii. (1906), pp. 202-7; *Analecta Bollandiana,* 1907, no. 1. [The 3d ed. omits the reference to Rendel-Harris' 1906 work, and to Thurston's article; it adds: This is a veritable obsession of Dioscures. *Analecta Bollandiana,* vol. xxvi, p. 332-33; vol. xxxviii, p. 182-3.]

19th April.—St. Dioscorus.

19th May.—St. Polyeuctes.

18th June.—SS. Mark and Marcellianus.

19th June.—St. Judas-Thomas and SS. Gervase and Protase.

18th August.—SS. Florus and Laurus.

18th September.—St. Castor.

18th December.—St. Castulus.

19th December.—St. Polyeuctes.

I have shown elsewhere that not one of the above saints has anything whatever in common with the Dioscuri.[1] Nearly all of them are clearly defined historical personages, while their cultus is regularly established and rests on a traditional basis. Add to this the fact that no Dioscuri are to be met with in the martyrologies for 19th April. It is the 18th May that must be meant, for on that date the memory of St. Dioscorus, lector, was celebrated in Egypt. The 19th of May is not the date of the martyrdom of St. Polyeuctes. This saint is the second in the group of Timotheus and Polyeuctes inscribed in the Syriac martyrology for 20th May, and it is only by the commonplace blunder of a copyist that the names have been repeated among the martyrs of the 19th.

But putting aside all these difficulties, admitting even that there may have been some sort of link—which as a matter of fact there was not—between the Dioscuri and the saints already enumerated, let us suppose that their feasts were all celebrated on the same day of the month, the 18th. Should we be justified in concluding that in all probability the festival of the Dioscuri was fixed for the 18th of every month? Far from it, for it is obvious at a glance that the date of the 18th in the

---

1 *Analecta Bollandiana*, vol. xxiii., pp. 427-32.

Julian Calendar does not correspond with the 18th in the Greek, Syrian or Asiatic calendars, in accordance with which the festival of Castor and Pollux, had it been celebrated monthly, would in the first instance have been fixed.

We have here a further example of the necessity of not being satisfied with a mere coincidence of dates.[1] One of the arguments brought forward to prove that SS. Florus and Laurus are merely the Dioscuri under another name, is the date of their feast, 18th August, for St. Helena is also commemorated on this same day. Helena, in the fable, is the sister of Castor and Pollux. Give Florus and Laurus their correct names, and you will then discover in the martyrology an authentic feast of the Dioscuri and their sister.

The matter, however, is not quite so simple as it appears. It so happens that the collocation of Florus and Laurus with Helena is entirely fortuitous. No single Latin martyrology makes any mention of Florus and Laurus, who are only known to Greek tradition, whereas no Greek synaxary names Helena on 18th August ; she is always associated with Constantine on 11th May, and does not appear in any other place. It was the accidental result of a compilation composed of Greek and Latin elements that brought Helena and the Greek martyrs together at the same date in the martyrology. This fortuitous collocation does not go back further than the sixteenth century, a simple observation which should suffice to eliminate from the ancient calendar the supposed festival of the Dioscuri corresponding to 18th August.

We shall have something to say later concerning the

---

[1] Harris, *op. cit.*, pp. 1-19. See also *Analecta Bollandiana*, vol. cit., pp. 428-29; and compare *The Month*, March, 1907, pp. 225 ff.

theory which has resulted in fixing 7th January as the date of the festival of the "Epiphany of Dionysus" in Bithynia.

In order to establish a connection between St. Pelagia, specially honoured on 8th October, and Aphrodite, much emphasis has been laid,[1] among other reasons, on the date of the festival, supported by the text of an inscription at Aegæ in Cilicia, in the following terms:—

Θεῷ Σεβαστῷ Καίσαρι καὶ Ποσειδῶνι ἀσφαλείῳ καὶ Ἀφροδείτῃ Εὐπλοίᾳ.[2]

Euploia is the title of the Aphrodite of Cnidus. It might at least be expected that the first thing to prove would be that the goddess was honoured on 8th October. Not at all. One solitary date has been verified in connection with the worship of the Pelasgic Venus,[3] and that has reference to a local festival, the dedication of a temple and statue to the goddess at Nigra Corcyra (Curzola) on 1st May, in the year 193 of the Christian era. But it is pointed out that Poseidon is mentioned in the same votive inscription, and that in point of fact the 8th of each month was dedicated to Poseidon. I must confess that the argument would make but a feeble impression upon me, even if it could be proved that the God of the sea had his festival on the 8th of the month in Cilicia as well as at Athens.

1 H. Usener, *Legenden der heiligen Pelagia*, Bonn, 1879, p. xxi.
2 C. I. G., 4443.
3 C. I. L., iii., 3066, *Signia Vrsa Signi Symphori templum Veneri Pelagiæ a solo fecit et signum ipsius deæ posuit Falcone et Claro cos. k. mais.*

V.

The legends which offer the most vulnerable points, those which in their entirety or in certain portions appear to reflect pagan traditions, are those which have most attracted the attention of critics, and it is in fact mainly through such legends that they have attempted to connect a certain number of the saints—and not the least celebrated among them—with paganism.   We must follow them upon their own ground and attempt to outline the methods which should be applied to this branch of research.

If people merely wish to assert that among a series of legends certain features are to be found that were already in circulation among the nations of classical antiquity, we have nothing to say against their view, and indeed when we ourselves were treating generally of the origins of our hagiographic narratives we quoted sufficient examples of such adaptations to leave no room for doubt on the point.[1]   The further our researches in the domain of comparative literature can be carried, the greater will be the number of these parallels, and people will be surprised to discover in mediæval lore so many remnants [2] of classical antiquity.

[1] See above, pp. 30-35.

[2] In order to convey some idea of the discoveries that may still be made in this direction, I will quote a page from the collection, justly celebrated in the Middle Ages, in which St. Gregory has brought together so many quaint narratives, stories of saints, pious anecdotes, visions and revelations with which, with charming can-dour, he entertains his deacon Peter. The thirty-sixth chapter of book iv. of the *Dialogues* bears the curious title, *De his qui quasi*

But whether such material was used in its raw state or whether it was first given a Christian colouring, there is, as a general rule, no reason for talking of pagan infiltration or even of pagan survivals. It is not the religious element which is responsible in these cases, it is the stream of literary activity carrying along with it the debris of earlier ages.

The problem to be solved is whether a Christian legend perpetuates in any sense a religious incident appertaining to paganism, in other words, whether it is the expression of an ancient cultus, surviving under a Christian form. One must, therefore, in the first place, put aside all legends that are independent of any religious observance. In hagiographic collections such as menologies and passionaries and in compilations such as synaxaries and martyrologies there are many names and documents which represent merely a literary tradition. These may well date from classic times

---

per errorem educi videntur e corpore. One of the incidents related by St. Gregory thoroughly illustrates the title. The saint had gathered it from the lips of a certain Stephen who related it as his own experience. Stephen had died and saw his soul conducted to hell. Brought before "the judge who presided there" he was refused admittance. "That is not the man I sent for," said the judge, "it was Stephen the blacksmith." Forthwith the soul of the dead man was returned to his body and the blacksmith, his namesake and neighbour, died (Migne, P. L., vol. lxxvii., p. 384). It is impossible to be mistaken in this matter. The friend of St. Gregory was an unscrupulous person who boasted of being the hero of a tale he had read in some book. Without speaking of St. Augustine, he might have read it in Plutarch, or still better in Lucian's *Philopseudes,* in which Cleomenes relates in similar fashion how having been taken to Hades before the tribunal of Pluto he was sent back to earth again, and one of his friends, the blacksmith Demylus, was taken in his stead. See E. Rohde, *Psyche,* 2nd edition, vol. ii., p. 363; L. Radermacher, *Aus Lucians Lügenfreund* in *Festschrift Theodor Gomperz dargebracht,* Vienna, 1902, p. 204. [The 3d ed. adds a reference to A. Jülicher, *Augustinus und die Topik der Aretalogie,* in Hermes, vol. liv, 1919, p. 94-103.]

without our having to discuss the possible influence of paganism.

Our business is with saints whose cultus is proved by a church erected in their honour, by a regularly observed festival or by relics offered to the veneration of the faithful.   Such cases may come under three categories.

In the first place, it may happen that legends whose dependence upon pagan antiquity is admitted to have been purely literary may end by giving birth to a cultus.   In its origin the History of the Seven Sleepers was a pious romance which, little by little, left the sphere of literature to pass into the domain of liturgy.[1]   The heroes of this wholly imaginative work end by being honoured as saints of whom the burial-place is shown, and whose relics are in request. Similarly, Barlaam and Joasaph, the principal personages of a Buddhist romance, eventually, after long delays, attained to similar honours.   But their artificially created cultus does not bury its roots in the distant past of Buddhism any more than that of the Seven Sleepers is a continuation of a religious episode of the polytheism of Greece.

In the second place, a legend possessing pagan features may have for its subject an authentic saint whose cultus dates from a period anterior to the legend and is quite independent of it.   The problem suggested by these circumstances is not always easy to solve.   It may be that the fabulous element has become mingled with the history of the saint merely in virtue of that inevitable law which connects legendary incidents totally devoid of any special religious interest with the name of any illustrious personage.   But it is also possible that the

1 *Acta SS.*, July, vol. vi., p. 376.

saint has inherited the attributes of some local deity together with the honours paid to him. No point is more difficult to unravel in practice.

We must not indeed forget that a great number of practices and expressions and stories, beyond doubt religious in their origin, and implying, if we press them, doctrines that were clearly polytheistic, have by degrees wholly lost their original significance, and have become either mere embellishments or conventional formulæ devoid of objectionable meaning. The graceful little genii that painters and sculptors love to set climbing among the festoons and vine-branches are mere decorative motifs, just as the *Dis Manibus Sacrum* was written quite guilelessly at the head of Christian inscriptions on tombs without people seeing in the fact anything save the obligatory prelude to an epitaph.[1]

Indeed the history of the saints supplies many examples that allow us to appreciate the exact value of certain facts which at first sight would appear to be dependent on religion and worship but which in reality are only connected with them by a very slender thread.

The Byzantines sometimes named stars after the saints whose feasts corresponded with their rising. Thus the star of 26th October became the star of St. Demetrius, that of 11th November was named after St. Menas, that of the 14th was the star of St. Philip.[2] It is difficult to see in these appellations anything further than the expression of a date, and I should not like to assert that the Byzantines believed that the

[1] F. Becker, *Die heidnische Weiheformel, D. M.,* Gera, 1881, pp. 65-67.

[2] *Catalogus codicum astrologorum græcorum II.: Codices venetos descripserunt,* G. Kroll and A. Olivieri, Brussels, 1900, p. 214.

saints ruled over the stars or that they attributed to them in the firmament functions from which the gods had been deposed.[1]   It seems to me clear that, putting aside certain superstitious customs,[2] they talked of the star of St. Nicholas just as we should speak of the Michaelmas term.   When sailors referred to the autumn equinoctial gales as the " Cyprianic winds" the expression [3] no doubt testified to the popularity of St. Cyprian, but in no way implied any practice of piety.

Hence it does not follow because some characteristic belongs both to mythology and to the legend of a saint that therefore the saint must be regarded as a deity in disguise.   It would scarcely be logical to raise doubts concerning the existence of St. George merely because of his legend, and it is highly temerarious to affirm positively that in his person "the Church has converted and baptised the pagan hero Perseus".[4]   When the origin of the shrines of St. George has become better known we shall perhaps be enabled to replace him on the historical footing which hagiographers have done so much to undermine.   No one has, however, been able to prove hitherto that his cultus among Christians was a mere prolongation of some pagan devotion.[5]

The majority of the hagiographic legends that are adorned with mythological rags and tatters appertain in all 'probability to saints who have nothing else in

1 Cumont, *Catalogus*, etc., vol. iv., 1903, p. 159.

2 See above, p. 159.

3 Procopius, *Bell. Vand.*, i., 21; Τὸν χειμῶνα οἱ ναῦται . . . ὁμωνύμως τῇ πανηγύρει προσαγορεύειν εἰώθασιν, ἐπεὶ ἐς τὸν καιρὸν ἐπισκήπτειν φιλεῖ ἐφ᾽ οὗ ταύτην οἱ Λίβυες ἄγειν ἐς ἀεὶ τὴν ἑορτὴν νενομίκασι. *Cf.* i., 20, Dindorf, pp. 393, 397.

4 E. S. Hartland, *The Legend of Perseus*, vol. iii., London, 1896, p. 38.

[5 In the 3d ed. these two sentences have been further developed and he draws upon his *Légendes grecques des saints militaires*, pp. 45-50, and 75; the cultus of St. George is perfectly localized at Lydda in Palestine, and the episode of the dragon, he pointedly observes, does not enter into any of the ancient legends of St. George.]

common with pagan deities. Yet this is not a universal law. Certain very well-authenticated saints have developed in certain shrines such special features that in the cultus paid to them it is difficult to deny the survival of a pagan ritual or belief. Whatever may have been the primitive history of SS. Cosmas and Damian they were represented at an early age as the successors of the Dioscuri, and the honours paid to them at certain of their shrines undoubtedly betray points of contact with pre-existing forms of worship.[1]

For a long time sailors also had their own special ways of honouring St. Nicholas[2] and St. Phocas,[3] and of attributing to them powers which remind one of the heroes of antiquity. One might therefore describe these saints as the successors of Poseidon. No doubt little by little the figures of the holy protectors took the place of the sea god, but the phenomenon is due to accidental circumstances, and even 'when heir to a pagan god the saint none the less preserves his individuality.[4]

We have still to consider a third case, that of the legend which reveals purely and simply the continuity of a religious tradition, to-day Christian, yesterday idolatrous and superstitious. It is no longer a question of deciding whether an authenticated saint has assimilated some of the characteristics or even the general physiognomy of an earlier deity, but of ascertaining by a careful study of all the narratives concerning the saint

[1 See *Les recueils antiques de miracles des saints*, p. 8-18. 3d ed.]

2 The sailors of Aegina wish each other a good crossing in the formula, "May St. Nicholas be seated at thy helm". E. Curtius, *Die Volksgrüsse der Neugriechen*, in *Sitzungsberichte der k. Preussischen Akademie*, 1887, p. 154.

3 L. Radermacher, *St. Phokas*, in *Archiv für Religionswissenschaft*, vol. vii, 1904, p. 445-452.

[4 The scholarly author of *Hagios Nikolaos*, Leipzig, 1913-17, M. Anrich, arrives at the same conclusion after a thorough examination of the question — vol. ii., p. 505. 3d ed.]

whether he himself is not a god or pagan hero raised to the altars after a decent transformation.

The distinctions we have sought to establish may seem to some over-subtle, but to ourselves they appear indispensable unless we wish to be satisfied with superficial resemblances and far-fetched comparisons. In order to realise the difficulties of mythological investigations, based upon the analysis of legends of saints, it will suffice to examine thoroughly one or two individual cases over which scholars have already exercised their wits and to measure the results of a criticism as searching as it is ingenious. We propose to restrict ourselves to the legends of St. Lucian [1] and St. Pelagia, [2] and the interpretation which we shall suggest is very different from that which has been current for some years past.

St. Lucian is one of the most celebrated martyrs of the fourth century. He died at Nicomedia, 7th January, 312, and his body was conveyed to Drepanum, a town on the coast of Bithynia which was re-named Helenopolis by Constantine in honour of his mother. Nothing could be better authenticated than the fact of of his martyrdom, nothing more firmly established than his cultus, witnessed to by the basilica of Helenopolis as well as by literary documents.

Among the principal testimonies to the history of St. Lucian we have that of Eusebius, [3] a panegyric by St. John Chrysostom, [4] and a celebrated legend [5] incorporated in the menology of Metaphrastes, but dating undoubtedly from a much earlier period.

---

1 H. Usener, *Die Sintfluthsagen*, Bonn, 1899, pp. 168-80.
2 *Id., Legenden der heiligen Pelagia*, Bonn, 1879, xxiv., 62 pp.
3 *Hist. Eccles.*, ix., 6.
4 Migne, P. G., vol. 1., pp. 519-26.
5 *Ibid.*, vol. cxiv., pp. 397-416.

We need not stop here to discuss the life of St. Lucian [1] in its general features, but it is necessary to dwell upon certain details of the legends which have been made use of in support of the theory which it is our intention to examine.

In the first place, the author of the passion relates that the martyr suffered torture by hunger for fourteen entire days: τέσσαρες καὶ δέκα τὰς πάσας ἡμέρας. [2] After the first few days he announced to his disciples that he would celebrate with them the Feast of the Theophany and would die on the following day. This prophecy came true: in the presence of the emperor's representatives, filled with amazement at his prolonged endurance, he repeated three times " I am a Christian," and expired. [3]

Others affirm, writes the chronicler, that while still alive he was flung into the sea. The Emperor Maximian, exasperated by his constancy, had commanded that he should be cast into the waves with a heavy stone fastened to his arm, so that he should be deprived for ever of the honours of Christian burial. And he remained in the sea fourteen days, the precise number he had spent in prison; τέσσαρες καὶ δέκα τὰς ὅλας ἡμέρας. On the fifteenth day a dolphin is supposed to have brought his sacred body back to land, and to have died immediately after depositing his precious burden. [4]

No one can fail to recognise in this marvellous incident one of the most popular of all legendary themes of classic antiquity. The dolphin, the friend of man,

---

[1] The best work we possess on the Acts of St. Lucian is that of Pio Franchi, *Di un frammento di una Vita di Costantino*, taken from *Studi e documenti di storia e diritto*, vol. xviii., 1897, pp. 24-45.

[2] *Passio S. Luciani*, n. 12, Migne, P. G., vol. cxiv., p. 409.

[3] *Ibid.*, n. 15.

[4] *Ibid.*, n. 16.

who bears him, living or dead, upon his back, is the
subject of more than one poetic fable and of a whole
host of works of art.[1]   Melicertes, Hesiod, Arion—in
this latter case also the dolphin expired on the sand—
were all popular types, and there is nothing surprising
in the fact that so poetic a legend should have passed
into the realms of hagiography.   The dolphin further
plays a part in the lives of St. Martinian,[2] St. Callis-
tratus,[3] St. Arianus [4] and others.   This circumstance
alone is sufficient to prove that the dolphin episode in
the legend before us is purely adventitious and has
only an accidental, and in no sense a mysterious, connection with its history, even should we fail to ascertain the precise circumstances under which St. Lucian
came to be associated with this reminiscence of a
classical myth.

It has been suggested that dolphins may have been
carved on the sarcophagus of the martyr, and that
this decorative design may of itself have sufficed to set
popular imagination working.[5]   This explanation combined with the mythical tradition which had not been
lost at that period and which the sight of the dolphins
would recall, is not lightly to be set aside.   But it has
the disadvantage of being a pure hypothesis suggested
by the necessities of the case.   In point of fact we

---

[1] O. Keller, *Thiere des klassischen Alterthums*, Innsbruck, 1887,
pp. 211-35 ;A. Marx, *Griechische Märchen von dankbaren Tieren*,
Stuttgart, 1889, p. 1 ff.

[2] *Acta SS.*, Feb., vol. ii., p. 670.

[3] *Ibid.*, Sept., vol. vii., p. 192.

[4] *Ibid.*, March, vol. i., p. 757; *Synaxarium ecclesiæ Constantinopolitanæ*, p. 308.

[5] P. Batiffol, *Étude d'hagiographie arienne. La Passion de saint
Lucien d'Antioche*, in *Compte-rendu du Congrès scientifique international des catholiques*, Brussels, 1894, vol. ii., pp. 181-86.

possess no information concerning the decoration of the sarcophagus of St. Lucian.

A second explanation has been brought forward which possesses the merit of being at least founded on fact.[1] St. Lucian was martyred at Nicomedia, yet his basilica is situated, not in that town, but across the gulf, at Helenopolis. The translation of the sacred remains probably left no impression on popular memory, and later on the inhabitants explained the anomaly by the familiar device of a miraculous intervention of which tradition furnished them with so many examples.

The presence of the dolphin in the Nicomedian legend has, however, suggested conclusions of a far more radical nature to our school of mythologists.

Note, they say, the persistence with which the number 15 recurs in connection with the name of St. Lucian. Putting aside, suggestive as it is, the fact that among the Greeks his feast has been transferred to the 15th of October, let us study the legend itself. The saint expired after fifteen days of suffering; the dolphin brought his body to shore on the fifteenth day; he died the day after the Epiphany which was the 15th of the month of Dionysius, and observe that at Helenopolis his feast is celebrated on the eve which is precisely the 15th of the month of Tishri.[2]

And what meaning has the dolphin? It is one of the attributes of Dionysus. And why is it connected with the memory of St. Lucian? Because his feast coincided with the feast of Dionysus which was observed in Bithynia on the 15th of the month of Dionysius. Therefore it was a pagan feast which the people

---

[1] P. Franchi, *op. cit.*, pp. 39-43.
[2] In the Syriac Martyrology. See De Rossi-Duchesne, *Martyrologium Hieronymianum* in *Acta SS.*, Nov., vol. ii., p. lii.

still remembered and which they associated with this Christian commemoration.   The dolphin of the legend of St. Lucian is a witness to the affection of the new converts for their ancient superstitions.

Such is in brief the reasoning of these learned critics.

One would of course be bound to discuss these weighty conclusions, if in point of fact we knew from other sources that the great solemnity in honour of Dionysus was really celebrated on the 15th of the month, coinciding with 7th January, and also that a legend of Dionysus, current in Bithynia, was one of the numerous replicas of the history of the dolphin bringing to shore the body of Melicertes.   But we know nothing of the kind.   It is to the legend of St. Lucian itself that we are referred for the evidence of these statements.[1]

What can we think of this logical structure save that it is destitute of any sound basis and that not only do we discern no sort of link between St. Lucian and Dionysus, but, in studying the matter closely, we find that Dionysus disappears completely from the scene, to leave us in the presence of one of the most ordinary phenomena of folk-lore in all countries?   It seems superfluous to insist on the feebleness of the argument—it should rather be called the suggestion—drawn from the number 15, which itself has not even been established beyond question.   The Arian commentary on Job, which would appear to contain an echo of the same tradition

1 "Durch die legende des Lukianos wissen wir das die Bithynier die epiphanie des Dionysos am xv. des auf wintersonnenwende folgenden monats Dionysios feierten. Wir wissen daraus auch, unter welchen mythischen bilde die erscheinung des gottes geschaut wurde. Als entseelter auf dem rucken eines gewaltigen delphin zum lande gebracht, das war das bild Bithynischer epiphanie." Usener, vol. cit., p. 178.

as the passion of St. Lucian, bears another figure: *Hic namque beatus duodecim diebus supra testas pollinas extensus, tertia decima die est consummatus.*[1]

Thus the legend of St. Lucian involves no sort of reflection upon the Christians of Bithynia. It would justify no one in suspecting the purity of their faith or in attempting to prove that they had more difficulty than other people in forgetting Dionysus. Moreover, it remains to be proved that the great festival of the god really did coincide with the day after the Christian Epiphany, the day of the martyrdom of St. Lucian. For, so far, neither his own legend nor any historical text has furnished any proof of the assertion.

The legend of St. Pelagia has been the starting-point of a most laborious inquiry, conducted on the same principles, of which the results, although accepted by many scholars who have not felt bound to investigate them further, are certainly surprising. Its authors profess to have discovered that the Church continued, though admittedly under a very modified form, to pay homage to Aphrodite, to Venus, to the goddess of carnal pleasure and animal fecundity.

Pelagia, known also as Margarito, was, owing to the splendour of her pearls and jewels, one of the most celebrated as also one of the most corrupt of the dancing-girls of Antioch. One day she entered the church while Bishop Nonnus was exhorting the faithful. Touched by grace she begged for baptism, and when she quitted the white robe of the newly baptised she donned a hair shirt and a man's tunic, and left Antioch in secret in order to hide herself on Mount Olivet

---

[1] "For this blessed saint after lying for twelve days upon a bed of minute shells breathed his last upon the thirteenth day." Migne, P. G., vol. xvii., p. 471.

outside Jerusalem. There she lived for three years in a little cell under the name of Pelagius, after which she entered upon the reward of her life of penance. The Greek Church celebrates her feast on 8th October.

Under this form, and taken by itself, the history of Pelagia offers no very improbable features, and it would certainly not be easy to draw from it any conclusions favourable to a mythological survival. But its critics compare it with other legends with which it constitutes a whole, of which the pagan origin and character are according to them clearly manifest.

In the first place, on 8th October, a commemoration is made of another Pelagia of Antioch, a virgin martyr, whose heroic death was related by St. John Chrysostom in a panegyric preached in her honour.

The same day recalls the martyrdom of a third Pelagia, of Tarsus, who preferred death by fire in a brazen bull to the love of the emperor's son.[1]

Pelagia of Tarsus reappears at Seleucia on 22nd August under the name of Anthusa, with a history[2] of which the incidents, if not the closing scenes, recall the preceding version.

St. Marina of Antioch, in Pisidia, commemorated by the Greeks on 17th July,[3] and St. Margaret of Antioch by the Latins on 20th July,[4] suffered death like Pelagia of Tarsus, for having scorned the advances of the judge, the prefect Olybrius.

---

1 The three legends are summarised in *Synaxarium ecclesiæ Constantinopolitanæ*, pp. 117-20. The sources in *Bibl. hag. græc.*, pp. 105-6.

2 Published by H. Usener in the *Analecta Bollandiana*, vol. xii., pp. 10-41.

3 H. Usener, *Acta Sanctæ Marinæ et Christophori*, Bonn, 1886, pp. 15-46.

4 The different versions of the Passion of St. Margaret, *Bibl. hag. lat.*, 5303-10.

It is easy to trace the connection of yet another group of saints with the preceding.

St. Margaret, commemorated on 8th October, flies from her nuptial chamber disguised as a man. She hides herself in a monastery where she passes under the name of Pelagius. Accused of having seduced a nun she suffers the penalty for a sin she could not have committed. Her innocence is only established after her death. She receives the name of Reparata.[1]

Maria, or Marina (12th Feb.), also enters a monastery disguised as a man. One day the daughter of an innkeeper travelling in the neighbourhood accuses the supposed monk of being the father of her baby. Marina is driven from the monastery and forced to maintain the child. The severity of her penances re-open the doors of the cloister to her, but only after her death is the discovery made that she has been the victim of calumny.[2]

St. Eugenia (24th Dec.) ruled as abbot over a monastery of monks. She also was falsely accused by a woman before the tribunal of her father who was prefect of Egypt.[3] It is also in Egypt that we meet with a St. Apollinaria (5th Jan.) who hides herself under the name of Dorothea, and suffers a similar misfortune.[4] Euphrosyne of Alexandria (25th Sept.) adopts the name of Smaragdos and lives peacefully in a community of monks until at length she is recognised by her father.[5]

Theodora of Alexandria (11th Sept.) convicted of infidelity, retires into a monastic house for men in

---

[1] *Acta SS.,* Oct., vol. iv., p. 24.
[2] Migne, P. G., vol. cxv., p. 348 ff.
[3] *Ibid.,* vol. cxvi., p. 609 ff.
[4] *Acta SS.,* Jan., vol. i., pp. 257-61.
[5] A. Boucherie, in *Analecta Bollandiana,* vol. ii., pp. 196-205.

order to do penance.   She is denounced for misconduct
and rehabilitated after her death.[1]

It is clear that all these legends are interconnected,
as may be seen partly by the similarity in the names :
Pelagia, Marina, Pelagius or Margaret recalling the
surname of Margarito given to the courtesan of Antioch,
and partly by the theme: a woman disguised as a
monk and keeping the secret of her sex until death.
Sometimes the theme is complicated by the further
theme of calumny, which, under the circumstances, is
only a logical development of the main idea.

Before indicating the series of deductions by means
of which folk-lorists have succeeded in recognising
Venus or Aphrodite in the person of St. Pelagia, let
us try to determine the starting-point of the whole
series of legends which we have just summarised.

In the fourth century the Church of Antioch celebrated on 8th October the feast of a St. Pelagia,[2] a
quite historical personage, concerning whom both St.
John Chrysostom[3] and St. Ambrose[4] have furnished
us with information.   But her history in no way re-
sembles that of the penitent courtesan, and there is
nothing in it to suggest anything in the nature of mas-
querading.   Pelagia is a maiden of fifteen who sees

1 K. Wessely, *Die Vita S. Theodoræ*, Vienna, 1889, pp. 25-44.
We refrain from mentioning Porphyria of Tarsus, who is not a saint,
or Andronicus and Athanasia who, in our opinion, burden M.
Usener's list quite superfluously. He might, however, have included
in it St. Papula who lived with some monks of the diocese of Tours
and was placed by them at the head of their monastery. Gregory
of Tours, *In gloria confessorum*, xvi.

2 Date furnished by the Syriac Martyrology, *Acta SS.*, Nov., vol.
ii., p. lxi.

3 Migne, P. G., vol. l., pp. 579-85.

4 *De virginibus*, iii., 7, 33; Migne, P. L., vol. xvi., p. 229; *Epist.*
xxvii., *ad Simplicianum*, 38; *ibid.*, p. 1093.

her father's house in the hands of the soldiery. To escape from their outrages she begs for a delay, the time to array herself in her finest robes. And while the soldiers are waiting below for their victim she flings herself from the roof and preserves her virginity by a voluntary death.

Should we then admit the existence of a second St. Pelagia of Antioch, the penitent sinner? The identity of dates, 8th October, gives food for reflection. An admirable passage from St. John Chrysostom may profitably be recalled at this juncture.

In his sixty-seventh Homily on St. Matthew, the saintly doctor recalls the history of a celebrated actress whose name he does not give, and who came to Antioch from one of the most corrupt cities of Phœnicia, having become so notorious, thanks to her evil life, that her fame had spread as far as Cilicia and Cappadocia. She brought ruin to a large number of persons, and the very sister of the emperor fell a victim to her seductions. Suddenly she resolved to reform her life, and, under the influence of grace, she wholly renounced her evil ways. She was admitted to the sacred mysteries, and after her baptism lived for long years in the strictest austerity, wearing a hair-shirt, and shutting herself up in a voluntary prison, where she allowed no one to visit her.

Nothing justifies us in assuming that this anonymous penitent became after death the object of an ecclesiastical cultus, indeed the way in which St. John Chrysostom speaks of her seems to imply the contrary. But it may be taken as certain that the narrative known under the name of Pelagia's Repentance is neither more nor less than an adaptation of the incident related by St. John Chrysostom. The editor, who bestows on himself the name of James, no doubt considered it too simple and therefore introduced into it the idea of the disguise with which more than one tale would have made him familiar.

It is very difficult to decide whether the so-called James originally intended to write an edifying romance in which a heroine named Pelagia should play the leading part, or whether, by means of fresh data, he proposed to write the legend of the venerated saint of Antioch. We know from illustrious examples both how quickly historical tradition concerning local saints may disappear beneath the action of legendary compositions, and also how little hagiographers hesitate in making alterations that render their subjects almost unrecognisable. However this may be, whether or no in the mind of the so-called James there was any identity between his heroine and St. Pelagia of Antioch, it was inevitable that such identity should soon be assumed to exist.[1]

The further legend of Pelagia of Tarsus in Cilicia appears to us to be the result of the double tradition that surrounded the name of Pelagia. In certain aspects she recalls the courtesan of Antioch, whose reputation, as we are expressly told by St. John Chrysostom, had penetrated as far as Cilicia, and who had also had relations with the imperial family. On the

---

[1] It must not be maintained that no confusion has existed, nor can the three saints bearing the name of Pelagia, and entered in the synaxaries for 8th October, be produced in support of such a contention. The similarity of the date is in itself sufficient to explain the error. The three notices referring to the three namesakes are the outcome of a very ordinary proceeding among compilers of synaxaries. Whenever they met with two traditions concerning one and the same saint which were not easy to reconcile, they had no hesitation in resolving him into two distinct people.

other hand, Pelagia of Tarsus was a virgin, and in that, as in her martyrdom, she recalls the primitive Pelagia whose cultus was established as early as the fourth century.

The history of Pelagia in its double form proved highly successful and gave rise to an amazing wealth of legendary lore of which other examples may be found in hagiographic literature. The version by the self-styled James, at once the most interesting and the most highly coloured, is that which has enjoyed the greatest popularity. The true personality of the saint of Antioch, shadowy at the outset, soon disappeared entirely in the interest taken in her legend. This latter lost by degrees every vestige of historic fact; even the account of the conversion became eliminated and the purely legendary residuum passed under various names, thus degenerating into the primitive form of a tale strictly so called, thanks to which we have the saints Mary or Marina, Apollinaria, Euphrosyne and Theodora, who are simply literary replicas of the Pelagia of the self-styled James; or else, as in the case of St. Eugenia, the theme of a woman hiding her sex was tacked on to other narratives having for their hero some historic personage.

We have dealt at length with this development, which we regard as a somewhat commonplace phenomenon to be explained by the normal action of the legendary ferment. If there is any item of religious interest to be deduced from all this, it is the fact that a traditional cultus may have the life crushed out of it by legend. But the cultus in this instance was Christian, so too was the subsequent legend, although mingled with elements drawn from the domain of general literature. Nowhere does a pagan influence make itself felt.

Such, however, as may be supposed, is not the interpretation accepted by those who profess to identify Pelagia with Aphrodite.

After having glanced over the series of narratives of which we have given a summary, the conclusion is arrived at that "this bird's-eye view must give rise, even in the most prejudiced minds, to the conviction that one and the same divinity reappears in the multiple variety of these legends like a trunk despoiled of its branches; thus the image that was profoundly impressed upon the soul of the people, though banished from its temples, continued to draw from its secret roots sustenance for the new branches that were shooting out on every side. . . . The Hellenism of the Imperial epoque contained but one conception which could have produced all these legendary forms: that of Aphrodite. It was necessary to tear from the hearts of the faithful the dangerous image which personified carnal beauty; it was accepted as it was, but purified in the fire of repentance and suffering in order to render it worthy of heaven." [1]

Clearly the point now is to prove that Aphrodite or Venus is indeed no other than the heroine of our legends.

Nothing, it seems, is more simple. Aphrodite was the goddess of the sea, and she is known under a profusion of titles which recall this quality: Aigaia, Epipontia, Thalassaia, Pontia, Euploia, and finally Pelagia, of which Marina is merely a translation.

And this is the whole kernel of the demonstration; and as, in point of fact, nothing is to be drawn from the dates of the festivals it is the whole of the argu-

[1] Usener, *Legenden der heiligen Pelagia*, p. 20.

ment.[1] Is it needful to add that I consider it a weak one?

If only the name of Pelagia had been a rare or unusual one among women, if it had been less well known at Antioch, the common home of the various versions, or again, if the title of Pelagia had been one of the popular epithets applied to Aphrodite, there might have been some excuse for this loose reasoning. But only one solitary example [2] of a Venus Pelagia and two of a Venus Marina, both supplied by Horace,[3] are to be discovered, whereas there is every reason to believe that Pelagia was quite a common name both at Antioch and elsewhere.[4]

Doubtless we shall be excused from dwelling on other comparisons which are intended to support the main contention. Thus *Anthusa* of Seleucia is compared with the Aphrodite *Anthera* of Knossos; *Porphyria* of Tyre with the Venus *Purpurina* of Rome; *Margarita* with the Venus Genitrix because Cæsar dedicated to her a cuirass studded with pearls.[5] What erudition wasted on a futile task!

We cannot however neglect a further consideration produced in support of the theory we are combating, one that is really ingenious and intended to demonstrate an unequivocal trace of the worship of Aphrodite under one of its most monstrous developments, in the very heart of Christianity. Attention is specially

1 The question of the date has been already discussed, p. 185.

2 C. I. L., iii., 3066. *Cf.* Preller-Robert, *Griechische Mythologie,* vol. i., 1894, pp. 364-65. Nothing on the subject among the Greek poets, C. F. H. Bruchmann, *Epitheta deorum quæ apud poetas græcos leguntur,* Leipzig, 1893, p. 68.

3 See T. B. Carter, *Epitheta deorum quæ apud poetas latinos leguntur,* Leipzig, 1902, p. 102.

4 C. I. G., 3369, 3956, 9497.

5 Usener, *op. cit.,* pp. xxi-xxii.

drawn in the Pelagian legends to the contrast between pleasure and penance, between lust and chastity, and to the ever-recurrent theme of sex-disguise. The object of this is to bring us back to the goddess of Amathus in Cyprus, who could be regarded at will as Aphrodite or Aphroditos, and who wore the dress of a woman with the beard of a man. In the sacrifices offered at this shrine the men were dressed as women and the women as men.[1] It was the worship of the Hermaphrodite. The legend of Pelagia, it is suggested, has retained the imprint of this; but the cultus continues formally within the Church; the bearded woman has been raised to the altars. In Rome it is St. Galla;[2] in Spain, St. Paula;[3] and in other places SS. Liberata, Wilgefortis, Kümmernis, Ontkommer, etc.[4]

I have already pointed out that the incident of sex-dissimulation is a most ordinary theme in circulation in every literature; and as for the supposed replicas of the Hermaphrodite, they could not have been more ill-chosen. Can any one seriously bring forward the case of Galla, whose history, told by St. Gregory, is of the most vulgar kind? Physicians, in order to induce her to marry again, assured her that if she did not do so she would grow a beard, and so it came to pass.[5] Paula is an obscure saint of Avila whose history is a repetition of that of Wilgefortis. This grotesque legend, however, is very far from possessing the mysterious origin which some people are anxious to attribute to it. It took its rise, as has already been shown, from the diffusion of the picture of the *Volto*

1 Usener, *op. cit.*, p. xxiii.
2 *Acta SS.*, Oct., vol. iii., pp. 147-63.
3 *Ibid.*, Feb., vol. iii., p 174.
4 *Ibid.*, July, vol. v., pp. 50-70.
5 St. Gregory, *Dial.*, iv., p. 13

Santo of Lucca, and is merely a coarse interpretation of an unusual iconographic type.[1]

VI.

Mythological names—Other suspicious names—Iconographic parallels
—The Blessed Virgin—"Saints on horseback".

In the preceding pages it has been made clear that saints' names play a certain *rôle* in the researches of mythologists, and that not infrequently a real importance is attributed to them in the question of pagan survivals. Thus we have been assured that "the Greek nations of the continent, the Islands and Asia Minor turned with ardour towards the ancient gods of the Hellenes, on whom they were content to bestow new and often very transparent names: Pelagia, Marina, Porphyria, Tychon, Achilleios, Mercurios," etc.[2] It is easy to show that assumptions based merely upon the name are, in the present instance, particularly misleading.

From very remote times the Romans were in the habit of bestowing the names of Greek divinities more especially upon slaves and newly enfranchised persons; later, the names of Roman gods became equally popular. The Greeks conformed to the custom which became more prevalent as polytheism died out. Hence the frequency with which one meets with the names of gods and heroes such as Hermes, Mercurius, Apollo, Aphrodite, Pallas and Phœbus,[3] as well as with derivatives from mythological names, such as Apollonios,

[1] See above, p. 110.
[2] Gelzer, *Die Genesis der byzantinischen Themenverfassung*, p. 54.
[3] The sources are given by H. Meyersahm, *Deorum nomina hominibus imposita*, Kiliae, 1891.

Pegasios, Dionysios, etc.[1]   Several of these are the names of quite authentic saints, and this fact should suffice to show that, in a general way, a pagan name should not throw suspicion on the saint who bears it.   Certain names, moreover, are only mythological in appearance.   St. Venera, for example, whose name recalls that of Venus, is no other than St. Paraskeve, *vendredi*, in its Latin or Italian form.[2]

This is not to say that in the calendar of saints we do not come across strange names which may give rise to legitimate suspicions.   In Corfu (Corcyra) honour is paid to an obscure female saint named Corcyra, Κέρκυρα, who plays a part in the legend of the Apostles of Corcyra, Jason and Sosipater.[3]   It would be difficult not to believe that this St. Corcyra stands in the same relation to the Island as Nauplius to Nauplia,[4] Romulus to Rome, Byzas to Byzantium, or Sardus to Sardinia,[5] and that she is simply the product of the brain of the hagiographer.   A study of the Acts of SS. Jason and Sosipater entirely confirms this impression.[6]

There is yet another class of names which may well excite distrust.   I refer to those which express a quality or function such as Therapon, Sosandros, Panteleemon and others.   It is almost always to saints with a

[1] H. Usener, *Götternamen*, Bonn, 1896, p. 358 ff.

[2] A fact admitted by Wirth himself, *Danae in den christlichen Legenden*, Vienna, 1892, pp. 24-26.

[3] *Acta SS.*, June, vol. v., pp. 4-7. Compare *Synaxarium ecclesiæ Constantinopolitanæ*, pp. 633-36.

[4] A. Boeckh, *Encyklopaedie der philologischen Wissenschaften*, 2nd ed., Leipzig, 1886, p. 560.

[5] "Sardus Hercule procreatus. . . . Sardiniam occupavit et ex suo vocabulo insulæ nomen dedit." Isidore, *Etymol.*, xiv., 6, 39, Migne, P. L., vol. lxxxii., p. 519. Isidore's compilation is rich in analogous examples.

[6] Mustoxidi, *Delle cose Corciresi*, Corfu, 1848, pp. xi.-xx.

marked reputation as thaumaturgists that names of this character are applied, nor is it always the result of chance. I am well aware that people have denounced, and with reason, the mania for transforming into myths all personages whose names correspond with the activity attributed to them. "It would be quite easy," writes Boeckh, "considering that nearly all names in classical times possessed a meaning, to explain the greater number of them by myths, and it would be somewhat embarrassing to decide how the Greeks should have named their children in order to guard them from the danger of losing their identity and seeing themselves reduced to a state of myth. Sophroniscos, the father of Socrates, would fall under grave suspicion, for it is Socrates who makes men wise, σώφρονας; his mother Phænarete has in point of fact been suspected by Buttmann, for Socrates is ὁ φαίνων τὴν ἀρετήν." [1]

The matter could not be expressed better. But, in the case before us, the existence of the saints who appear to be the personification of attributes is frequently only guaranteed by strange legends, and we know, moreover, that people are quick to bestow on the saints they invoke, names in keeping with the *rôle* they are presumed to play. St. Liberata, Ontkommer or Kummernis offers an example of this. The homage paid to her was in reality addressed to Christ, as originally it was the crucifix of Lucca that people venerated before the transformation wrought in accordance with the data of the legend. The cultus of other saints of the same stamp may possibly have veiled a worship of a very different character, difficult to specify and connected by mysterious links with some pagan supersti-

[1] Boeckh, *Encyklopaedie*, p. 581.

tion. Such an hypothesis cannot be wholly excluded, but it certainly cannot be asserted as a general principle. It is, for instance, very improbable that it is applicable to St. Panteleemon whom Theodoret places among the most celebrated martyrs of his day [1] and who possessed many famous shrines in the time of Justinian.[2]

We cannot bring this chapter to a close without touching cursorily on a point which will illustrate in some degree the ideas we have already developed. Just as, in the domain of legend, certain scholars have been eager to mark the stages of a sort of Christian metamorphosis having its starting-point in absolute paganism, so certain Christian pictures and statues appear to them simply as the Christianised interpretation of an idolatrous idea. In such a matter the danger of assuming the existence of a real dependence from certain outward resemblances becomes particularly evident, the more so because the arts afford after all only a narrow range of expression.

In point of fact it may be said that the few timid attempts in this direction that have hitherto been undertaken have been remarkably unfortunate, and that, in almost every instance, a simple confrontation with definite historical data has proved sufficient to shatter all the conclusions drawn from the vague analogy between certain Christian compositions and figures of admittedly pagan origin. Need we recall the extraordinary pretension of a certain learned person to trace the type of the Virgin with the seven swords, so popular in Catholic countries, back to the Assyrian goddess Istar ?[3] As it so happens the genesis of this representation of Our Lady of Seven Dolours, as indeed of the devotion

[1 See our *Origines du culte des martyrs*, p. 220. The 3d ed. deletes the phrase about Theodoret placing St. Panteleemon among the most celebrated martyrs of his day.]

[2] *Acta SS.*, July, vol. vi., p. 398.

[3] H. Gaidoz, *La Vierge aux Sept Glaives* in *Mélusine*, vol. vi., 1892, pp. 126-38.

itself, is known in all its details, both the time and the place of its origin having been accurately ascertained. We have evidence that it does not date back farther than the sixteenth century, and that it comes from the Low Countries.[1]

Another writer has professed to discover numerous analogies, indicative of a common origin, between the worship of the Madonna and the worship of Astarte. He has even gone so far as to recognise in those pictures of the Virgin to be seen in our churches adorned with a long triangular embroidered robe a continuation of the sacred cone which represented the Eastern divinity.[2]

Again, an effort has been made to prove the descent of the Madonnas of the thirteenth century from the type of Gallic mother-goddesses " through the medium of Gallo-Roman types of a more skilful execution which already wear a virginal expression ".[3] This channel of transmission is supposed to be found in statues representing goddesses in the form of a woman nursing her child. Surely every one can see that such a group would very easily suggest the mother of God, and that it is in no way surprising if here and there our forefathers were deceived by the resemblance. But so far were they from needing a model from which to represent the Blessed Virgin in that attitude, that this is precisely the type of the most ancient Madonna known to us, that painted on a wall of the catacomb of Priscilla.[4]

---

1 *Analecta Bollandiana,* vol. xii., pp. 333-52. [P. Soulier, *La confrérie de Notre-Dame des Sept Douleurs dans les Flandres,* Brussels, n.d., 71 pp.; A. Duclos, *De eerste eeuw van het broeder-schap der Zeven Weedommen van Maria,* Brussels, 1922, 142 pp.]

2 See *Mélusine,* vol. iii., 1887, p. 503; also G. Rösch, *Astarte-Maria in Theologische Studien und Kritiken,* vol. lxi., 1888, pp. 265-99.

3 J. Baillet, *Les Déesses-Mères d'Orléans,* Orleans, 1904, p. 14.

4 It is more surprising that archæologists of eminence should have allowed themselves to be mistaken concerning the significance of

From the fact that Horus is always represented on horseback, piercing a crocodile with his lance, we must not rush to the conclusion that St. George, who is equally represented on horseback, killing a dragon, is identical with the Egyptian divinity.[1] Apart from the fact that the great majority of warrior-saints are represented on horseback,[2] and that the sight of an equestrian statue might suggest this iconographic type, the legend of St. George, the dragon-slayer, a legend without any sort of link with the god Horus, would naturally induce Christian artists to confer upon the image of the saint what has come to be its consecrated form. St. Menas with the two camels, his indispensable companions, equally recalls Horus and his crocodiles. It may well be that Coptic sculptors derived their inspiration from so widely spread a representation and in this way helped to create the popular type of the great martyr. But it does not follow that he should therefore be regarded as a pagan divinity, and made into a sort of

an Egyptian stele representing Isis with Horus at her breast. M. Gayet in *Les monuments coptes du musée de Boulaq* in the *Mémoires de la mission archéologique du Caire*, vol. iii., pl. xc., p. 24, has no hesitation in recognising it as the Blessed Virgin giving suck to the Holy Child, although with the proviso "that this representation must belong to the earliest times of Coptic evolution when the antique manner was still predominant". G. Ebers, *Sinnbildliches, Die Koptische Kunst*, etc., Leipzig, 1892, has also adopted the explanation. But M. C. Schmidt had only to turn round the stone of which the reverse side had served for a Christian epitaph to eliminate the stele from the series of Coptic monuments, and restore it to the worship of Isis and Horus. C. Schmidt, *Ueber eine angebliche altkoptische Madonna-Darstellung* in the *Zeitschrift für aegyptische Sprache,* vol. xxxiii., 1895, pp. 58-62.

[1] Clermont-Ganneau, *Horus et saint Georges* in the *Revue Archéologique*, N.S., vol. xxxii., 1876, pp. 196-204, 372-99, pl. xvii.

[2] See J. Strzygowski, *Der koptische Reiterheilige und der hl. Georg* in *Zeitschrift für aegyptische Sprache*, vol. xl., 1902. pp. 49-60.

understudy to Horus.[1]   The classical origin of the type
of St. Peter seated on a throne with the keys in one
hand and the other raised in blessing is beyond dispute.
But is St. Peter in consequence to be ranked entirely
with the personages represented in a similar attitude?[2]

[1] I. A. Wiedemann, *Die Darstellungen auf den Eulogien des
heiligen Menas* in the *Actes du sixieme congrès des Orientalistes*,
vol. iv., Leiden, 1885, pp. 159-64.

[2] H. Grisar, *Analecta Romana*, Rome, 1899, pp. 627-57.

CHAPTER VII.

CONCERNING CERTAIN HAGIOGRAPHIC HERESIES.

Direct relation established between the history of a saint and his
legend — Exaggerated confidence in hagiographers — Ill-con-
sidered appeals to local tradition—Confusion between a probable
and a truthful narrative—Excessive importance attributed to the
topographical element—Legend held in utter contempt.

To draw up a catalogue of the principal errors committed by hagiographers and critics ever since the world
has studied the lives of the saints would be indeed an
onerous task.   There is no form of literature into which
people rush so frequently without any sort of preparation, and if it be true that goodwill is sufficient to give
pleasure to the saints, it is less true that nothing more
is needed in order to praise them worthily, or to appreciate at its true value the quality of the praise bestowed
upon them.   Hagiographers, alas, have sinned greatly,
and the only consolation left us is to believe that much
will be forgiven them.

But if it be futile to hope that we may draw them all
back into the straight paths of historical criticism, let
us try at least to warn them against certain gross errors
which have become accredited among them, and which
day by day render the misunderstandings between
history and poetry more serious, and the conflict between science and piety more acute.   These erroneous
beliefs usually circulate in a nebulous condition.   In

the light of the principles which we have attempted to lay down, it should suffice in most cases to reduce them to precise terms in order to expose their falsity forthwith.

The first and most widely spread error consists in not separating the saint from his legend. A narrative will be accepted because it refers to a well-authenticated saint, while the very existence of another saint will be held in doubt because the stories concerning him are improbable or even ridiculous. It is one and the same principle which may, according to the school that acts upon it, lead to either of these equally absurd conclusions.

It will not take us long to demonstrate its falseness. The various divisions of our own work go to show that the saints run a continual risk of being compromised by the literature written in their honour, for the very reason that the people on the one hand and the hagiographers on the other are much in earnest in singing their praises. Moreover the documents concerning them are exposed to all the perils of transmission. Thus there is no sort of immediate proportion between the legitimacy and popularity of the cultus of a saint and the historical value of the written documents which attest its existence. One martyr whose cultus has never spread beyond the narrow walls of his basilica, may live for us in authentic Acts of an incomparable beauty. Another, whose tomb attracts pilgrims from the whole world, is only known to us from narratives whose interest is far inferior to that of the Arabian Nights but whose historical value stands on much the same level.

Dare I say that the value of the Acts of the saints is in inverse ratio to the celebrity of their cultus? As a general proposition this perhaps would not be quite accurate. But it cannot be denied that legend having been most active round the most popular saints, historical tradition has been more difficult to preserve in much-frequented sanctuaries than elsewhere. And this is true of all great pilgrimage centres. Except in certain quite special cases, we know nothing either of their origin or their patrons save the most fabulous reports.

We are therefore fully justified in looking with suspicion upon the legend, while retaining full confidence in the saint.

I will not go so far as to maintain that one should admit the existence of a saint whatever his legend may be. It will be remembered that we have come across more than one hagiographic narrative having reference to an imaginary personage, and yet bearing all the appearance of an authentic document. Some other evidence is therefore needed in order to establish the real existence of the object of the cultus. If it is a fact that, in the course of centuries, every other trace of his career has become obliterated then we may reasonably entertain doubts on the subject. When we affirm that a particular saint has never existed we simply assert the fact that he is only known to us by a legend of insufficient authority to prove his existence.

A second very common error is to place an exaggerated confidence in the biographers of the saints. People seem to transfer to these pious writers something of the respect due to the saints themselves, and the oft-repeated phrase, "We read in the Lives of the Saints," without any one taking the trouble to specify the biographer referred to, shows clearly that people implicitly attribute the highest qualities of the historian to every member of the fraternity.

If one insists upon knowing upon what grounds so much faith is placed in the author of the life of a saint, one is probably told that by his piety, his reputation or the dignity of his office he was one of the remarkable men of his day. People forget to add whether there is any reason for believing him to have been well-informed, and capable of making the most of the sources he had at his command. And while the known writers are accepted thus uncritically, the anonymous ones—and the great majority of legends bear no name by which to authenticate them—are allowed to benefit by the reputation for science and integrity which has been conferred on the whole corporation of hagiographers, a reputation, as we have seen, wholly unmerited.

Need we dwell, at this juncture, on the injustice done to the saints themselves, by quoting, as their authentic utterances, the words some obscure scribe has placed on their lips after having evolved them laboriously from his own mediocre intelligence?

I shall be told that these remarks can only apply to readers wholly destitute of critical sense or of literary pretensions. Not at all. What is true is that in more scientific circles the same monstrous error is found under another name: it is the confusion between authenticity and veracity. The first step is to prove that the Acts are authentic, that, for instance, St. Eucherius is incontestably the author of the Passion of the Martyrs of Agaunum, the second is to make use of the Passion as though it were a document of the first value, and with it to encumber the history of the later persecutions; and so on.

We shall not be wandering from our subject if we call attention to the further illusion of those who pro-

fess a sort of blind admiration for that highly respectable collection known as the *Acta Sanctorum* and who
have developed the unfortunate habit of quoting it as
though it were the Gospel. How frequently have we
not read concerning some strange miracle or some suspicious revelation for which the writer was anxious to
gain credence, this naïve remark, "This fact is admitted by the Bollandists".

The uninstructed reader would of course assume that
after having submitted the incident to a minute examination, these "pitiless critics"—this is the consecrated phraseology—have allowed themselves to be dis-
armed, and that, in the face of the evidence, they have
been unable to deny the correctness of the narrative,
or to contest the supernatural character of the event.

Need we point out that it would be paying too much
honour to any group of men, however learned, who
merely apply methods that are known to and at the
command of every one, to attribute to them a decisive
authority in questions of infinite delicacy and not easily
susceptible of hard and fast rulings? Neither Bol-
landus, nor Papebroch, nor any of their successors
have ever entertained any such pretensions. As a
general rule they have abstained from attempting to
solve insoluble problems, holding it to be a sufficient
task to classify the hagiographic texts, to print them
with scrupulous care, to make known with all attainable
exactitude, their origin, their sources, their style, and if
possible to pronounce upon the talent, the morality and
the literary probity of their authors.

Should therefore some honest writer experience the
desire of conciliating his public by making it known
that he has not neglected to turn over "the vast collection"—the epithet is once more *de rigueur*—of the *Acta*

Sanctorum, I must beg him at least not to make the editors responsible for all that it contains. Let him content himself with a formula that can compromise no one, such as : " The account of this incident has been published by the Bollandists ". But to infer from this that the Bollandists guarantee its authenticity is to draw an unwarrantable conclusion. " If the Bollandists," writes one of their number, " believed definitely in all the miracles and all the revelations they publish, there could not be men of more robust credulity." [1]

We now come to a third error which consists in setting the tradition of the church in which a saint is specially honoured in opposition to the solid conclusions of scientific research.

Among those who make use of this argument are some who, without knowing it, confuse apostolic tradition, the rule of faith for all Christians, with the popular tradition of their particular church. Such persons should be sent back to their theology in order to learn not to use the word " tradition " in an unqualified sense save in dogmatic matters.

But without going to this extreme, a considerable number think themselves justified in contesting the results of criticism by pleading respect for local traditions. Unfortunately what it is usual to dignify with the title of the tradition of a particular church, is merely the current version of the legend of the patron saint, and the form of respect claimed on its behalf is to consider it straightway as a tradition of historical value : an inadmissible pretension if it is hoped by these means to evade the necessity of weighing the evidence. In order to do that it is essential to go back to the begin-

[1] Ch. de Smedt, *Des devoirs des écrivains Catholiques,* Brussels, 1886, p. 16. [This last sentence is deleted in the 3d ed.]

ning.   If the history of the saint, as officially accepted, belongs to one of the three first categories of hagiographic texts enumerated in an earlier chapter, it may be conceded that at least in its main outline local tradition is an historical tradition ; if not, then it is no use quoting it at all.   Historical tradition is that which goes back to the event itself; popular tradition often arises several centuries later, and sometimes even unceremoniously dislodges the most solidly established historical tradition.

History informs us that St. Procopius of Cæsarea belonged to the priesthood.   Legend, as accepted throughout the East, transformed him at a later date into an officer, and soon he was universally known under the title of *Procopius dux*.

Current tradition describes Pope Xystus as dying on the cross, and every one is familiar with the verses on St. Laurence by Prudentius :—

> Fore hoc sacerdos dixerat
> Jam Xystus adfixus cruci.[1]

Yet we know for a fact from a letter by St. Cyprian, who was not only a contemporary, but a well-informed contemporary, that Xystus died by the sword.[2]

Concerning St. Agnes there were current, as early as the fourth century, the most contradictory reports, every one of which would probably be disproved by history, if unhappily history had not been wholly silent where she is concerned.[3]

The traditions of the various churches in France which claim apostolic descent only date from the

---

[1] "'Twas this his bishop had foretold, Xystus when fastened to the cross." *Peristeph.*, ii., 21-22. [Instead of "current tradition" ("la tradition courante") the 3d ed. reads "Prudence fait mourir": "Prudentius has Pope Xystus . . ." *Ed.*]

[2] *Epist.* lxxx., Hartel, vol. iii., p. 840.

[3] Pio Franchi de' Cavalieri, *S. Agnese nella tradizione e nella leggenda*, p. 26.

period at which these legends, on which their pretensions are based, first won acceptance. This period is, in most cases, quite easy to ascertain, and it is simply arguing in a vicious circle to seek to authorise the legend by the tradition of which it was itself the source.

And yet the argument is pressed: "Are you unaware," these writers say to us, "of what took place in the churches in the fifth and sixth centuries when, in response to the eagerness of the faithful to listen to the acts of the martyrs in religious assemblies, the ancient and venerable narratives of an earlier period were collected from all parts, and recorded in a more methodical and oratorical style? The new editors, writing under the very eyes of the bishops, would certainly have abstained from introducing into their narrative any important circumstances up to that time unknown to the people." [1]

This manner of looking at the problem fails to correspond in any way with the actual facts.

It is assumed, what has to be proved in every individual case, that the Passions of a debased age were, in fact, derived directly from "ancient and venerable narratives of an earlier century," whereas we know how rarely the hypothesis can be verified.

Further, it is assumed that the Acts of the Martyrs were very generally read aloud at the liturgical Offices. We know that in the very great majority of churches such was not the case, and consequently that we can count neither on the vigilance of the bishops nor on the sensitive ears of the faithful for the maintenance of historical traditions concerning the martyrs.

[1] [Dom Guéranger,] *Les actes des martyrs depuis l'origine de l'église chrétienne jusqu'a nos temps,* vol. i., Paris, 1856, p. xxxiv.

Hence episcopal control over local hagiography and the devotion of the people to a received version of the history of a saint constitute facts that require demonstration and can in no sense be accepted as an hypothesis to be taken for granted.

In point of fact wherever we are in the position to trace the diverse phases of the genesis of a legend, we are able to demonstrate in the clearest possible way the lack of this double conservative influence. The case of St. Procopius which we have studied in detail is sufficiently conclusive on this point. Could it be said that the priests and the faithful of the diocese of Lyons kept jealous guard over the memory of the curé d'Ars if they in any way countenanced a biographer who represented him as being, not at home in his presbytery, but at the head of an army?

The hagiographic legends of antiquity belong incontestably to popular literature. Not only do they bear no official hall-mark, but what we have been able to ascertain concerning their origin and their development affords us no guarantee of their historical value. The faithful found in them a means of edification and they required nothing further. Even in our own day, how many people are quite satisfied with those deplorable compilations known as the *Petits Bollandistes* or the *Grande Vie des Saints* in which history holds but an inferior place, but of which the narratives serve as food for piety!

A fourth error consists in accepting a hagiographic narrative as historical merely because it contains no improbabilities.

I may say at once that mediæval hagiographers intent on impressing their readers with what was marvellous and extraordinary, have so encumbered their passionaries with fabulous tales, that the absence of any extravagant element of itself creates a favourable impression. If people went no further than that we should have nothing to complain of.

But we must first examine in what form the document has come down to us. Many Passions of martyrs have been transmitted to us in texts of varying lengths, some developed, others obviously abridged or even cut down to a short lesson. Now the abridged texts frequently make a more favourable impression than the originals, the developments which betray the methods of the compiler having largely disappeared. One may compare, for example, the short Passion of St. Theodotus with the longer version that has also been preserved.[1] On the evidence of the abbreviated version alone, one might perhaps pronounce a very different judgment on the hagiographer and his work. It would be easy to apply a similar test to many other abridged narratives of which the original is still in existence.

Unhappily the confusion between what is true and what is probable may frequently be recognised even in the methods of that higher criticism by means of which students have professed to disentangle the historical narrative concealed from our view beneath a confused mass of legendary, lore. Supposing it to be true that all the improbabilities of a narrative are interpolations : it will then suffice to exclude this extraneous element in order to bring the document back to its primitive condition.

The process may appear somewhat naïve ; nevertheless it has been put into operation by men who were

[1] Both have been published by M. Pio Franchi de' Cavalieri, *I martirii di S. Teodoto e di S. Ariadne* in *Studi e testi,* vol. vi., pp. 85-87, 61-84.

far from simple themselves. I will only quote, as an interesting example, the case of a scholar like Lami who by making a judicious selection from the fabulous legend of St. Minias, succeeded in compiling a reasonable history, but one that was as little veracious as its predecessor.[1]

If it is rare for historians ostensibly to indulge in practices of this kind, they frequently apply the method in all unconsciousness. Thus they are guilty of doing so whenever they make use of suspicious documents on the specious plea that they contain "good parts". Le Blant was guilty of the practice on a large scale when he was hunting up "supplements to Ruinart". If these "good parts" are anything except portions of the original historical record which the compiler had before him, they are of no possible use—as any one can see—for rehabilitating the document.

A fifth error consists in classifying a document as historical merely because the topographical element can be certified as correct.

This blunder has been committed hundreds of times, and it must be admitted that in many instances the argument to be drawn from topographical precision is, at first sight, beguiling. How often does it not occur that this is the one point capable of verification, and if the document is found to ring true in this respect what more natural than to assume the excellence of the whole?

And yet we may go very far astray by relying too

1 *Sanctæ ecclesiæ Florentinæ monumenta,* vol. i., Florence, 1758. This is how he expresses himself: "Eius actis insinceris et apocryphis fides adhiberi ab homine cordato non potest; tentare nunc juvat an ea defæcare, et fabellis, quibus scatent, purgare et ad verosimilem historiam redigere, mihi res ecclesiæ Florentinæ inlustrare adgresso fortunate liceat". (p. 589).

much on topographical tests! It would be easy to quote many wholly psychological novels, the wanderings of whose heroes through Paris could be traced without difficulty. When the world has forgotten that Bourget wrote novels, we should be compelled, according to this theory, to accept his stories as real history, and the problem as to whether or no *David Copperfield* is compiled from autobiographical memoirs would be solved by the fact that all the hero's journeys can be verified on the map. All that scientific criticism may assume from a narrative topographically correct, is that the author had familiarised himself with the places in which his personages reside, which in most cases simply means that he wrote at Rome, Alexandria or Constantinople, according to the special knowledge he may display, and that he had seen the tomb or the basilica which he describes.

Bearing this in mind it is easy tó appraise the value of certain archæological discoveries which have seemed to justify what had hitherto been regarded as somewhat dubious acts of martyrs. It has become possible to prove that these Acts have been written—a fact that is in no way surprising—in the vicinity of the sanctuaries whose origins they were supposed to relate. But the authority of the narrative gains nothing thereby, and after, as before, the "confirmation" supplied by the monuments, we are free to assert that the whole legend had its birth in the imagination of a poet.

There was much excitement some years ago over a discovery which was held to have rehabilitated the Acts of SS. John and Paul. This is how M. Le Blant [1]

---

[1] *Les persecuteurs et les martyrs,* p. iii.. See also P. Allard, *La maison des martyrs,* Paris, 1895. Taken from the *Correspondant,* 39 pages.

describes the circumstances : " Little reliance was placed on a text which was thought to be founded in part on original documents but to have been corrupted by the introduction of some wholly inadmissible details. Nevertheless the tradition of the martyrdom inflicted on the two saints in their own house continued to survive. Indeed the precise spot where they were executed was shown, and in the sixteenth century a marble slab was let into the pavement towards the centre of the church, bearing these words, *Locus martyrii SS. Ioannis et Pauli in ædibus propriis.* One of the Passionist fathers attached to this church, the Rev. Dom Germano, whose intelligent initiative cannot be too highly praised, was anxious to ascertain whether the conformation of the ground was in accordance with the belief to which the inscription testified. He set about excavations and explored the soil beneath the church, and almost at once he made the discovery, beneath the high altar, of two rooms of a house, which from the materials out of which they were constructed as well as from their interior decoration, undoubtedly belonged to the beginning of the fourth if not to the end of the third century. Hence it is clear, as the *Passio* relates, that the church was built on the site of an ancient house."

It is useless to continue the quotation, for we have arrived at the one definite result of these excavations. They have in no way solved the problem as to whether the hagiographic text was founded on original documents in spite of its containing some " inadmissible details ". Since then proof has been forthcoming that the story of SS. John and Paul does not depend on any historical source, but is merely an adaptation of the

history of SS. Juventinus and Maximinus,[1] and in spite
of all the interest that surrounds the "house of the
martyrs" none of the difficulties of the legend have
been solved by it. Indeed the only solution to which
no serious objection can be taken is that the patrons
of the title of Pammachius are the holy apostles
John and Paul transformed by legend at an early date
into officers of Julian's court, after the pattern of
other similar transformations with which we are by
this time familiar.

We have now pointed out to the reader various
vicious methods in order to put him on his guard
against over-confidence in hagiographic legends. We
have been exclusively occupied with the historical
point of view, and it must be admitted that only too
often the history of the saints has been obscured by
legend. But it would be a fresh error to assume from
this that the legends of the saints—I refer here to
legends in general—are unworthy of attention. A comparison will at once make my meaning clear.

Let us suppose that an artist and an archæologist are
both standing before a religious picture, some great
work by an Italian or Flemish master.

The artist would rave enthusiastically of the beauty
of the conception, the skill in the composition, the
intensity of the expression, the depth of the religious
feeling.

If the archæologist were one in whom the æsthetic
sense is lacking, he would give vent, before the masterpiece, to a series of criticisms, possibly accurate in themselves, but which would have the effect of exasperating

---

[1] P. Franchi de' Cavalieri, *Nuove note agiografiche* in *Studi e testi*,
vol. ix., Rome, 1902, pp. 55-65. See also *Analecta Bollandiana*, vol.
xxii., p. 488. [The sentence following — "Indeed . . . familiar."
— was deleted in the 3d ed. *Ed.*]

his artist friend. Here we have a fantastic landscape absolutely at variance with what we know of the physical features of the country; there a style of architecture unheard of in that region, while the costumes belong neither to the period nor to the people. His feelings would be outraged to see St. Lawrence wearing a dalmatic when before the tribunal, and he might possibly ridicule that charming scene in which St. Peter preaches from a pulpit in a Roman piazza while St. Mark sits at his feet and takes down the sermon, dipping his pen in an inkstand respectfully held for him by a kneeling disciple.

This is the sort of criticism which our archæologist might pass upon Fra Angelico, Van Eyck or Perugino. No doubt he would study with curiosity the robes worn by the holy women at the tomb, the weapons of the soldiers escorting our Lord to Calvary, and the buildings by the roadside, because he would recognise in them contemporary documents of the time of the painter, and he would perhaps grow indignant with the art connoisseur, indifferent to these antiquarian details, and wholly absorbed in that which constitutes the true value of the work, the expression of the ideal.

Which of the two is the more just appraiser of this legend in line and colour, the enthusiast who seeks to penetrate into the inspired soul of the artist, or the unfortunate being who experiences precisely the same emotions before a great work of art as before a case of antiquities in a museum?

I would not be so bold as to transfer this comparison in all its rigour to the two camps that have grouped themselves round the hagiographic literature of the Middle Ages, that of the simple readers and sincere admirers, and that of the despisers of these legends. It must be admitted that the pious chroniclers of the lives of the saints have not, as a general rule, been as happy as the painters, and that they have produced few master-pieces, few works even which, taken alone and judged on their own merits, would have attracted any notice or held public attention.

And yet, who can deny that in spite of all the ignorance of technique and the clumsiness of execution, there is exhaled, not indeed from each individual legend, but from out the store-house of mediæval lore, something of that mysterious and sublime poetry which pervades the walls of our ancient cathedrals? Who will dispute the fact that these legends give expression with unparalleled vigour to the beauty of Christian faith and the ideal of sanctity?

Let us not forget that there is frequently a notable difference between what our worthy hagiographers wished to say and what, in point of fact, they have succeeded in saying. Their amplifications are often cold, the attitudes of their personages awkward and formal, their situations forced. But the thought which inspires them is noble and elevating, and their eyes are fixed on that perfect beauty of which pagan antiquity was wholly ignorant, the beauty of the soul filled by the grace of God, while their very helplessness in reproducing it in all its glory only aids us to esteem it the more.

For a long time the Golden Legend, which is so accurately representative of the hagiographic labours of the Middle Ages, was treated with supreme disdain, and scholars showed no mercy towards the worthy James de Voragine. "The man who wrote the

Legend," declared Louis Vivès, "had a mouth of iron and a heart of lead."

It would in fact be hard to speak of it too severely if it were conceded that popular works are to be judged according to the standards of historical criticism. But people are beginning to realise that this is an injudicious method, and those who have penetrated into the spirit of the Golden Legend are very far from referring to it in scornful terms.[1]

I confess that, when reading it, it is somewhat difficult at times to refrain from a smile. But it is a sympathetic and tolerant smile and in no way disturbs the religious emotion excited by the picture of the virtues and heroic actions of the saints.

In this picture God's friends are represented for us as what is greatest on earth; they are human creatures lifted up above matter and above the miseries of our little world. Kings and princes honour and consult them, mingling with the people in order to kiss their relics and implore their protection. They live, even here on earth, in God's intimacy, and God bestows upon them, with His consolations, something also of His power; but they only make use of it for the good of mankind, and it is to them that men have recourse in order to be delivered from sufferings both of body and soul. The saints practise all the virtues in a superhuman degree; gentleness, mercy, the forgiveness of injuries, mortification, renunciation, and they render these virtues lovable, and they urge Christians to practise them. Their life is, in truth, the concrete realisation of the spirit of the Gospel, and from the very fact that it brings home to us this sublime ideal, legend, like all poetry,

---

[1] *Analecta Bollandiana*, vol. xxiii., p. 325.

can claim a higher degree of truth than history itself.[1]

1 In a letter to Count John Potocki Joseph de Maistre quotes, with comments of his own, an example of what he calls "Christian mythology". We cannot do better in order to elucidate our own thought than cite this eloquent passage: "Listen and I will give you one of these examples. It is taken from some ascetical work the title of which I forget. A saint, whose name I have also forgotten, had a vision in which he saw Satan standing before the throne of God. And listening, he heard the evil one say: 'Why hast Thou damned me, I who only offended against Thee once, whereas Thou hast saved thousands of men who have offended against Thee many times?' And God replied, 'Hast thou asked for pardon even once?' Such is Christian mythology! It is dramatic truth which preserves its value and its effect quite independently of literal truth, and would indeed gain nothing by it. What does it matter whether the saint in question did or did not hear the sublime words I have quoted? The great point is to know that *forgiveness is only refused to him who has not begged for it.*" See Count Joseph de Maistre, *Lettres et Opuscules inédits,* vol. i., Paris, 1851, pp. 235-36.

INDEX.

233